Edmund Clifford

The Life and Reign of Edward I.

Edmund Clifford

The Life and Reign of Edward I.

ISBN/EAN: 9783337012427

Printed in Europe, USA, Canada, Australia, Japan

Cover: Foto ©ninafisch / pixelio.de

More available books at **www.hansebooks.com**

PREFACE.

THE volume entitled " The Greatest of the Plantagenets," was correctly described in its title-page, as " an Historical Sketch." Nothing more than this was contemplated by the writer. The compilation was made among the manuscripts of the British Museum, in the leisure mornings of one spring and summer; and so soon as a fair copy had been taken, it was handed to the printer. The work was regarded as little else than a contribution towards an accurate review of what is both the most interesting and the most neglected period of our English history.

Its reception exceeded by far the author's anticipations. Very naturally—it might be said, quite inevitably—many of those who admitted the general truth of the narrative, were ready to charge the writer with " partisanship," and with taking a " one-sided view " of the question. It is not easy to see how this could have been avoided. A great literary authority has said, that the first requisite for a good biography is, that the writer should be possessed with an honest enthusiasm for his subject. And in the present case his chief object was to protest against what he deemed to be injustice. It was his sincere belief, that for about a century past an erroneous estimate of this great king's character had been commonly presented to the English people. He endeavoured to show that this had been the case; to explain the causes, and to lead men's minds to what he deemed to be the truth. Such a task could hardly be performed without giving large opportunity to an objector to exclaim, "You write in a partisan spirit."

When a new view of any passage in history is presented, many fair and honourable men, while they yield to the force of evidence, cannot help feeling some reluctance—some dislike to the sudden change of belief which is asked of them. Such men will often be found to object to the manner in which their old opinion has been assailed, even while they admit that that opinion was erroneous, and can no longer be maintained.

So, in this case, even those who advanced this charge of partisanship were generally ready to concede, that an altered view of Edward's character had been not only propounded, but in a great measure established. Thus the Dean of Chichester, Dr. Hook, while he "differs widely from some of the author's conclusions," admits that "his argument is always worthy of attention," and describes the volume as one in which "everything that can be advanced in favour of Edward is powerfully stated." * So, too, the Oxford Chichelean Professor of History (Mr. Montagu Burrows), speaks of the book as

---

* Lives of Archbishops, vol. iii., p. 401.

"a bold, and on the whole, successful attempt to reclaim for him; who is perhaps the only sovereign of England since the Conquest who has a right to the title of 'Great,'—that position of which he has been deprived for more than a century."* And Sir Edward Creasy calls it "an earnest, elaborate, and eloquent defence of Edward I. against all the imputations that have been made upon him;" and adds, "my frequent references to this volume will show how much I value it." †

The success, then, of the author's attempt to rectify a prevalent error, has been clear and indisputable. All that he proposed to do has been done—the estimate of this great king's character which prevailed a dozen years ago, has been considerably elevated—the justice which the writer claimed for him is now almost universally conceded.

But a desire is expressed by most of these critics—and it is a natural and laudable desire—that, as a result of the whole, a history, in the ordinary sense, of this great sovereign, and of the remarkable period in which he lived, might be given to the British public. The writer has entirely sympathized with this desire, and he has waited several years in earnest expectation of the appearance of some such work. Nothing of the kind, however, has yet been given to the world; nor is there any announcement of such a purpose. It seems to him, therefore, that it is in some sort his duty to review his former work; to

---

* Oxford Hist. Society, 1864, p. 322.
† History of England, vol. i., p. 406.

consider how far it is justly chargeable with "partisanship," and to reduce it, so far as he is able, to the proper form and proportions of a permanent history.

He feels the more impelled to attempt this, from an increasing conviction that not the sovereign only, but the time in which he lived and reigned, alike present to the mind of the dispassionate student, a subject meriting and richly repaying a careful examination. The chief features of the period in which this prince was born, and in which he lived, are more remarkable than even that union of great qualities by which he himself was distinguished.

This fact—the unusual concurrence of many symptoms of advance and of excellence at that period—has already been noticed by more than one writer. Lord Macaulay said: "It was during the thirteenth century that the great English people was formed. *Then* first appeared with distinctness that Constitution which has ever since preserved its identity; then it was that the House of Commons, the archetype of all the representative assemblies which now meet, held its first sittings; then it was that the Common Law rose to the dignity of a science; then, that our most ancient colleges and halls were founded; and then was formed a language, in force, in richness, and in aptitude inferior to the tongue of Greece alone." Another writer adds, that "it was *this* age of all ages, to which every Englishman ought to look back with the deepest reverence. In this thirteenth century our Constitution, our laws, and our language, all assumed a form which left nothing for future ages to do, but to improve the detail."

This language is strong, and yet it does not fully describe the fact. The union of solid and real advance with more ornamental characteristics is very remarkable. It is true, as the writers whom we have just cited observe, that this thirteenth century—the life-time of Edward the First—saw the rise into existence of the English people, of the English language, and of the English constitution; but there were also several other appearances which were stranger than these. The realm had been, for many years, almost destitute of a settled government; it had suffered from something nearly approaching to anarchy. The Norman dukes who domineered over it only vouchsafed to their province of England an occasional visit; often manifesting very little care for it. Richard I., out of a reign of nine years, spent only a few months in this island. His successor was the worst king that England ever saw, and did his utmost to plunge the realm into ruin and absolute confusion.

It fills us, therefore, with wonder, to observe that so soon as these two pernicious rulers had departed, and the land was left in the hands of a weak and incompetent, but well-meaning youth, symptoms of revival of all kinds became perceptible. Not only did the English people and the English language come to light in this realm, but mind, and intellect, and taste all uprose together. "It is curious," says Lord Campbell, "that in this turbulent reign (of Henry III.) there should have been given to the world the best treatise upon law of which England could boast, until the appearance of Blackstone's Commentaries. For comprehensiveness, for lucid arrangement, for logical precision, this author, Henry de Bracton, was unrivalled for many ages."* Nor did this great lawyer stand alone. The same period gave us Roger Bacon, and, with him, Antony Beck and Chancellor Burnel, two of the greatest statesmen that England has ever known.

In the fine arts, also, England, though not yet rid of tumult and civil war, made equal or still greater advances. Henry really valued the arts; his wife was a cultivator and a patroness of poetry, and he himself resolved to raise, at Westminster, a new and splendid shrine for the remains of the last of the Saxon kings; ornamenting it, also, with pictures of great Saxon achievements. This royal taste for architecture was in accordance with the popular feeling. It was in the latter half of this century that Westminster Abbey, the old St. Paul's, the Temple church, and the cathedrals of Salisbury and Norwich were built, while during the same period, the churches of Lincoln, Ely, Ripon, Exeter, and Wells, all received important enlargement. Nor was Edward himself, though a soldier and a statesman, at all indifferent to these matters. He raised in Westminster Abbey two monuments to his father and his consort, of which an eminent critic of our own day says: "Few figures can surpass, in simplicity and beauty,

* Campbell's Chancellors, vol. i., p. 159.

the effigy of queen Eleanor, and those on the crosses erected to her memory are almost equally fine."*

The last words remind us, naturally, of another comparison. The king of England, in A.D. 1290, lost his dearly-loved consort; and he paid to her memory every tribute of affection and of sorrow that he could conceive, or that could be suggested to him. Her funeral " presented one of the most striking spectacles that England ever witnessed."† And he then strove to perpetuate that memory by monumental works, both within the Abbey and in twelve other places. In our own day we have witnessed a similar bereavement. We have been conscious, too, of the existence of a sorrow as deep and as enduring as that of the Plantagenet king. But have we, with all the wealth and all the refinement of this nineteenth century, been able to exceed, or even to equal, those outward and permanent expressions of sorrow which king Edward conceived and compassed in the earliest days of the English people and kingdom?

A consummate judge of these matters has truly said that "The reign of Edward I. is the period of the most perfect and beautiful Gothic buildings, when English art attained to the highest eminence it has ever yet reached."‡ And do we not all know, as a simple matter of fact, that if we, after a lapse of six hundred years, wish to raise a

* Parker's Gothic Architecture, p. 161.
† Archæologia, vol. xxix., p. 174.
‡ Parker, p. 253.

building of more than ordinary beauty, we are compelled to have recourse to the noble works which were achieved in the days of Edward I.? there being within our reach no purer or loftier models.

The age, then, in which this great monarch lived was a very extraordinary age. To ascribe its singular fruitfulness in every department of human excellence to his influence, would be altogether irrational and absurd. He himself was only one fact or feature among many. But it crowns the whole edifice with singular grace, to find—in the days which produced a Bracton and a Roger Bacon, a statesman like Burnel, a divine like Grosstete—the throne filled by a man like Edward, whose first thought was of uprightness,* whose mind was a "legislative mind,"† and who wrestled and fought his way through a period of no common difficulty and trouble, with such " cleanness of hands" as to leave him, at last, one of the noblest examples that it is possible to adduce, of a ruler " fearing God and working righteousness."

Those who are acquainted with the former publication will recognize in the present, whole pages, sometimes whole chapters, which merely reproduce what had been therein said. Perhaps one third of the book is thus composed. Wherever a passage of plain and simple narrative, disputed by no one, occurred, there seemed to be no

* " *Pactum serva.*" † Mackintosh.

good reason for merely putting it into new phraseology. But all the more important and controverted questions have been reconsidered, and the chapters which concern them almost entirely rewritten.

The portrait which faces the title-page is given because there seems good reason to think that it is, substantially, a true representation. England possessed, as we have said, in the days of Edward, good sculptors as well as good architects; and it is tolerably certain, that the artist employed to erect at Carnarvon a statue of the king, would be a man competent to execute that work in a creditable manner. It is true that at the present moment, the hand of time has nearly destroyed every feature. But a century and a half ago, the statue was, doubtless, in a better condition. An artist accustomed to detect, with a practised eye, not only what *was*, but what *had been*, might gather from the brow, from the mouth, from the chin, and from the general contour, a tolerably accurate idea of the general portraiture. George Vertue, in his researches for the illustration of Rapin's history, visited Carnarvon, believed that he gained from the statue a just idea of what Edward had been, and brought away a drawing of it, which he carefully engraved. From that portrait the present frontispiece has been taken.

CONTENTS.

		PAGE
I.—BIRTH AND EARLY YEARS	. . . . .	1
II.—ACCESSION TO THE THRONE—EDWARD'S EARLIEST PROCEEDINGS	. . . .	17
III.—THE FIRST SEVEN YEARS	. . . .	36
IV.—MIDDLE PERIOD OF EDWARD'S LIFE, A.D. 1279—1290		50
V.—RETROSPECTIVE VIEW	. . . . . .	87
VI.—SCOTTISH AFFAIRS—THE ARBITRATION—THE WAR A.D. 1291—1296	. . . .	101
VII.—TROUBLES WITH FRANCE—WAR IN SCOTLAND	.	128
VIII.—THE WAR WITH FRANCE, AND VARIOUS TROUBLES AT HOME, A.D. 1297	. . . . . .	157
IX.—WILLIAM WALAYS, A.D. 1297, 1298	. . .	176
X.—PROLONGATION OF TROUBLES IN SCOTLAND—PARLIAMENTARY DISCUSSIONS IN ENGLAND, A.D. 1299—1302	. . . .	203

	PAGE
XI.—THE DISAFFORESTING QUESTION—THE COMMISSION OF TRAILBASTON, ETC., ETC., A.D. 1299—1305	226
XII.—THE SETTLEMENT OF SCOTLAND, A.D. 1303—1305	265
XIII.—BRUCE'S REBELLION: THE WAR WHICH FOLLOWED.—THE DEATH OF EDWARD: HIS CHARACTER	290
APPENDIX	347

THE

LIFE AND REIGN OF EDWARD I.

I.

BIRTH AND EARLY YEARS.

ON the night of June 17-18, 1239, Queen Eleanor, the consort of Henry III., presented her husband with a son, who was born in the Palace of Westminster, and who was instantly, says the old chronicler, named by the king, "Edward, after the glorious king and confessor, whose body rests in the church of St. Peter," immediately adjoining. The event was greeted by the nobles and by the people of London with great manifestations of joy: by the citizens more especially, because the young prince was born among them. The streets of the city were illuminated at night with large lanterns, and music and dancing marked it as a day of general rejoicing.

Such a birth was a new thing, in those days, to Englishmen. They had passed nearly two centuries under the dominion of the dukes of Normandy, whose home was in France, and whose sojourns in England were merely visits paid to a conquered territory. During the later years, indeed, of that Norman tyranny, two or three of its princes, though still deeming themselves Normans, had first seen the light on English ground;* but now, by his own choice, the reigning king had ordained that his eldest son should receive his birth in the metropolis of his kingdom, and had named him after the lamented and venerated " Confessor," the last of the Saxon sovereigns. All this was gratifying to the Anglo-Saxon mind, and how it was received and felt we can discern in a chronicle of the period, which gladly accepts and records the birth of an English or Anglo-Saxon prince, narrating that, "on the 14th day of the calends of July (June 18), Eleanor, queen of England, gave birth to her eldest son, Edward ; whose father was Henry, whose father was John, whose father was Henry, whose mother was Matilda the empress, whose mother was Matilda, queen of England, whose mother was Margaret, queen of Scotland, whose father was Edward, whose father was Edmund Ironside, who was the son of Ethelred, who was the son of Edgar, who was the son of Edmund, who was the son of Edward the Elder, who was the son of Alfred." †

In this manner the chronicler, who doubtless gave utterance to a common feeling among Englishmen, manages to drop out of view almost entirely the Norman dukes, who had overrun and subjugated the land for more than one hundred and fifty years, and whose yoke had been felt to be indeed an iron one. Among those sovereigns there had been some men of talent and prowess, and one or two of good and upright intentions; but the general character of their rule had been hard and despotic. " The people were oppressed; they rebelled, were subdued, and oppressed again.

* Henry I. at Selby, Richard I. at Oxford, and Henry III. at Winchester.
† Florence of Worcester, A.D. 1239.

After a few years they sank in despair, and yielded to the indignities of a small body of strangers without resistance. The very name of Englishman was turned into a reproach; their language, and even the character in which it was written, were rejected as barbarous. During a hundred years, none of their race were raised to any dignity in the State or the Church."* The old "Saxon Chronicle" tells us how the Norman soldiers "filled the land with castles,—forcing the poor people to toil in their erection; and then, when these fortresses were built, they filled them with devils and wicked men. They took those whom they supposed to have any goods, and shut them up, and inflicted on them unutterable tortures."

The dawn of a better state of things was seen, when, in 1204, under the weakest and worst of all these alien despots, Normandy was separated from England. To the Norman knights who had settled upon their English possessions acquired by the sword, this separation must have seemed a dire calamity, but to Englishmen it was the reverse. England rose once more to the rank of an independent kingdom. Her sovereigns, Norman dukes no longer, must henceforward be really kings of England if they would be anything; and thus Henry III., born at Winchester, and living all his life in England, came to feel for the land and the people far differently from any of his progenitors. He was a prince, too, who, with many faults, had some real virtues. He was kind-hearted and liberal. He was, too, the first of his race who knew by experience the value of home affections. From the Conqueror downwards, all the Norman kings had been men of license, and their households the abodes of jealousy, hatred, heart-burnings, and conspiracies. Henry III. was a faithful

* Macaulay.

husband and an affectionate father; and he owed it to these virtues that, after many errors and many follies, he descended at last into a quiet and not unhonoured grave. The first of all the Conqueror's descendants to feel himself merely "king of England," he was the first, also, to desire to gain the good will of the English people, and the first to stand before them as one knowing the value and the duties of an English home. Henry had married a woman of talent, one who stands high in mental rank among English queens. One of our old chroniclers speaks of her as

> "The erle's daughter of Provence; the fairest May of life:
> Her name is Helianore, of gentle nurture;
> Beyond the seas there was none such creature."

A poem from her pen is said to be preserved in the Royal library of Turin; and it is in this reign that we first hear of a poet laureate in England. It was probably from his consort, to whom he was all his life devotedly attached, that Henry learned that fondness for the arts and that cultivated taste which are often discernible in his proceedings. Painting and architecture, as well as poetry, always interested him. Over the Confessor's tomb he resolved to raise a noble edifice; and to that resolve we owe the Abbey Church of Westminster. Several of our finest ecclesiastical buildings were commenced about this time, and it is now that the Norman style of architecture disappears, and the early English comes in its room. Both the Temple Church, and the great cathedral of St. Paul which perished in the fire of London, were upreared in Henry's reign. There can be no doubt that his liberal and often lavish expenditure on objects of this kind was one among the various causes of that long series of pecuniary troubles and embarrassments, which brought upon him all the chief disasters of his reign. Thus, in passing through Paris in 1255, Henry thought that it became him to give a banquet to the French king and his nobles, at which banquet twenty-five dukes, twelve bishops, and eighteen countesses, with a host of illustrious knights, were present; and the next day he sent to his distinguished guests, at their dwellings, " rich cups, gold clasps, silken belts, and other princely presents." And very naturally, the chronicler next tells us that he landed at Dover oppressed with a burden of debt, which he himself described as " horrible to think of." Then followed exactions, forced loans, and applications to a " great council " for aid ;—mutual reproaches, disputes, and at last a civil war.

But we must return to our subject—the earlier years of Henry's distinguished son. Edward's childhood appears to have been spent principally at Windsor. In his third year, 1242, we find an order in these terms: " Pay out of our treasury, to Hugh Giffard and William Brun, £200, for the support of Edward our son, and the attendants residing with him at our castle of Windsor."* Four years later, Matthew Paris notices the death of this Hugh Giffard, whom he calls " a nobleman of the household, and preceptor to the princes." In the following year, prince Edward was seized with a dangerous illness, and the king wrote to all the religious houses near London, requesting their prayers for his recovery.

Of Hugh Giffard's successor we find no record; but as the prince's education now became a matter of importance, we may be sure that a competent instructor was provided. Two very able men are found in habits of friendship with him through life, and it is probable that one or both of them had a share in his early training. Robert Burnel was the

* Devon's Issues of the Exchequer, p. 18.

prince's chaplain and private secretary, and he and Anthony Beck accompanied Edward in his expedition to Palestine, and were named executors in the will made at Acre, in 1271, after the attempt on his life. Burnel afterwards became chancellor and bishop of Bath and Wells, and Anthony Beck received the bishopric of Durham. But whoever it was that gave to Edward's mind its earliest bent and bias, he has a right to our sincere respect and gratitude.

High and noble principles, both of religion and morals, are exhibited in every act and word of his after life. He was at all times devout; frequent in pilgrimages, religious retirements, and similar observances, and fond of using scripture language and citing scripture precedents: yet there was nothing of the monk or the ascetic about him. Throughout his life he was pre-eminently a man of action, but in every action recollections of duty and principles of rectitude were always perceptible.

Young Edward begins now to be spoken of as a youth of fine stature, often described as "Edward with the flaxen hair." The king showed great fondness for him, and evidently felt a natural pride in his son. Long before the youth could be competent for such a post, he endeavoured to make him the lieutenant or governor of Gascony, and involved himself in quarrels both with his brother Richard the earl of Cornwall, and with earl Simon, by these attempts. He was at last obliged to go over to Gascony to arrange these quarrels, which had arisen from his own imprudence; and we read of his embarkation at Portsmouth on the 6th of August, 1253, when we are told "the prince, after his father had kissed and wept over him at parting, stood sobbing on the shore, and would not leave it so long as a sail could be seen." The deep and ardent affection which subsisted in both father and son, is visible in many other incidents of the following twenty years, and it constitutes an important feature in Edward's character.

Henry, when in Gascony, had an object in view beyond the adjustment of the existing differences. He sent two of his confidential servants, the bishop of Bath and John Mansel his minister, into Spain, to propose to king Alfonso the Wise a marriage between Alfonso's young sister Eleanor and his son Edward. By this marriage certain claims which the Spanish king had, or was supposed to have, on Gascony, were to be adjusted; such claims being made over to Eleanor as a kind of dowry. A treaty on this basis was made, sealed with gold, and brought over to England, where it is now preserved among our ancient records.

The Castilian monarch, however, with the stateliness and dignity of his nation, claimed that Edward "should be sent to him, that he might examine into his skill and knowledge, and confer knighthood upon him." The queen of England resolved to visit Alfonso with her son, and personally to assist at the betrothal. She reached Burgos, with the young Edward, on the 5th of August, 1254. Alfonso was pleased and satisfied, and we know, from the after history, that the two persons most interested in the question became sincerely attached to each other. Throughout a wedded life of six-and-thirty years, we observe the prince and princess scarcely ever separated. When Edward goes to Palestine, Eleanor accompanies him; when a painful operation is to be performed, she can only by force be removed from the apartment. Wherever he journeys she is ever by his side: when fever seizes her, he is her faithful attendant; and when at last the tomb must receive her, he will give her such honours and follow her with such grief, as few women of the most exalted rank or character have ever been the occasion of.

The prince and princess reached England in the autumn of 1255, and took up their abode in the palace of the Savoy. In the following year, Edward's sister, the young queen of Scotland, paid them a visit, and the palace of Woodstock became the scene of royal festivity;—Oxford and all the neighbouring villages being filled with distinguished guests.

The king had professed to give his son, on his marriage, the government of Gascony and of Ireland, and the earldom of Chester, guaranteeing to him a revenue of 15,000 marks, or £10,000, which would be equal to £150,000 in the present day. But with these great revenues still larger expenses accrued. In 1257, the Welsh, always unruly, made an inroad into the English counties on the border, and the king, when appealed to, threw upon Edward the task of restoring order. The prince was obliged to borrow of his uncle, the earl of Cornwall, a sum of 4000 marks, and he began to organize a military force. But the Welsh, who were fond of marauding expeditions into England, were too numerous to be kept in order by a few hundred horsemen; and the prince began to understand by painful experience, how unsatisfactory and how injurious to both countries was the existing state of the relations between Wales and England.

We shall not dwell upon the last eighteen years of Henry's reign—years of trouble, disgrace, dissension, and civil war. The young prince took just that part in these painful transactions which might have been expected of him. He was sincerely attached to his father; he was also a firm supporter and assertor of the royal rights; but his ruling principle through life was an inflexible adherence to rectitude;—a resolve to do justice alike to all men.

Hence he could not approve or maintain many of his father's proceedings. As early as the period at which we have arrived, differences arose between the father and the son on these questions. Henry had professed to make his son the lieutenant or governor of Gascony. Yet the king's officers still continued to seize, for the king's use, quantities of wine at Bordeaux. The Gascons appealed to the prince, and he went to the king to claim redress for them. He told his father plainly that he would not tolerate such proceedings. "The king," says the chronicler, "with a sigh exclaimed, 'My own flesh and blood assail me; the times of my grandfather, whose children fought against him, are returning!'" But the prince felt assured of the justice of the cause he had espoused; he was firm, and Henry was compelled to promise that these acts of oppression should cease.

This same sort of struggle between the rights of the people and the assumed privileges or encroachments of the crown, now began to grow into a serious and prolonged strife in England. One historian remarks, that "It was not that Henry was by inclination a vicious man; he had received strong religious impressions; though fond of parade, he avoided every scandalous excess; and his charity to the poor and attention to public worship were deservedly admired. But his judgment was weak, and his will, it must be added, was often at the command of others."

He had also the disadvantage of committing faults and falling into errors, in the presence of one who was well qualified to take advantage of both.

Simon de Montfort was one of the greatest among the great Norman knights of that age. It has been well said of this remarkable class of men, that "The ideal perfection of the knight-errant was to wander from land to land in quest of renown; *to gain earldoms, kingdoms, nay, empires, by the sword*, and to sit down a settler on his acquisitions, without looking back on the land which gave him life. Every soil was his country; and he was indifferent to feelings and prejudices which promote in others patriotic attachments." *

The earls Simon de Montfort, grandfather, father and son, were pre-eminently soldiers of this class. In 1165 Simon the Bald obtained in marriage a daughter of Blanchmaines, earl of Leicester, and his son and grandson always put forward a claim to that earldom. The son of Simon the Bald went to France, took up the crusade against the Albigenses, and died count of Toulouse. One of his sons, calling himself "earl of Leicester," came to England and gained, some said clandestinely, the affections of the princess Eleanor, daughter of king John, and sister of Henry III. Thus connected with the royal family, we find him, all through the middle portion of this century, either trusted and employed by the king, or else heading a combination of the barons against him. He became at last a popular leader, admired and sometimes almost idolized by the people; and when he died, he was held by them to have been a martyr to their cause. We are scarcely able to form a decided opinion of his whole character. Some of his later acts are not reconcilable with the obligations of loyalty to his sovereign, who was also, by marriage, his relation; but we must admit that the difficulties of his position were considerable. The most favourable feature in the case is, that this great soldier seems to have possessed and valued the friendship of Grosstête, "holy bishop Robert," who is, perhaps, the purest and brightest character presented to us in the records of that day.

Up to a certain point the prince concurred with the discontented faction among the barons, and with earl Simon their leader, whose consort was his aunt. But, as we might have anticipated, when their plans and purposes began to

---

* Walter Scott's Hist. of Scotland, vol. i., p. 68.

border upon treason, Edward, whose affection for his father never varied, soon withdrew from their society. "The Barons' war," as it has been called, lasted from 1258 to 1265. "A concilium," held in London in the first of these years, led to a much larger and more important assembly at Oxford about Midsummer. The barons came to that city with great numbers of armed retainers, and forced from the king an assent to "the provisions of Oxford," which did, in effect, put the royal authority "into commission," or share it with a selected number of great lords. The prince, we are told, "being brought to it with great difficulty, at last submitted himself to the ordinance and provision of the barons." He saw, we cannot doubt, the degradation of the royal authority which was implied in those provisions; but he saw no available way of escape. He consented, therefore, though unwillingly; but a pledge once given was, with him, a solid reality.

Through life, the motto which, doubtless by his own command, was afterwards inscribed upon his tomb, was his constant rule: *Pactum serva*. Having entered into an engagement, he would adhere to it. Accordingly, we find that in 1259 the poor king was alarmed by rumours that the prince and the barons were confederating for his dethronement. One chronicler tells us that certain evil advisers created distrust between the father and the son; and that when the prince would have vindicated himself, the king exclaimed, "Let him not approach me, for if I were to see him, I should not be able to help kissing him."* Such was the affection which had always existed between the two.

But again we find, about a year later, that the uprightness of the prince, and his adherence to his engagements,

* "Annals of Dunstable."

created a new difference between Henry and his son. Matthew of Westminster tells us, that "Edward, receiving full information concerning the king's vain counsels and counsellors, became enraged against the latter, and withdrew himself from his father's sight, and in all good faith declared his adherence to the barons, in conformity with his oath. The king shut himself up with his evil advisers in the Tower, and Edward remaining outside with the barons, things assumed a threatening aspect."

Two years of fluctuating prospects and of great trouble followed. But Edward began to see, on the part of earl Simon, designs which he could not possibly approve or tolerate. The earl, on one occasion, actually threatened Windsor Castle; and when the prince agreed to meet him at Kingston to confer upon the position of affairs, the earl "was too circumspect to allow him to get into Windsor again." He "detained the prince" until, to regain his liberty, he consented to surrender the royal fortress to the earl.

Such proceedings as this must have alienated the prince from earl Simon and the barons; and at last, in 1263, it was agreed that all questions should be submitted to king Louis of France (St. Louis), to whose decision all parties bound themselves to conform. At the commencement of 1264, Louis held a great court, and heard the arguments on both sides; and then, by his final sentence on the 23rd of January, he "annulled and made void the provisions of Oxford," and discharged all persons from any obligations to the same.

At last, then, the prince was morally and legally at liberty. The obligation by which he had so long felt bound was at an end; but earl Simon and the discontented barons refused to abide by their engagement. They had sworn that "whatsoever the king of France should ordain concerning the matters in dispute they would faithfully observe," but when the decision was against them, they refused to submit to it. From this moment Edward takes his place by his father's side. Hostilities commenced in April, 1264, and in May a battle was fought at Lewes. The prince defeated the forces opposed to him, but earl Simon broke up and dispersed the centre and left wing of the royal army, and forced the king to shut himself up in the Priory of Lewes. Edward, to extricate his father, agreed to terms; and for a time both the king and the prince were in a sort of honourable captivity, attended everywhere by earl Simon, who now acted in the king's name, and did, in almost every matter, merely what he pleased.*

This state of things lasted about a year, when at last the prince escaped from the guards whom earl Simon had placed around him, was joined by the earl of Gloucester and Roger Mortimer, and once more raised the royal standard. At Evesham, in August, 1265, the final struggle took place. Earl Simon, seven lords of his party, and one hundred and sixty knights, perished, and "the Barons' war" was ended. A year or two was required to restore tranquillity; but during the rest of Henry's life, which lasted seven years longer, the realm was for the most part at peace.

A parliament was held at Marlborough in 1267, for the settlement of questions arising out of the civil war. And now, seeing the country again in tranquillity, Edward listened to the earnest entreaties of Louis of France, and consented to accompany him on the last great Crusade.

* The Chronicle of Mailros describes a messenger coming to Edward from his sister, the queen of Scotland; and tells how earl Simon took care to be present, observing every word and gesture that passed between the two.

He embarked at Portsmouth in the spring of 1270, accompanied by his faithful Eleanor. The princess was with him when, at Acre, his life was attempted by an assassin. The romantic story of her extraction of the poison from the wound with her own lips, is not found in authentic history; but one chronicler narrates how, when a painful operation became necessary, the surgeon requested Edward's brother and the lord de Vesci to carry the princess away; "so she was carried out, weeping and crying aloud."

The support of the French army failing him, Edward quitted Palestine in July, 1272, and at Sicily he met the news of his father's death and of his own accession to the crown of England. The king of Sicily was surprised at the grief which these news excited—a grief more poignant and more visible than that caused by an earlier despatch which mentioned the death of one of Edward's children. The prince made the natural reply, that other children might replace the one which he had lost, but that he never could have another father. The warm and sincere affection which always subsisted between these two very different men, is proved by incidents which meet us at every turn; and our estimate of king Henry's character is considerably raised by the fervour and the permanence of his son's attachment to him.

Of Edward's own character we have already seen something. In two chief characteristics, it is fully developed long before he reaches the royal dignity. He was in a more than ordinary degree a man who could love, and who was beloved. His father, his mother, his wife, his friends, were the objects of his unvarying attachment. This feature of his life is constantly apparent.

But he was also a man of honour and of integrity. He looked, in all matters, more to the question of *right* than to that of *expediency*. Born to wear a crown, he was careful to do nothing to diminish the royal dignity; but not even for the maintenance of his father's privileges, would he do that which he did not believe to be just and right; and, above all things, the one principle, *Pactum serva*, was never to be departed from. A prince's word, once given, must be held sacred. One other feature in his character is noted by the historians of his day. He was of an irascible temper, easily excited to anger; but his anger might be as quickly calmed as it was aroused. Walsingham tells us how, on one occasion, the prince was amusing himself with his hawks, and one of the lords in attendance overlooked a falcon which had made a stoop on a duck among the willows. The prince spoke sharply to him, and the other answered, with some pertness, that "he was glad the river was between them." In a moment Edward had plunged into the stream, and was urging his horse up the opposite bank, in pursuit of the offender. But the attendant, knowing with whom he had to deal, flung off his cap, bared his neck, and threw himself on the prince's mercy. Edward's wrath was gone in a moment, he sheathed his weapon, gave instant forgiveness, and the two rode home in perfect amity together.

In like manner, while engaged in the pacification of the country after "the Barons' war," he found, in a forest in Hampshire, a noted captain of free-lances, one Adam Gordon, or Gourdon, whose deeds made him the terror of all the country round. The prince sought him out, and met with him one evening when he and his followers were returning to their fastnesses. Edward at once singled Gordon out, and engaged him in single combat. Both being skilled in arms, and of tried valour, the contest was an arduous one. At last Gordon was wounded, and yielded himself. Edward respected his valour and his knightly prowess, received his submission, had his wounds attended to, took him into his favour, and presented him that night to his mother, the queen, at Guildford Castle. Gordon proved faithful, and remained long attached to Edward's service.

A similar clemency marked all Edward's proceedings. To "seek his grace" was always to find it. The few exceptions, in his whole life, are those of men who had "broken covenant," and proved false and treacherous after confidence had been placed in them. Even Hume, generally unfriendly to Edward, is obliged to confess of the pacification which followed the victory of Evesham, that "The clemency of this victory is remarkable. No blood was shed on the scaffold; no attainders, except of the Montfort family, were carried into execution."

And if we examine his conduct through life with an unprejudiced eye, we shall find this attribute of clemency —a' very uncommon one in those days—distinctly perceptible in all his proceedings. A firm and resolute and warm-tempered man, he could sometimes punish; but his general rule of conduct was once expressed by himself in a hasty exclamation: "*May* pardon him! Why, I will do that for a dog, if he seeks my grace!"

II.

ACCESSION TO THE THRONE—EDWARD'S EARLIEST PROCEEDINGS.

THE death of Henry III. took place in Westminster on the 16th of November, 1272, and he was buried on the 20th, in front of the great altar in that noble church, on the uprearing of which he had lavished so much treasure. At the close of the funeral, earl Warenne, the earl of Gloucester, and all the chief of the clergy and laity there present, went forward to the high altar, and swore fealty to king Edward. Three guardians or regents immediately entered upon the government of the realm—namely Edmund, the king's cousin, son of the late earl of Cornwall, brother of Henry III.; Walter, the archbishop of York; and Gilbert, earl of Gloucester. No difficulty of any kind appears to have occurred; the submission of all classes was entire; and we may assume that a regular correspondence was at once established between the regents and the king. We find him showing no signs of haste, but remaining abroad until sundry matters of importance were arranged, and then taking his journey homewards with royal state and deliberation.

He was in Sicily when the tidings of his father's death reached him. Before his visit to the pope had terminated, he was known throughout Italy to be king of England; and as he proceeded homewards through Northern Italy, he met with a royal reception in many of the cities;

the people coming forth to receive him with processions, and blowing of trumpets, and acclamations of "Long live king Edward." At Chalons a grand tournament had been prepared for him; which, however, was not without sinister design; "the Burgundians bargaining over their wine-cups, for some days before, for the horses and armour of the English knights, whom they confidently reckoned on overcoming."* The English, however, were not overcome. The gigantic count of Chalons, failing to dismount Edward, tried, by main force, to pull him from his horse; but he was thrown to the ground, chastised, and made to give up his sword. Ill blood and exasperation arose; the English had to fight their way out of the town; and the tournament was remembered as "the little battle of Chalons."

Edward next visited the king of France, and did homage for his French possessions. Passing into Gascony, he found it needful to subdue and bring into subjection a fractious noble, Gaston de Bierne. Thence he proceeded to the courts of the countess of Limousin and the countess of Flanders, with each of whom he had business to transact. At last, in July, 1274, he set his face towards England, landing on the 2nd of August at Dover. The two great earls, Warenne and Gloucester, were awaiting his arrival, and he became, in turn, the guest of each, at their castles of Reigate and Tunbridge. Meantime, preparations were making for his immediate coronation; and, on the 19th, this ceremony took place. In the abbey-church of Westminster Edward and Eleanor were crowned king and queen of England by Robert Kilwardby, archbishop of Canterbury. There were present, besides all the great men of the realm, Edward's two brothers by marriage—Alexander, king of Scotland, and John, duke of Bretagne—with their consorts,

* Hemingford.

the sisters of the king. On the following day, king Alexander of Scotland paid his accustomed homage.*

The ceremony was attended with many circumstances of rejoicing and exhibitions of munificence. While the nobles and citizens made the conduits flow with wine and the streets gleam with tapestry, scattering silver in handfuls, the princes showed a royal liberality. King Alexander of Scotland, "when the king was seated on his throne, came to do him worship, and with him an hundred knights, mounted and accoutered; and when they had lighted off their horses, they let the horses go, and they that could catch them, had them for their own behoof. And after these came Sir Edmund, the king's brother, and with him the earl of Gloucester; and after them the earl of Pembroke and the earl Warenne, and each of these led an hundred knights, who, when they alighted, let their horses go, and they that could take them had them to their liking."

The feast was a right royal one. We shall find, throughout Edward's reign, that none ever practised a truer or a wiser economy. His habits were simple and plain, his household well regulated. A friend once expressed wonder at the plainness of his dress. His answer was, "And what good, think you, would fine clothes do me?" But he well understood his royal estate and office. When he had to come before the people as their king, his doings were always kingly. The coronation-banquet was a noble one. New buildings were erected in the court-yard of Westminster, to accommodate the guests; and the provision made shows how numerous these guests must have been. The details are still preserved, and we find that the principal items were— " 380 oxen, 430 sheep, 450 pigs, 18 wild boars, 278 flitches,

* The extent of this homage became a matter of negociation, and the question was not finally adjusted until some three or four years after.

and nearly 20,000 fowls." Such a prodigious supply was not provided for one day's festival; the feast was prolonged through a whole fortnight. Edward's friends and chief counsellors, such as Anthony Beck and Robert Burnel, were churchmen; and we find, in every part of his personal history, frequent reference to Old Testament precedents. In the present instance they seem to have followed a notable example—" At that time Solomon held a feast fourteen days."—1 Kings viii. 65.

And now Edward was on his throne,—was dwelling in his palace, ruling over the people of England. The work before him was an arduous one; his chief advisers were men suited to the times; and his own strength of purpose, sagacity, and perseverance were precisely what the land needed at that peculiar juncture.

England had long been in a state of extreme disorder, and it required a clear head and a strong right arm, to bring it into a condition of health, and comfort, and security.

One change of vast moment, indeed, had been effected in the course of the protracted reign which had just ended. From the time of William until the end of the reign of John, during one hundred and fifty years, the people had felt that they were under the yoke of alien lords. The Normans, men of iron, people of another land, and who spoke another language, ruled over them; but the half-century of Henry's reign gradually lightened, and at last removed the weight of this oppression.

The two races, Saxon and Norman, began to know a real amalgamation. In the eleventh and twelfth centuries, "those Saxon swine" was the usual appellation employed by a Norman knight when speaking of the people of the land; and, " Do you take me for an Englishman?" his form of indignant disclaimer. In the thirteenth, we find both Normans and Saxons agreed in a league to expel "all foreigners." And thus it was that, at last, "in the thirteenth century, the great English people was formed." * A nation more warlike and more enterprising than the Saxons, and more fond of home life and of personal liberty than the Normans, gradually appeared. It was in Henry's reign that the English tongue, and the English desire for laws suited for free men, began to be seen and heard: but that weak though well-meaning sovereign was not a leader or a ruler who could direct his subjects in such a path as this.

The order and the governance of law scarcely existed in Henry's reign. When the sovereign needed corn or wine, or any other commodity, his usual course was to seize it. On one occasion he angrily asked of his earl marshal, "Cannot I send and seize your corn, and thresh and sell it?" "And cannot I send you the heads of the threshers?" was the earl's angry reply.

One of the judges, accused of corrupt practices, came to court to defend himself, attended by armed friends, one of whom offered wager of battle. The king, exceedingly enraged, publicly declared, that "if any one would kill Henry of Bath, (the judge,) he should have pardon for the crime!" When even the bench of justice was thus occupied by violent and corrupt men, it is no wonder that we hear that "the whole county of Hampshire swarmed with felons and murderers," or to find that "the king himself was obliged to hold a court of justice at Winchester, trying and sentencing the offenders, many of whom were wealthy, and some of them his own servants."

Several years after this, we find one of the greatest nobles in the land setting an example of disorder. Matthew Paris narrates how, "in consequence of some hasty words

* Macaulay.

which passed between them, John de Warenne, earl of Surrey, slew with his own hand, in Westminster Hall, Alan de la Zouch, the king's justiciary." Probably, had Henry been at that time without assistance, this outrage, committed by so potent a nobleman, would have escaped retribution; but the prince was now at his right hand. Collecting a sufficient force, Edward pursued the earl to Reigate, besieged his castle, brought him to London a prisoner, tried him, and only spared his life, after much deliberation, in consideration of an enormous fine, equal to £100,000 of our present money.

Nor was violence, even of the extremest kind, a privilege of the nobles only. In July, 1263, during the excitement of "the Barons' war," queen Eleanor desired to leave her residence in the Tower of London, and to remove to Windsor Castle; but as her barge approached London Bridge, she found that it was occupied by a crowd of earl Simon's adherents, who assailed her with cries of the grossest abuse, among which, " Drown the witch! " was one of the mildest. Huge stones, as well as all kinds of filth, were hurled at the barge, and the queen was glad to accept of the protection of the mayor, who conveyed her to the house of the bishop of London. Not many months after, when a body of these Londoners took part in the battle of Lewes, prince Edward rejoiced to avenge these insults, and to drive them in confusion at the spear's point off the field.

But more than ten years had passed since these calamitous times, and most of those years had been spent in peace. No voices but those of acclamation now greeted Edward and his queen in their progress through the metropolis; and we may easily believe, without any violent stretch of the imagination, that among the London citizens who partook of the coronation-banquet in 1274, there were many who, in the rawness of their youth, had crowded London Bridge to cast stones at Edward's mother, and had fled before his vehement charge on the downs at Lewes in 1264.

Such was the realm of England, and such was its state and condition, over which Edward was now called to rule. It needed such a regulator, such an organizer; and he, perhaps, could hardly have found anywhere a better raw material out of which to build up a nation.

To him, in some measure, we owe the production and the formation of the men who fought and conquered at Crécy, Poictiers, and Agincourt; but we should be lothe to indicate this as his chief glory. We deem the work performed in his reign in establishing law, and in giving England a free legislature, to have been far more noble, far more glorious, than the achievement of brilliant but barren victories on distant battle-fields.

England needed, most of all, at that peculiar conjuncture, precisely what, in Edward, God gave to her, " a legislative mind." The king seems to have entirely appreciated the necessities and the difficulties of his position; and to have applied himself to the great task, of bringing everything into order, and of establishing the dominion of wise and equitable laws.

At the same time we must not forget, that such a work, and one embracing such a variety of details, could not have been performed by any single mind or single hand. Edward must have been aided by one or more of the most sound and competent of advisers. We cannot doubt that in Robert Burnel he had found such an assistant. And it is, perhaps, the best proof of the perfect unity and harmony which always existed between the king and his wise and able chancellor, that we find it difficult to separate the one from the other.

We cannot tell when the king himself speaks, and when we are listening to his chancellor. We find, indeed, sometimes, language so evidently personal, as to make us feel that it must have been the king's own; but at other times we seem to hear the great lawyer, the jurist, who is fitly interpreting his master's will. Take, for instance, that noble opening of Edward's reign, which we find in the preamble of the first statute of his first parliament :—

"Because our lord the king hath great desire to redress the state of the realm in such things as require amendment, for the common profit of the holy church and of the realm ; and because the state of the holy church hath been evil kept, and the people otherwise entreated than they ought to be; and the peace less kept, and the laws less used, and offenders less punished than they ought to be—the king hath ordained by his council, and by the assent of archbishops, bishops, earls, barons, and all the commonalty of the realm, these acts under written, which he intendeth to be necessary and profitable to the whole realm."

We cannot doubt that this high and kingly purpose was truly Edward's; but we may with equal reason believe, that this right royal declaration came immediately from the pen of Robert Burnel.

There is, however, another feature of this reign which ought never to be overlooked. To frame good laws is a great merit in a ruler; but it is a still higher merit to devise and to create a legislature. And this is, in fact, the principal achievement of this sagacious and high-minded sovereign.

Until his time the nation, at least for centuries, had known no such thing as a law-making, still less a representative, body. Under the Norman kings, from A.D. 1066 to 1216, every now and then, "great councils" were held. The military despot who sat upon the throne, often found it convenient and necessary to summon together his barons, the great captains of his Norman soldiery, to ask an aid or contribution from them. But nothing like the construction of a law is ever heard of in these assemblies. At last, towards the end of the reign of John, " Magna Charta " is extracted from him; but this is not so much a statute as a treaty, dictated at the sword's point by his armed barons.

Then followed the fifty-six years of Henry's reign. In the first forty years of this reign, several " great councils" were held, usually, as in Norman times, to consult about " granting the king an aid." Once in 1236, we find " The provisions of Merton," which commences " It was provided in the court of our lord the king." In the same year we find a " royal ordinance " concerning Ireland; and twenty years later, in 1256, "a provision for leap year," also a " royal ordinance."

About this time the chroniclers begin to borrow the term "parliament" from France, and we hear that " a parliament was held at Oxford," at which the barons dictated to the king certain " provisions," which were afterwards cancelled and set aside by king Louis of France.

Seven years after this, earl Simon, in the king's name, summonses a meeting in Westminster, and, as many of the nobles kept aloof from him, so that only five earls and seventeen barons were called to this " concilium," he orders the sheriffs to send knights from the counties, and burgesses from certain towns, so as to form a sufficiently numerous body. But the earl's object was merely to dictate certain terms to the king. No such thought as that of a legislature—an assembly for agreeing upon necessary laws—is anywhere to be perceived.

After the death of earl Simon, we hear of " a concilium" at Kenilworth; which, like earl Simon's parliament, is only a council for agreeing upon certain terms, between the king on the one part and the barons on the other. These terms are embodied in "the Dictum of Kenilworth."

But at last the realm is quieted; king Henry is once more at peace upon his throne, and his son, now arrived at the full manhood of his twenty-eighth year, is naturally the guide as well as the protector of his weak though well-meaning father. And now, in the year 1267, all enemies and all perils having vanished, and the king and the prince being left to their own free will, we hear, doubtless from Edward's lips, words, which for two centuries at least, had never been used in this realm of England. The first document we possess, bearing the name of a "Statute," is "the Statute of Marlborough," and of this, the opening sentences run thus:—

"Our lord the king, providing for the better estate of his realm of England, and for the more speedy ministration of justice, as belongeth to the office of a king; the more discreet men of the realm being called together, as well of the higher as of the lower degree; it was provided, agreed, and ordained," etc.

Here we have the first rough sketch or outline of what we now call "the British Constitution." This constitution, we are often told, was wrung from the unwilling hands of successive sovereigns by the urgent demands of the people, in times of royal exigency. With respect to some later details, this may be true; but not less true is it, that the main and general outline was freely given to the people by the "legislative mind" of Edward, aided by his great chancellor, Robert Burnel.

Four hundred years after Edward's day we had a philosopher in England, John Locke, who had read and pondered much, and who explained to us that the very nature of a civilized and free society is " to have a standing rule to live by, common to every one of that society, and made by the legislative power erected in it." The very object, he adds, " of civil society is to authorize a legislature to make laws for us, as the public good shall require." These principles, as we have said, arose in John Locke's mind, in the course of study and cogitation. But several centuries before this, the same thoughts had occurred to an English prince, to whom " study," as we understand the word, was impossible, and who must have owed these conclusions, in a large measure, to that sagacity and true nobility of soul with which God had endowed him. Yet we ought not to overlook the fact, that in Edward's youth one of the earliest of our great lawyers, Bracton, had thus written:—

" The king ought not to be subject to man, but to God, and to the law; for the law maketh the king. Let the king, therefore, render to the law what the law hath invested in him with regard to others, dominion and power; for he is not truly king where will and pleasure rule, and not the law." And again, " The king also hath a superior, namely, God, and also the law, by which he was made a king."

Just while Edward was rising into early manhood, did this great lawyer appear, and the probability surely approaches to something like a certainty, that Robert Burnel had been a student of Bracton's writings, had felt the truth and force of the above words, and had made the young prince acquainted with those invaluable pages.

Edward's coronation had taken place in August. His four years' absence on the Continent must have occasioned an accumulation of matters needing regulation; his castles and palaces, his forests and royal domains, would require to be visited and brought into order. A new state of things must be established. We see immediately an important change in the "Exchequer Issues." In Henry's reign, we read: "To Humphrey de Rohan, earl of Hereford, £120 for 50 casks of wine, *taken from him* by Imbert Pugeis (a soldier), for the king's use." "To Gerard de Bosco, a merchant of Bordeaux, 70 marks, for 20 casks of wine *taken from him* for the queen's use." But on Edward's accession these seizures disappear, and the entries run thus, "To Raymund de Alemaunt, of Bordeaux, £46 13s. for 20 casks of wine, *purchased from him*, for the king's use, by Gregory de Rokesle and Matthew de Columbius, the king's butlers."

The royal revenues and the royal expenditure were now, for the first time for a century, to be brought into order and under proper regulation. Christmas would naturally approach, long before all this business could be despatched, and it is not surprising that, however he may have desired it, Edward found it impossible to convene his first parliament earlier than the February of 1275.

In that month—the same which, in modern times, has been found the most suitable and convenient, did this first of English parliaments assemble.* And when the clerk, sitting at the chancellor Burnel's feet, took pen in hand to record its proceedings, his entry ran in the following terms:—

"These be the acts of king Edward, made at Westminster, at the first parliament-general after his coronation; by his council, and by the assent of archbishops, bishops, earls, barons, and all the commonalty of the realm, thither summoned."

Here we find, set forth rather more fully, the same idea and purpose which we had seen expressed at Marlborough in 1267;—a legislature, a council summoned for the purpose

---

* "The first mention of the term, 'parliament,'" says Blackstone, "is in the preamble to the 'Statute of Westminster,' A.D. 1275."

of making and establishing laws; which council was not to consist of great barons only, or of barons and prelates only, but, "of the lower as well as of the higher degree," of "bishops, earls, barons, *and all the commonalty of the realm.*"

This idea was, as yet, but vaguely expressed. In Edward's after years we shall see it more fully worked out, until the whole British Constitution rises to completeness under his creative hand. In this first attempt he merely recognizes the principle that the "lower degree as well as the higher" ought to be present,—ought to be consulted. What "the commonalty of the realm, hither summoned," may mean, we cannot now define with any certainty. The most probable view of the matter is, that the London corporation, then fully existing and on the spot, was invited to represent "the commonalty of the realm," and did appear, doubtless with awe and reverence, as a portion of the first parliament, the first real legislature, that had been assembled in England in Anglo-Norman times.

But what was the work which this first "parliament of England" had to do? And the answer to this question reveals to us the real greatness of Edward's wise counsellor. Robert Burnel, who had accompanied his master to Palestine, and who had, at Acre, been named one of his executors, seems to have been despatched to England, when the king, on his homeward journey, was delayed by business in Gascony and in Flanders. We find him in England, acting as one of the regents or guardians of the realm, several months before the king landed at Dover. He, doubtless, possessed his master's entire confidence, maintained a regular correspondence with him, and was fully occupied in bringing all things into order, before Edward himself appeared at Dover. To some such mind as this we owe it, that so soon as the king had landed, and had conferred on two of his greatest nobles the honour of a visit while passing from the coast to London, he found, on reaching the metropolis, the whole ceremony of the coronation, with its great banquet and rejoicings, only awaiting his arrival. Can we see there assembled, awaiting the king's arrival, the king of Scotland, the duke of Bretagne, all the nobles of the land, with their countless retinues; can we remark the new buildings prepared, and the vast provision for the banquet, and all these and many other preparations, all concentrating to one point, and all involving a large expenditure—without acknowledging that in bringing such a variety of affairs to a ripeness on a day before appointed, there is visible the mind of a man of vast ability? All, at last, is in readiness. The king arrives at Dover, passes on with kingly state and deliberation to the castle of his greatest subject, the earl of Gloucester; then to Reigate, to earl Warenne's,—then to the metropolis, and to his own palace of Westminster. He rests apparently but a single night, and then proceeds from his palace into the abbey, and is at once crowned king. And his very first act, after thus taking his rightful place, is, to make his trusted friend and most able counsellor, Robert Burnel, the chancellor of England.

To this great man, we doubtless owe that noble production, the "Statute of Westminster." In the five or six months which intervened before the meeting of parliament; while the king was examining and regulating the condition of his castles, palaces, establishments, and household, his chancellor, looking forward to the great event which was to follow immediately after Christmas, was occupied, we may safely assert, with the preparation of the work of legislation; a work then to be commenced, but never afterwards to be discontinued in this realm.

Parliaments, such as we now possess, were new things in England. The "concilium," or great council, which we find in Anglo-Norman history, was a gathering of earls, barons, and prelates, for the decision, usually, of a simple question—most generally, of granting an aid to the king. All through the long reign of Henry III., the idea that it was necessary occasionally to meet for the purpose of making laws, never once appears in any record. Of course parliaments holding protracted sittings, for weeks or months together, were wholly unthought of. Provision for the residence and maintenance of the prelates and barons would have been difficult. All that was contemplated was, one meeting, to do one thing and then to separate. Very naturally, therefore, Chancellor Burnel, while he had discovered the need of several laws on different subjects, combined his various reforms in one great statute. Lord Campbell observes that, "The 'Statute of Westminster' deserves the name of a code, rather than an act of parliament. Its object was, to correct abuses, to supply defects, and to remodel the administration of justice." * * * "It protects the property of the church from violence and spoliation; it provides for the freedom of popular elections; it contains a strong declaration to enforce the enactments of 'Magna Charta' against excessive fines; it enumerates and corrects the great abuses of tenure, particularly with regard to the marriage of wards; it regulates the levying of tolls; it corrects and restrains the power of the king's escheator, and other officers under the crown; it amends the criminal law; it embraces the subject of procedure, both in civil and criminal matters, introducing many regulations with a view to render it cheaper, more simple, and more expeditious."

This great measure was in fact the beginning of English

legislation. Up to this period, for centuries, the law of England had been a mere tradition, an unwritten collection of rules and principles, handed down from one generation to another, and deposited in the minds and memories of the judges and students of law. Recollections and traditions of Saxon laws, confirmed in " Magna Charta," doubtless constituted its substance. Such a traditionary code is now of great value, under the name of " common law," because it is expounded in books, and administered by judges of known integrity. But in the days of which we are speaking, books, *i.e.*, manuscripts, were rare and of great price, and the judges, as a rule, were corruptible. Hence, Burnel, having observed and learned what provisions were chiefly needed, began, in this first of parliaments, to apply the remedy of written and authoritative law. A legislative system, worked by a new power; a real legislature, meeting usually every year, but in some years twice or thrice, began now to be known in England. This legislature, under Edward's watchful eye, was enlarged and strengthened from time to time, until, before his reign had closed, we find it closely resembling the parliament of our own day—consisting, in 1304, of "the prelates, nine earls, ninety-four barons, the knights of the shire, and the burgesses sent by 159 towns."

In the great " Statute of Westminster "—the beginning of our English Statute law—there is one provision which, if the mind dwells upon it, suggests many inquiries. It runs thus :—

" And because elections ought to be free, the king commandeth, upon great forfeiture (*i.e.*, penalties), that no man by force of arms, nor by malice nor menacing, shall disturb (or hinder) any to make free election."

Almost six hundred years after, in the parliament now

sitting, serious and prolonged inquiries have been entered into, as to how "elections can be free," and how to provide that neither "by force of arms, nor by menace" shall any be hindered from making a free choice or election. Thus, after so many centuries of parliamentary legislation, we find ourselves again trying to effect that which Edward and his great chancellor commanded in the very first law that they placed upon our statute-book.

But does not the question naturally arise, "What were these elections which Robert Burnel thus saw to need protective legislation?" After all the violence and disorders of such reigns as those of Stephen, Richard, and John, the idea of " a free election" seems a strange one to have existed in this realm of England.

Yet elections there must have been, of two kinds. The Londoners had preserved from days long preceding the Conquest, their " hustings," both name and thing, and one of the laws in use in the days of Edward the Confessor, fixes the time for holding these meetings.

Henry I., a son of the Conqueror, again recognizes the London hustings and the folk-motes; and he grants the citizens the right of electing and appointing a sheriff of Middlesex. And in various charters and other records we find traces of elections frequently occurring in the city of London. These elections, too, were liable, as now, to be disturbed by force of arms and menaces. "Several of the great barons and prelates had their palaces or castles in or near the city. Baynard's Castle, in the days of king John, was the stronghold of Robert Fitzwalter, castellan of the city, who doubtless lacked neither the will nor the power greatly "to disturb free elections." Mobs, too, were frequent and unruly in those days. Fitz-Albert, called Longbeard, in 1196, had more than fifty thousand of the people at his command, and at last fortified himself in Bow Church, whence he was taken and executed. Still more recently, indeed, just about the time of the holding this parliament of Westminster, a feud broke out in the city, concerning the election of a mayor. The candidate properly chosen was Philip le Taylour, but the mob insisted on having Walter Harvey. The king was obliged to interfere, and to appoint a *custos* of the city until an election of mayor could be well and properly holden. This fact, occurring very shortly after Edward's arrival and coronation, of itself explains the insertion of this clause in the statute. Doubtless, also, the elections of " knights of the shire," an institution which dates from the two preceding reigns, would give occasion to many disorders. The great men of a county would often attempt to carry the election " by force of arms ;" the populace would resist ; " menacing" would be heard on both sides ; and complaints would reach the ear of the king and his chancellor. Now both Edward and his great minister were upright and honourable men. Being therefore engaged in the great work of establishing the dominion of wise and equal laws, they insert in this statute, which, as Lord Campbell says, " rather deserves the name of a code," this brief but pithy declaration : " And because elections ought to be free, the king commandeth, under great penalties, that no man disturb such elections, either by menaces or by force of arms."

One other curious circumstance connected with this first parliament of England deserves a mention. Edward always regarded himself as the rightful champion and protector of his people in all just quarrels. The countess of Flanders, in Henry's old age, had taken the violent course, upon some quarrel, of confiscating all English property in the warehouses of Flanders. Edward on his way home heard of this, and sent immediate orders to stop the export of wool; thus reducing the manufactories of Flanders to a state of paralysis. He then met the son of the countess and concluded a treaty, by which the English merchants received full restitution. This settlement of the quarrel was received in England with great satisfaction, and the parliament of Westminster at once granted to the king a customs' duty of half a mark on every sack of wool exported, and a mark on every bale of leather. These duties were recorded, in the spirit in which Edward always acted, as " granted by the archbishops, bishops, earls, barons, and communitates of the kingdom of England." Always and on all occasions does the king associate with himself in public acts, " the commonalty of the realm, the lowest as well as the highest."

III.

THE FIRST SEVEN YEARS.

The key-note struck by Bracton seems never to have ceased vibrating in the minds of Edward and his chancellor. "Let the king render to the law, what the law hath invested in him with regard to others, dominion and power." "The king hath a superior—namely, God—and also the law, by which he was made a king." Duty, the pressure of moral obligation, is as constantly present in Edward's mind as, six centuries after, it was in the mind of Arthur Wellesley. We have seen it recognized at Marlborough, in 1267, in his father's day, when the Statute so named is thus prefaced —"Our lord the king, providing for the better estate of this realm, and for the more speedy administration of justice, as *belongeth to the office of a king*," etc. We find it again in the opening of the Westminster Statute—"Because our lord the king hath great desire to redress the state of the realm, in such things as require amendment." And a little later, in the "Statutes of Gloucester," we hear the same strain—"The king, providing for the amendment of his realm, and for the fuller administration of justice, as the *good of the kingly office requireth*," etc.

Thus, from time to time, we hear from Edward's lips the frank confession, "I hold an office, and that office has its duties; let me look to it that those duties are rightly discharged." He proceeds, after the great "Parliament of Westminster, 1275," to enter in earnest on the important work of regulation, organization, and the removal of abuses and disorders. Just as the owner of a large estate, on coming into full possession after a long minority, sets to work, if he rightly comprehends his position, first to examine and then to regulate every portion of his inheritance, so does Edward give the earlier years of his reign to a similar though larger work. He shows his consciousness that the weakness of a long period of misrule had filled the land with disorders, and that "the kingly office requireth" that he should, in a variety of particulars, introduce new laws and a purer administration. He had seen and regretted, in his father's reign, the fearful weakening of the royal authority which accompanied a system of pecuniary improvidence. At once, therefore, without waiting for the assembling of his parliament, he issued a royal commission to inquire into, and ascertain, the royalties and revenues appertaining to the crown, the state and particulars of the crown-lands, with the names of the tenants and the terms of their tenure.* He rightly judged that on this point—the regulation of the royal revenues—largely depended the just fulfilment of "the office of a king." He soon made himself acquainted with the extent and particulars of his possessions; and so well were these administered, throughout his whole reign, that his applications to parliament were few, and always based upon public grounds,—the acknowledged requirements of the state. Yet he was never wanting in a

* "He issued," says Rapin, "writs of enquiry to two commissioners in every county, to enquire what his royalties, and the liberties and prerogatives of his crown were; who were his tenants *in capito*; and how many and what fees they held of him. Also of his tenants in ancient demesne—how they had behaved themselves, and in what condition the lands were. Also of the sheriffs, coroners, and bailiffs, and their clerks—whether they had extorted money, or had wronged any one, or had taken bribes. This first step," says Rapin, "produced a wonderful effect upon the people."

truly royal munificence; exhibiting liberality on all fitting occasions, and a never-ceasing kindness to the poor.

In the course of these investigations, touching the royalties and revenues belonging to the crown, it would naturally happen that legal questions and doubts would arise, as to the respective boundaries of possessions belonging to the crown, and those belonging to the great barons who had received grants from former sovereigns. The king soon came to the conclusion that, rightly to define these limits, it would be necessary to refer, in all cases, to the original grants. He issued, therefore, after the lapse of two or three years, which the first investigation must have required, another order or commission, that all parties who were in possession of any estates of doubtful title, should lay their grants or charters before the judges, that their validity might be ascertained by competent authority.

In taking this step, Edward was actuated by those motives of frankness and rectitude which were never absent from his mind. He evidently thought that the same sort of investigation to which he had submitted the rights of the crown might fairly be applied to the grants under it; but he soon found that he was likely to involve himself in a serious peril. During such disorderly times as those of Stephen and John, many of the great barons had seized upon estates, the owners of which had perished in the field or on the scaffold. Those great proprietors would very naturally shrink from any sort of legal examination or inquiry. They would have been prompt to combine in a league of resistance to any such investigation. One of the greatest of them, the earl of Surrey, John de Warenne, who had fought at Edward's side at Lewes, and had entertained him in 1274 at Reigate, on his landing,—took an early and a very peremptory position of resistance. He doubtless was one of the first to whom the royal commissioners addressed their inquiries. His answer was that of a rough, bold, and impetuous soldier. He unsheathed an ancient sword, exclaiming, " It was by *this* that my forefathers won these lands, and it is by *this* that I mean to maintain my title."

Edward was wise, as well as frank and noble. A little reflection would enable him to perceive, that if he pressed his demand upon this irascible and powerful soldier-baron, he might soon discover that there were hundreds of other land-owners who felt a sympathy with the earl, and that thus he might be engaged in a strife of a very serious character. His object and his motives had been pure, but prudence evidently dictated a moderate and cautious course. The resistance of this great earl materially affected the whole inquiry. The intended investigation was, for a time at least, suspended. On this, as well as in two or three other passages of his life, Edward showed that even when his first determination had been just and reasonable, he could exercise a thoughtful self-control—that he knew how to waive his rights, when prudence so counselled, as well as how to assert them on all fitting occasions.*

One of the chief matters, however, on which Edward had evidently set his heart, was that of bringing the relations of England and Wales into a better condition. It was on the Welsh border that the first years of his public life had been spent. As early as in his eighteenth year, his father had given him the charge of " the Welsh Marches ;" and he had had the grief of witnessing, again and again, inroads of the Welsh into Cheshire and Herefordshire, in which

* " But Edward never faltered in his purpose, and the inquiry went on, at intervals, through a period of more than twenty years."—Pearson's Hist. Eng., vol. ii., p. 298.

maraudings whole districts were desolated, and the poor English farmers of those counties reduced to beggary. Matthew Paris says: "The Welsh carried fire and slaughter into the border counties. They gave themselves up to incendiarism and pillage, till they had reduced the whole border to an uninhabitable desert." Edward had seen these things with pain and with resentment, and he had evidently resolved to bring the relations of the two countries into a more satisfactory state.

It has suited the purposes of those who wished to represent Edward as an ambitious and designing man, to assume, throughout, that Edward's object, from the beginning, was the conquest of Wales. But the facts of the case, if patiently examined, tell a very different tale. They rather justify our old chronicler Fabyan's description of him. Writing more than three hundred years ago, and conveying down to us the old English belief and tradition, he says: "This prince was slow to all manner of strife, discreet and wise, and true of his worde." And, assuredly, the plain facts of this Welsh controversy justify entirely Fabyan's words.

That Llewellyn owed homage to Edward as his superior lord—just as Edward, for his French possessions, owed homage to the king of France—has never been questioned. Llewellyn himself never denied the obligation. Yet, at Edward's coronation, while the king of Scotland was present and paid his homage, there was no attendance, either personally or by deputy, of the prince of Snowdon.

The Welsh prince pleaded, in excuse, that there was so much enmity between him and some of the lords of the Marches, that he could not safely visit London. Edward met these excuses with forbearance, and even offered to take a journey to Shrewsbury to receive the homage there,

But Llewellyn still raised new difficulties. Had Edward been the ambitious and designing man that he is often represented, he might now, without further parley, have peremptorily summoned Llewellyn, and on his non-appearance, might have declared him contumacious, and his fief a forfeiture. Such had been the course taken by Philip of France, when in 1202 he summoned John, pronounced him contumacious, and at once took possession of Normandy.

Edward's course was equally clear. There was nothing to prevent the immediate annexation of Wales, except the single let or hindrance of the English king's conscientiousness. But Edward would take no hasty or violent step. He reserved the question for his parliament, and at one of the sessions of 1275 it was decided that the Welsh prince should be summoned a third time, and that now the king should even go to Chester to meet him; that being the nearest point to Llewellyn's home.

"Slow to all manner of strife" was written on all these proceedings. Edward knew well that there were precedents in abundance which would have justified him in declaring the Welsh prince a rebel, and in entering into possession of his fief. He was also, we cannot doubt, fully alive to the great advantage which would result from the union of the two countries.

He earnestly desired to terminate the wretched border-warfare which had so long continued. But a leading principle of his whole life was, a constant respect for the rights of others. Again and again shall we meet with this rule of conduct in his after-life. In the present case he remitted to Llewellyn not only the summons to appear at Chester, which the parliament had directed to be sent, but also a safe-conduct for his coming, abiding, and return—a guarantee which the Welshman might know would be strictly fulfilled. But Llewellyn now raised his demands. He would give no attendance until the king should send to him, as hostages, his own son, the chancellor of England, and the earl of Gloucester!—a demand which the old chronicler justly terms "an insolent one," and which must have been intended to terminate the negociation.

About this time Eleanor de Montfort, Llewellyn's intended bride, was met with at sea, and brought into Bristol by an English vessel. As the prince was in contumacy, Edward ordered that the young Eleanor should be conveyed to Windsor, there to remain in the queen's charge until the dispute between England and Wales had been terminated. But the year 1276 had now opened, and parliaments were held, in the course of that year, at Westminster and at Winchester. A fifth and a sixth summons had been remitted to the prince of Snowdon. Some of the bishops now offered to mediate, and they were allowed to send the archdeacon of Canterbury into Wales, personally to confer with Llewellyn. But the Welsh prince merely advanced new claims; requiring now guarantees from two prelates, and from four of the greatest earls in the realm.

The English parliament finally, on the 12th of November, 1276, declared Llewellyn contumacious, and recommended that the military tenants of the crown should be summoned in the spring for the invasion of Wales. Meanwhile the archbishop made one more attempt at mediation, writing to the Welsh prince an earnest but fruitless letter. Another parliament was held, in which "a twelfth" was granted to the king for the expenses of the war. In the spring the royal forces began to assemble, and Roger Mortimer was appointed to the command. The chief men of South Wales sent in their submission, and were "received to the king's grace." David and Roderick, brothers to Llewellyn, joined the king, and were honourably received by him. Meanwhile, Llewellyn believed that his mountain-heights were inaccessible, and that he could never be brought to submission. Edward, however, was a different sort of leader from his father, who in 1257 had led an expedition into Wales, and had miserably failed. With the skill and foresight of a general, Edward had prepared a naval force, which sailed from the Cinque Ports, made a descent upon Anglesea, and took possession of that island. Llewellyn was now enclosed, and it was easy to prevent all supplies from reaching him. He remained obstinate for several weeks; but as the winter drew on he saw the probability of ultimate starvation, and asked for terms of surrender.

Again we see that Edward was not that ruthless and ambitious man which he is often represented. The Welsh prince had been formally declared contumacious, and the forfeiture of his fief was the ordinary penalty. There was no way of escape for him; Edward had only to maintain his blockade, and the surrender and banishment of the Welsh prince, and the entire conquest of the principality, were inevitable and close at hand.

But Edward's guiding principle in all such cases was that which we have already cited from his own lips, "*May show mercy!*—why, I will do that for a dog, if he seeks my grace!" Llewellyn had no sooner asked for mercy than it was granted to him. His offence had been great; to make war upon a superior lord was treason; and the king showed his sense of the offence by imposing hard conditions of peace.

Llewellyn must pay a fine of 50,000 marks for the heavy expenses he had caused the king; must cede to England the four "cantreds" lying between Chester and the Conway; must hold Anglesea of the king at an annual rent of 2000 marks; must do homage to the king, and deliver ten hostages for his fidelity. This was a just sentence, and Edward merely vindicated the majesty of the law by pronouncing it; but the natural generosity of his mind very quickly cancelled the hardest of the conditions. The very next day the fine was remitted. Soon after the rent to be paid for Anglesea was cancelled, and the ten hostages returned. And now that the Welsh prince had submitted, all was grace and favour on Edward's part. The young Eleanor de Montfort, who had been detained in the queen's household, was sent for, and in Worcester Cathedral, in the presence of the king and queen, Llewellyn received his bride. In another respect, the king conferred on the Welsh prince a very substantial benefit. David, Llewellyn's brother, had often been at variance with him. On one occasion the two brothers met on the battle-field, and David was taken prisoner. To remove David from Wales was to confer on Llewellyn a favour of a very important kind. The king took this hostile brother with him to England, gave him £1000 a year in land (equal to £15,000 a year at the present time), and married him to an earl's daughter. "Thus," says Lingard, "Edward flattered himself that what he had begun by force he had completed by kindness. To Llewellyn he had behaved rather with the affection of a friend than the severity of an enemy, and his letters to that prince breathe a spirit of moderation which does honour to his heart. To David he had been a bounteous protector. He had granted him the honour of knighthood, extensive estates in both countries, and the hand of the daughter of the earl of Derby."

Surely the prejudice must be of an extraordinary kind which can see in this first war in Wales, and in the manner in which it was terminated, any signs of an ambitious or overreaching disposition in the conqueror. He had voluntarily given away an opportunity of making Wales his own; he had preferred to endeavour to make the two Welsh princes his friends, by heaping kindnesses and benefits upon them.

The marriage of Llewellyn and Eleanor took place on the 3rd of October, 1278, and the bride and bridegroom spent the following Christmas with the king and queen at Westminster. As this year was the seventh of Edward's reign, and affords an opportunity of a pause in the story, we will briefly notice, before we close the chapter, a few events which occurred at various intervals between the coronation in 1275 and the Welsh prince's marriage in 1278.

In the autumn of 1276, to encourage his nobility and gentry in the practices and usages of chivalry, the king held in Cheapside a grand tournament, when such an assemblage of young nobles and gallant knights was seen as England had never before witnessed.

In Advent, 1278, the king and queen were present at the consecration of the new cathedral of Norwich. This ancient church had been destroyed by fire in a riot towards the close of king Henry's reign, and nearly seven years had been occupied in its restoration. A great gathering of prelates, earls, and barons attended Edward and Eleanor on occasion of this ceremony. A few weeks later, on Easter Sunday, the king and queen visited the renowned abbey of Glastonbury, where they remained several days. On the Wednesday of Easter week there was a solemn opening, in the king's presence, of the tomb which was deemed to be that of king Arthur. Edward deposited in the tomb, which was immediately reclosed, a record of his visit and inspection.

In the autumn, this revival of the memories and traditions of the famous British king bore fruit in an attempt, on the part of Roger Mortimer, to imitate the far-famed "Round Table." In Kenilworth castle, the king and queen were entertained for ten successive days, while a hundred knights and their ladies graced the tournament in the morning and the feast in the afternoon. The loyal host was greeted, before Edward had departed, with the title of "earl of March."

The remaining history of these three or four years is of a less pleasing character. It is evident, from the records of the first seven years of this reign, that foremost among all the disorders and grievances of the time, stood the extortions of the Jews. Again and again do we meet with inquiries and regulations intended to check these evil practices. Florence of Worcester tells us, under the date of 1275, that "the Jews throughout the realm were forbidden to lend money on usury; but were in future to gain their living by commerce, under the same rules and laws as Christian merchants. They were also ordered to pay to the king an annual capitation-tax of threepence for each person."

But we see various tokens of the uneasiness caused by the extortions of these people. In October, 1274, only two months after his coronation, we find Edward issuing an order concerning the Jews; in December, 1276, another; in May, 1277, a third; and in July, 1278, a fourth. All these mandates, we may be assured, were framed by his great chancellor—a man of a just and upright purpose. But it appears as if these restraints placed upon the open practice of usury, drove the Jews to secret devices of a still more nefarious kind. In the seventh year of Edward's reign the deteriorated state of the coinage had grown to be an intolerable evil. "The nation," says Carte, "had suffered for some time from the clipping of the coin; which had raised the price of all the necessaries of life, and had almost ruined its foreign commerce. The king saw the necessity of a great reform in this direction, and his measures were such as we might have expected from the decision which marked his character. To have merely ordered a new coinage, while these nefarious practices went on, would have been useless. The first thing to be done was to strike a blow at those who were depraving the coin—a blow which should inspire terror and crush the evil at once and for ever. On one evening in November, 1276, the houses of all the Jewish money-changers were visited and their private chambers searched. On a second evening all the goldsmiths received a similar visitation. Large sums of clipped money were found, with the tools and implements used in these evil works." The criminals thus detected and apprehended were very numerous. A Special Commission was issued for the trial of these malefactors; and its sittings, commencing after the Christmas holidays, were continued until Lent, and were resumed after Easter. Between two and three hundred were convicted and sent to execution, most of whom were Jews.* A terrible example was necessary to eradicate so serious an evil. When this severe check had been given to this sort of crime, immediate measures were taken for the issue of a new coinage. Exchanges were opened in various places, at which the old coin was taken in at its value, and new money issued. "Edward," says Rapin, "is supposed to

---

* This appears to us now a punishment of terrible severity. Yet we ourselves, in the days of George III., were in the habit of hanging men in great numbers for fabricating imitative bank-notes. All our modern civilization, at the beginning of the present century, had not carried us beyond the usages of Edward's day.

be the first king that perfectly fixed the standard of our coin."

Each of the years which had passed since Edward's landing at Dover, had witnessed the assembling of a parliament. The year 1275 saw the first of these gatherings which assumed that name, and which placed upon the statute-book of England the "Statute of Westminster." In October of the same year a second meeting of the same kind took place, at which the Welsh controversy was discussed. In 1276 a parliament assembled in Westminster, another at Winchester, and, towards the end of the year, a third was held in Westminster. In the sessions held this year, 1276, three new statutes were passed—that of Bigamy, that on the Office of Coroner, and one concerning Justices. In the next year, 1277, parliament was again convened, to grant the king an aid. Throughout the Welsh controversy, as well as on all the other " hard questions" of his reign, we see the king constantly resorting to the advice of his parliament. The maxim which he avowed in a public document several years after this, seems to have governed his thoughts and actions from the very beginning of his reign— that " what concerns all, should be by all approved."

In the year 1278, the war with Wales having terminated, the king visited Worcester to witness the celebration of the nuptials of Llewellyn and young Eleanor de Montfort. He then held a parliament in the neighbouring city of Gloucester, at which the important "Statutes of Gloucester" were placed upon our statute-book. One or two of our historians have described this reign, as if the ratification of the Great Charter and of the Charter of the Forests had been wrung from the king with great difficulty, and in the hour of his necessity. But for such a representation there is no foundation whatever. In 1276, being in a state of peace and of great popular esteem, the king issued, entirely of his own accord, a proclamation for the observance of the Charter of Liberties, and the Charter of the Forests.

At the same time we see in his whole conduct abundant signs of a feeling that these documents belonged to the past; and that his office was to open to the realm and people of England views of constitutional liberty, of which no mere observance of Magna Charta, in its largest interpretation, could ever have given them any idea.

IV.

MIDDLE PERIOD OF EDWARD'S LIFE.
A.D. 1279—1290.

The prime or maturity of Edward's life was spent in works of quiet usefulness. The rebellion and reduction of Wales formed, indeed, an apparent exception; but the period of actual hostility on this occasion was very short. Edward was forced by the sudden outbreak of Llewellyn and David, to draw the sword; but it was returned to its scabbard in a very few weeks. Prejudiced historians have delighted in describing this sovereign as a man who, like the great Corsican of the beginning of the present century, was ever plotting some new acquisition; ever coveting his neighbour's possessions. But in the actual records of his reign, we see him, from his fortieth to his fifty-second year, dwelling in peace, and "thinking no evil." The only instance in which we find him in the battle-field is just ' the exception which proves the rule.' He took arms because he was assailed; because his enemy had left him no option.

His fortieth year, the eighth of his reign, was distinguished in the way in which he best loved to distinguish it—by a great act of wise and useful legislation. Doubtless we owe its authorship mainly to the counsel and the legislative skill of Robert Burnel; but we must not refuse to the king the possession of that sagacious patriotism which we shall continue to discern in his actions long after that valued counsellor had been removed from his side.

The king and his chancellor were doubtless religious men. No Wiclif, no Latimer, had yet appeared; the twilight of the mediæval times was all the light they had to guide them. But we find Edward, without any asceticism, often giving days and weeks to religious exercises. His chancellor was a bishop, but he had been a statesman and a legislator before he became a bishop, and a statesman and a legislator he remained still. Both of these clear-sighted and sagacious men saw the perilous operation of the mediæval doctrine of Purgatory, and of the assumed power of the priesthood to open and shut the doors of that fearful abode. Month after month, and year after year, estates were constantly passing into the hands of the Church, for the supposed benefit of departed souls. The king himself could not throw off this belief, nor abstain from following in the practice which was universal in his day. When his beloved Eleanor was taken from him, we instantly hear of various manors given to the priests of Westminster for a long succession of masses to be said for the benefit of the poor queen's soul. And we may be sure that a delusion which ruled over so powerful a mind as the king's, was universal among his people, and that no man who had really loved his lost wife or parents would be backward in showing his solicitude by such donations of land or money as he could afford, " for their soul's benefit." As the Church was thus constantly receiving and never restoring, it seemed inevitable that in process of time it must become the sole landlord in the realm.

Hume tells us of one period when the clergy held one-third of the lands of the kingdom; and it is easy to perceive that had no Reformation occurred—had no violent redistribution taken place—that course of continual addition and accumulation must have left, by this time, very few estates in England in lay hands. The king saw this tendency, and he desired to check it. But he would not wrong the Church by any act of tyranny. He himself shared in the ordinary belief, and, as we have just said, when his queen was taken from him, he gave, like other men, large estates " for the good of her soul." But, while he questioned not the right of men in full possession of their faculties thus to deal with their own property, he saw an evident and a perilous abuse, grafted on this general belief and practice. Men in their latest hours—men, whose minds were clouded or prostrated by disease—bequeathed, they scarce knew what, out of sheer terror, or, in some cases, at the demand or dictation of some priest, who was zealous for " the good of holy Church." In all probability, Edward had heard the complaints of disinherited wives or children, who found their hereditary possessions suddenly wrested from them, and who knew that the expiring parent who had, they were told, so willed, was, for hours or days before his departure, scarcely conscious of the meaning of his own words or actions. Here, then, without interfering with the main question—the usual and generally admitted theory—was an evident and a very serious abuse.

A parliament was held in Westminster, in November, 1279, at which a great statute was passed—the far-famed law of *Mortmain*. It must have been passed in the presence and by the consent—apparent at least—of many prelates, whose desires " for the good of holy Church " it contravened. But the ascendancy of such a mind and will as that of Edward,—the legislative authority of the great chancellor, and the support, doubtless, of the earls and barons by whom the king was surrounded, prevailed; and the Church was compelled to submit to this limitation. Henceforth no man should be allowed " with dying hands " to will away his possessions " to holy Church." All such bequests were declared to be illegal and void. No more necessary statute could have been passed; and from that day to this—from 1279 to 1870—all England has honoured the name of the wise sovereign who devised and established the law of Mortmain.

Soon after this, Edward, finding all things at peace at home, paid a short visit to the continent. The death of the queen of Castile transferred to her daughter Eleanor, Edward's consort, the county of Ponthieu; and to obtain seizin of this territory, and to do homage for it, he visited the king of France at Amiens, where, however, his stay was but short. He brought back with him to England some fine jasper stones, which became part of the costly monument he was raising in the church of Westminster to the memory of the king his father. Not long after his return he found it necessary to repress some of the lofty pretensions of "holy Church." John Peckham, who had succeeded Kilwardby in the see of Canterbury, had convened a synod at Reading, in which various canons were adopted, tending to separate ecclesiastics and ecclesiastical property from the laity and their possessions, and to exempt them from the operation of the statute and common law. These attempts, fostered by such churchmen as Dunstan and A'Becket, had long been perplexing all the governments of Christendom. We shall meet with them, again and again, throughout this king's reign. But Edward was both clear-sighted and resolute, and we cannot doubt that his chancellor, though himself a prelate, supported him. The archbishop was at once called before a council, and commanded to revoke and cancel all canons which assumed or pretended to set aside the laws and ordinances of the realm.

Ireland began now to claim a share in the king's attention, and we may reasonably regret that the affairs of

Wales soon drew his thoughts another way. The fame of the enlightened legislation now going on in England had probably reached Ireland; for a petition was sent over to the king that they might be allowed the benefit of the English laws. They tendered, as a customary fine, or " benevolence," the sum of 8000 marks for the enjoyment of this privilege. Edward's disposition must have been, to comply at once with this request; but we shall find him, through his whole life, abstaining from all arbitrary or sudden decisions, and referring all public questions to his council or parliament. He wrote, therefore, to Robert de Clifford, chief justiciary of Ireland, desiring that steps might be taken to comply with the prayer of the petition. Some sort of an assembly or parliament was convened for the consideration of the question. But arbitrary power always finds some advocates, for there are never wanting persons who can turn it to their own advantage. The chief men in Ireland raised objections, and succeeded in postponing compliance with the king's wishes. Edward wrote a second time, in displeasure, ordering another council or parliament to be convened. But Wales now began to claim his attention, and the opponents of a wise and just policy in Ireland succeeded in their policy of procrastination.

The Principality had now remained at peace for more than four years. But there were various reasons for Welsh discontent. The king had established his authority on the border, and had put an end to those plundering inroads which had troubled the English frontier for many preceding years. To be thus kept in check would naturally vex and annoy the half-civilized tribes who had delighted, for half a century past, in burning and ravaging the farms and hamlets of the English frontier. "Edward," says Carte, "had thrown his newly-acquired territory into districts, had appointed sheriffs, and sent judges to administer justice. These things were not agreeable to the Welsh. They did not like counties or hundreds, courts or juries, or any institution, however beneficial, that was derived from England; —in fact, being used to a roving, disorderly, and plundering sort of life, they did not care to be kept in order." Both Llewellyn and David had also private grievances. The elder brother had a suit against Griffith Gwenwynn for some lands, and he was summoned to the hearing of the cause at Montgomery, which he deemed a great indignity. David was sued by one Venables, before the chief justice of Chester, touching the villages of Hope and Eston. Irritated by these proceedings, the two brothers made up their quarrel, and on Palm Sunday in March, 1282, David surprised the castle of Hawarden, seizing Roger de Clifford in his bed, wounding him, and carrying him off a prisoner, while several of the English garrison were put to the sword. The news of this sudden outbreak was carried to the king, who was keeping Easter at Devizes. Other messengers soon followed with the intelligence that Llewellyn had joined his brother, that the castles of Flint and Rhuddlan were besieged, and that the Welsh were rising in every quarter. Edward sent off immediately all the force he had with him to the relief of the besieged castles, and issued orders for the rendezvous of his military tenants at Worcester on the 17th of May. Before that time he had himself moved forward, and finding the insurrection to be growing general, he gave orders for a larger levy than he had at first intended; ordering his tenants to meet him at Rhuddlan on the 2nd of August. Llewellyn and his brother retired on his approach, taking refuge in the fastnesses of Snowdon. The king took the same precaution as in 1277, by sending a fleet to occupy Anglesea, which island at once submitted, and the possession of which enclosed Llewellyn on every side. Meanwhile, the archbishop of Canterbury visited the Welsh prince and tried to bring him to submission, but all attempts of the kind were fruitless. Llewellyn handed in a list of grievances, which were just such as might have been anticipated. "The four cantreds" between Chester and Conway, formerly the scene of continual strife, had now been ceded, by the treaty of 1277, to Edward, and the English laws had been established there. These laws were distasteful to the Welsh. By their own laws, such offences as murder or arson might be withdrawn from the courts by a payment to the chief lord of a fine of five pounds; but the English judges hanged such offenders. No doubt, some provocation had been given, some injuries inflicted, on both sides. But Llewellyn, who had twice been Edward's guest at Westminster, ought to have appealed to him for redress of any positive wrong. He might have known that it was not the king's habit to justify ill-doing. But the Welsh preferred to draw the sword, and now, when the archbishop strove to mediate, he found them obstinate and unbending.

At the outset of the war Edward had stormed and taken Hope Castle, had relieved Flint and Rhuddlan, and had driven Llewellyn back into the recesses of Snowdon. In November the English met with a disaster at the Menai Straits. They had constructed a bridge of boats, and a sudden attack of the Welsh, who rushed down with loud cries, created a panic; a rush was made for the bridge, it gave way, and thirteen knights and about two hundred men were lost in the waters.

Elated at this success, Llewellyn thought that as the bridge was destroyed, Snowdon was now safe for the winter, and he moved down into Cardiganshire, intending to rally and succour his friends in South Wales. Here, on the 10th of December, near Builth in Radnorshire, he came in contact with a party of the English, and one of them, Adam Francton, ran him through with a spear, in ignorance of his person or quality. After lying in the field some time, his body was searched, and his private signet and certain papers made his person known. His head was cut off and sent to the king, who, according to the custom of the period, ordered it to be sent to London and set up over the gate of the Tower.

The death of their prince seems to have so discouraged the Welsh that all opposition ceased, and Edward took quiet possession of the forfeited principality. From that day forward, England and Wales became one ;—subject to the same laws and ruled over by the same government. "This incorporation," says Mr. Sharon Turner, "was an unquestionable blessing to Wales. That country ceased to be the theatre of homicide and distress, and began to imitate the English habits. It was at once divided into counties, placed under sheriffs, and admitted to a participation in the more important of the English institutions."

The wretched beginner of this second Welsh controversy, David of Snowdon, contrived, for several months, to lead the life of an outlaw, and to evade the search of his pursuers. This unyielding contumacy completed his ruin. Had he frankly and immediately submitted to the conqueror, and besought mercy, all that we know of Edward assures us that his life, at least, would have been spared. But he remained an outlaw, and obdurate; until, after a concealment of several months, some of his own people seized and surrendered him. Then, when no choice remained, and when submission had no merit, he entreated to see the king. But

Edward doubted the propriety of granting forgiveness, and therefore refused to allow him an interview.

No one who has read the history of the ten or twelve succeeding reigns can doubt that such an offender as this David would, at any time in the fourteenth or fifteenth centuries, been quickly taken before some convenient tribunal and sent to the scaffold. He was an English subject; he had accepted wealth and honour at Edward's hands, and had then requited his benefactor by raising a rebellion and causing a civil war. At no period of our history, even in the gentle reign of Victoria, could such acts have escaped the highest degree of punishment.

But Edward, while he showed, throughout, his sense of the gravity of David's offence, never inflicted punishment in haste or in a passionate spirit. It is also a remarkable feature of his character that, though a man of unusual firmness and decision, and fitted above most men to act on his own judgment, he never found himself in the presence of any question of gravity, without instantly desiring to have it discussed in a council or parliament, or by conference with others. David's guilt and the gravity of his offence were abundantly evident, but the question of the extent of his punishment Edward desired to leave with some legal tribunal. He resolved to remit the whole subject to the decision of a parliament, and to summon that parliament to meet in Shrewsbury in October, 1283;—David having been given up to him in the course of June.

This "parliament of Shrewsbury" was one of a novel kind. It had two new features, and it seems to have held its sittings by adjournment, in two different places. Edward desired that the case of David should be considered and decided in a council. This was the first object of the assembling of that parliament. But his chancellor had seen the necessity of a new statute on commercial questions, and the framing of this statute formed the next matter for consideration.

As the first question would be a trial on which life or death depended, the king summoned no prelates to this parliament; probably feeling that in the discussion of such matters it was desirable that the clergy should take no part. The second subject to be brought under discussion was one relating to trade and commerce, and the king saw in it an opportunity of giving more form and substance than heretofore to that idea which had never been absent from his mind,—that, in a well-constituted parliament, "the lower as well as the higher estate" should be represented.

We have already said that we cannot doubt that, in the first parliament of Westminster, some citizens, under the name of " the commonalty of the realm," were present; but we find no record of any formal summoning of burgesses or borough-representatives. Now, however, the chancellor had a particular statute, relating to trade, to bring forward, and now, therefore, he could advise the king to summon, from the city of London and from twenty other great towns, from each two representatives, " de sapientioribus et aptioribus," for the consideration and discussion of the said statute. Here we have the real commencement of the borough representation of England. Let Simon de Montfort have all the merit which can justly be attributed to him, for having, in 1265, called to a council in Westminster some burgesses or borough-representatives:—that fact must always be taken with two qualifications: first, that earl Simon needed these borough-representatives to fill the empty benches, only five earls and seventeen barons attending at his call; and secondly, that that council was not what we now understand by the term, a "parliament,"—no legislation being attempted in it.

Some historians have been too ready to assume or assert, on all occasions, that our free constitution has been won by the repeated struggles of the people, who succeeded in wresting from their sovereigns one privilege after another. The whole course of Edward's government clears him from any imputation of this kind. At the opening of his political life, when he stood as a victorious leader at the head of an army, we find him again and again asserting the principle, that in a well-constituted parliament all classes should be represented; and now, when he orders these writs to be issued for the summoning of forty-two borough representatives to Shrewsbury, it is wholly of his own free will, and without the slightest "pressure of circumstances," that he acts. His chancellor feels the want of a new law for the regulation of commerce, and at once the idea seems to occur, and is forthwith acted upon, "Let all the principal towns, where the merchants and traders dwell—let them send representatives to this parliament, and let the new statute be passed with their help and in their presence."

The parliament of Shrewsbury met on the 30th of September, 1283, in that town. The business to be done consisted, first, of a criminal trial, and, secondly, of a statute on commercial matters. No prelates, as we have said, were summoned. To bring them from many distant places to Shrewsbury would have imposed upon them much trouble and expense, and for no fitting end. The persons summoned were—eleven earls, ninety-nine barons, two knights for each county, and two citizens from each of twenty-one great towns; and the writs themselves expressed, with all Edward's usual frankness, the purpose and the desire with which he called together this, the first complete parliament, though still in outline, that England ever saw. They remind the barons, knights, and citizens that they had seen " how Llewellyn and David his brother, spurning the obligations of fidelity into which they had entered, had, more treacherously than usual, suddenly set fire to villages, slain some of the inhabitants, burnt others, and shut up others in prison, savagely shedding innocent blood." The king desires those to whom the writs were directed to come to Shrewsbury on the day indicated, " there to determine what ought to be done with the said David, whom we received when an exile, nourished when an orphan, and enriched out of our own lands, placing him among the nobles of our court." " We charge you, therefore," the king concludes, " to meet us at Shrewsbury, on the day after the feast of St. Michael, to confer upon this and upon other matters."

Before this parliament, then, was David of Snowdon impeached. " He was tried," says the chronicle of Dunstable, " by the whole baronage of England." It is quite clear that Edward desired that others, and not himself, should decide upon the fate of the unhappy man. He appears to have retired to his chancellor's residence of Acton Burnel, and to have taken no part in these proceedings. The trial was entered upon, and, according to the custom of those days, the criminal was arraigned for several crimes, and for each crime a distinct punishment was ordered. As a traitor to the king, David was to be drawn to the place of execution; as the murderer of certain knights in Hawarden Castle, he was to be hanged; having sacrilegiously committed these crimes on Palm Sunday, he was to be disembowelled; and having conspired the death of the king in various places, he was to be quartered.*

---

* " Seldom," says Mr. Pearson, " has a shameful and violent death been better merited than by a double-dyed traitor like David, false by turns to his

This sentence, deliberately passed, was carried into effect, and many have been the exclamations of modern writers at its cruelty. One of the most moderate of these critics condemns Edward for " permitting his nobles and lawyers to devise and carry into effect such a barbarous sentence." In like manner is he censured for ordering Llewellyn's head to be set up over the gate of the Tower.

Such writers forget that a man must be judged, not by the ideas or usages of other times, but by those of the age in which he has been brought up and has lived. In our day, the thought of setting up a gory head over Temple Bar would horrify all men. But when the last rebellion was suppressed in England, little more than a century ago, the government of which lords Hardwicke and Chatham were members, beheaded men on Kennington Common, and sent their heads to Carlisle, to be set up over the castle-gates. Johnson and Goldsmith, Cowper and Whitfield, were accustomed to see human heads on Temple-Bar as they passed up and down Fleet Street.

The mutilation of the criminal's body is another feature of the case which shocks our modern notions, but it was a prevalent custom of those times. In 1238, before Edward was born, a man was found lurking in the palace, who confessed that his object was to kill the king. He had been guilty of no overt act, yet for this treasonable design he was sentenced first to be dragged asunder by horses, then to be beheaded, and his body to be divided into three parts, to be exposed in three cities.

Nor were these mutilations ordered in criminal cases

country and his king; nor could justice be better honoured than by making the last penalty of rebellion fall upon the guilty prince, rather than on his followers."
—" History of England," vol. ii., p. 330.

only. Robert Bruce, like many others, ordered his heart to be taken out after his death and carried to the Holy Land. Edward himself, if ever a man loved a wife, dearly loved his Eleanor. Yet, on her death, he ordered her heart to be interred in the church of the Black Friars, her bowels in Lincoln Minster, and the rest of her body in Westminster Abbey. Such were the habits and modes of feeling when a king could sleep in the open air on the night before a battle; when the gory head of an earl was thought a fitting present for a noble lady; and when even friendly sports often ended in slaughter.

"Sir Patrick Graham, a Scottish knight, having arrived from Paris, was invited to supper; and in the midst of the feast, an English knight turning to him, courteously asked him to run with him three courses. Next morning in the first course, Graham struck the English knight through the harness with a mortal wound, so that he died on the spot. Such were the fierce pastimes of those days." *

The sentence passed on David, then, and the exposure of Llewellyn's head, were merely the ordinary modes of procedure in those times; and would no more strike Edward as cruel, than like sentences inflicted on the adherents of the Stuarts seemed cruel to the kings and statesmen of the last century. Hume, however, tries to exaggerate the fact in the case of David, by styling him "a sovereign prince." This, however, is a fiction. Llewellyn did not die childless, and David was, neither in law nor in fact, his successor. And even had David been the next heir, there was no succession for him. Llewellyn, as vassal to the English crown, had committed treason, had forfeited his fief, and the superior lord was entering into possession. David was nothing more than an English lord; and as a subject to

* Tytler's History of Scotland, vol. i., p. 431.

Edward he had been guilty of open treason—treason against a sovereign who had been his benefactor. The justice of his sentence was altogether unimpeachable; the manner of his execution was merely conformable to the customs of those times. Both sentence and execution were dictated by the parliament, the king being merely an assenting party.

This, however, does not quite end the history of the two Welsh princes. Edward was ever a merciful and compassionate king, and having allowed justice to have its course with regard to the principal criminals, he did not forget that they both had children. We find a letter written by him on the 11th of November, 1283, to the prior and prioress of Alvingham, in the following terms:—

"Albeit, if we should turn our mind to past events, and should regard somewhat closely the deserts of certain persons, we should scarcely be bound to succour the children of Llewellyn, prince of Wales, or of David his brother, whose perfidy is fresh in the memory of all; nevertheless having the fear of God before our eyes, and compassionating their sex and age, lest perchance the innocent and unconscious should seem to pay the penalties of the crimes of the impious—we, from regard to charity, have thought fit in wholesome sort to make provision for them. Wherefore, being persuaded of your devotion, and specially considering the conversation of your order, we beseech you, brethren, that you admit to your order, and the habit of your house, any one or more of the said children of Llewellyn and David his brother, whom we shall name to you; and that you intimate to us what you shall think fit to do in this matter, before the feast of the Nativity next ensuing. Given under our private seal at Ludlow, on the 11th day of November."

Of the result of the application to the priory of Alvingham we find no record. But in the tenth year of Edward II. we find Wenciliana, a daughter of Llewellyn, spoken of as a nun of Sempringham; and we find her, also, receiving a pension of £20 a year (equal to £300 in the present day). Peter Langtoft speaks of her as personally known to him, and he mentions her death in June, 1337. He also mentions " her cousin Gladous, daughter of David," who was a nun at Sixille house, and who died in 1336. Evidently, "the innocent" were not left to suffer.

The first portion of the business allotted to the parliament of Shrewsbury had now been gone through; but the second remained. And, whether it was that the scene of an execution was not thought suitable for festivity, or that the chancellor wished to exhibit a noble hospitality, we cannot decide, but a removal of the parliament evidently took place. We find it sitting on the 12th of October, at Acton Burnel, the chancellor's home; and there was passed the Statute of Merchants, denominated by Lord Campbell " that famous law," " that most admirable statute." It doubtless had cost the chancellor much thought, and he piobably wished to connect his name with it. Accordingly it is sometimes called " the Statute of Acton Burnel."

So ended the year 1283; but the king had still a great work before him—a work of the kind in which he most delighted. Wales had been finally and entirely united to England; but it was still in an almost barbarous condition. The whole country was a scene of wildness and disorder, and Edward knew well that the first step in the regeneration of a country (so far as human government can regenerate it), is the establishment of just and well-considered laws. To this work, therefore, he immediately addressed himself. He did not, however, proceed as many would have done, by rashly ordaining that the laws of England should be henceforth the laws of Wales. He saw the necessity for first acquainting himself with the whole subject. "He was at great pains to gain a perfect knowledge of its ancient constitution and laws, and of the manners of its inhabitants."

With this view, he issued a commission to the bishop of St. David's and some others, to investigate these matters in the most careful manner. No fewer than one hundred and seventy-two intelligent persons were examined upon oath by these commissioners, who, upon this evidence, framed a report. Having thus obtained the necessary information, Edward held a parliament on the 24th of May, 1284, at Rhuddlan, in Flintshire, at which the "Statutes of Wales" were passed. The preamble to these statutes runs as follows:—

"The Divine Providence having now, of its favour, wholly transferred to our dominion the land of Wales, with its inhabitants, heretofore subject to us in feudal right, all obstacles ceasing; and having annexed and united the same unto the crown of the aforesaid realm, as a member of the same body; we therefore, under the Divine Will, being desirous that our aforesaid land should be governed with due order, to the honour and praise of God, and of holy Church, and the advancement of justice; and that the people of those lands who have submitted themselves to our will should be protected in security, under fixed laws and customs, have caused to be rehearsed before us and the nobles of our realm, the laws and customs in those parts hitherto in use; which, having fully understood, we have, by the advice of the said nobles, abolished some of them, some we have allowed, and some we have corrected; and we have commanded and ordained certain others to be added thereto."

It is in deeds and words like these that we see Edward in his real character. It was in such works that, in his hours of free choice, he always preferred to employ himself. Legislation—the taking care "that the people of these lands should be protected in security, under fixed laws and customs," " as becometh the office of a king:" this was his chosen employment. War might sometimes, as in the case of Wales, be forced upon him; but whenever it was so forced, "slowe to strife" was a rule which marked his every action.

He saw the necessity for a considerable stay in Wales for the thorough pacification and regulation of the country. He began at once the erection of the noble castle of Carnarvon. This work occupied several years. In 1283 queen Eleanor kept her court in Rhuddlan Castle, but in 1284, a portion of the castle at Carnarvon being completed, she removed thither, and on the 25th of April she gave birth, in a chamber of the Eagle Tower, which is still shown, to a prince—afterwards king Edward II. The king was at this time at Rhuddlan Castle, engaged in affairs of state. A Welsh gentleman, named Griffith Lloyd, was announced, who brought him the intelligence of the birth of a prince. Edward, in great joy, knighted Lloyd on the spot, making him a grant of lands. He soon hastened to Carnarvon to see his Eleanor and her son; and when a few days had elapsed, he was able to present to the Welsh chiefs "a prince born in Wales, and who could not speak a word of English."

He had now remained in Wales for more than two years, and the great work of union, and the establishment of peace, and the reign of law, seemed to be solidly advancing. At Newyn, in Carnarvonshire, in the summer of 1284, Edward held a grand tournament, with the usual festivities. Here were assembled, says Matthew of Westminster, "the great body of the knights of England, with many foreign nobles."

So splendid a spectacle was, at least, calculated to show the chiefs and gentry of Wales that the nation with which they had been incorporated was no mean one, and that the sovereign they had gained was a chief of might and power.

So ended the king's transactions in Wales in 1282, 1283, and 1284, and in the autumn of the latter year he proceeded slowly through Cardiganshire and Glamorganshire, reaching Bristol before the end of the year, and celebrating Christmas in that city.

So ends the brief history of the union of Wales with England. This war had been forced upon Edward, who evidently had no option in the matter. It was soon ended, and a single criminal—he who had caused the war—was the only victim claimed by the scaffold. The king's slowness and long deliberation show also that, could any reasonable plea for mercy have been found, even David himself would have been spared. A rather severe judge of Edward's whole career, says, of the annexation : " Never was conquest more merciful." * Yet some of the Scottish historians, while they endeavour to assume an air of impartiality when they speak of Edward's Scottish controversies, are eager to create a prejudice against him by giving the darkest complexion to his acts in Wales. Thus Hume, in narrating this portion of Edward's career, calmly tells us that " The king, sensible that nothing kept alive the ideas of military valour and of ancient glory so much as the traditional poetry of the people, which, assisted by the power of music and the jollity of festivals, made a deep impression on the minds of the youth, gathered together all the Welsh bards, and, from a barbarous but not absurd policy, ordered them to be put to death." And Gray, accepting the fiction as a fact, clothed it in noble

* Pearson's Hist. of England, vol. ii., p. 336.

verse, and his ode beginning " Ruin seize thee, ruthless king," fixed the alleged crime in the memory of every school-boy and school-girl in the realm.

And yet the whole charge was a mere calumny. These bards, who were said to have been extirpated, continued to sing and to write in such sort that " Mr. Owen Jones, in forming a collection of their productions, *after the time of Edward*, had to transcribe between fifty and sixty quarto volumes"; and "the work of transcription," said Sir Richard Hoare, " was not even then completed." *

A later Scottish historian than Hume—Sir James Mackintosh—admits the falsity of the charge. He says, " The massacre of the bards is an act of cruelty imputed to Edward *without evidence*, and it is inconsistent with his spirit, which was not infected by wanton ferocity."

Such an act as this slaughter, had it ever been committed, would have been nothing less than atrocious. But if so, what are we to say of a writer who coolly ascribes it to a king whom he dislikes, knowing that he is asserting it " without evidence," and in the teeth of such a practical refutation as Sir Richard Hoare has pointed out?

England was now again at peace, and with the assured prospect that the strife which had so long infested her western border was at last permanently ended. " The conquest of Wales," says Rapin, " and the universal esteem in which the king was held among his subjects, produced in England a profound tranquillity." Hence, as several questions of importance called Edward abroad, he began, about this time, to prepare for a visit of some length to various parts of the continent.

A singular application had been made to him while engaged in the affairs of Wales. Two princes—Peter of

* Hoare's edit. of Giraldus Cambrensis.

Aragon and Charles of Anjou—had each advanced a claim to the crown of Sicily. An appeal to arms appeared inevitable, when it was suggested by Charles, and agreed to by Peter, that they should decide the question by *single combat*. Arrangements were seriously made; twelve commissioners were appointed on each side, and these twenty-four drew up articles, which were afterwards ratified by both the princes. It was agreed that the combat should take place at Bourdeaux, whither the combatants were to repair on a certain day appointed, each to be accompanied by one hundred knights. But as all parties agreed in regarding Edward as standing at the head of the chivalry of Europe, it was made an essential point in the agreement that he should act as the umpire, and that the combat should take place in his presence.

These two princes had regarded Edward, evidently, as one of the same race with him of " the lion heart," who would, no doubt, have delighted in such a scheme. They thought of the English king as a man known to be "mighty in arms," and who had taken part in most of the great tournaments of his time. But they had overlooked, or not understood, that this was only the inferior part of his character; and that his nobler aspect was his wisdom, his statesmanlike sagacity, and, what a modern historian calls, " his legislative mind." The proposal, when made to Edward, only struck him as being eminently absurd. He was fond of martial sports and deeds of chivalry, but he had never dreamed that the affairs of the world could be carried on by tournaments. Questions concerning kingly rights and disputed successions were handled by him in courts and parliaments, on the ground of truth, and justice, and established law, with a deliberateness which disregarded the lapse of months and years. To leave such matters to be decided by, perchance, the possession of the strongest horse or the toughest spear, was not to be for a moment thought of. His instant reply was, "that if he were to gain by it both the kingdoms of Aragon and Sicily, he would not appoint the field of battle, or suffer the two princes to fight in any place within his dominions, nor in any other place, if it were in his power to hinder it." But he accompanied his refusal with offers of friendly mediation, which were afterwards carried into effect.

This frank and decided negative frustrated the whole plan, and Edward was soon requested to undertake a more pacific arrangement. In fact, throughout this whole affair, this sovereign of the mediæval times seems to have acted much as any modern king of sense and proper feeling would now act. To understand distinctly how great a superiority this implied over the prejudices and habits of thought of his own time, we should recal to mind the fact that, more than two centuries after Edward's day, two such monarchs as Charles V. and Francis I. actually contemplated, for a considerable time, a settlement of their disputes by this same absurd method of a royal combat! In truth, in this, as in many other passages of his life, Edward evinced the possession, as it were by intuition, of all the practical wisdom which the experience of nearly six centuries has given to the public men of our own day.

The king had now returned from Wales, and had received an urgent invitation from Philip of France to visit him at Amiens, in order that they might consult on the subject of this dispute. He accordingly set out on this journey, and had reached Canterbury, on his way to Dover, when tidings reached him of the illness of his mother, queen Eleanor of Provence, at the convent of Ambresbury, in Wiltshire. A messenger was immediately despatched to Amiens, with a letter of apology, and Edward forthwith turned his steps towards the west. On her recovery the king paid a religious visit to the abbey of St. Edmund's-bury, and spent a part of the season of Lent in this retreat.

On the 25th of March, 1285, a parliament was held at Westminster, at which the "Statutes of Westminster II." were adopted. "These statutes," says Delolme, "are the foundations of much of the law of the land, as it now stands." "They were framed," says Lord Campbell, "in a spirit of enlightened legislation, and admirably accommodated the law to the changed circumstances of the social system; which ought to be the object of every wise legislator."

In October, another parliament was held at Winchester, at which the "Statute of Winchester" was passed. This important enactment established an effective system of "watch and ward," for the protection of life and property; which, from the laxity prevalent through all the previous reign, had come to be greatly needed.

Two other parliaments appear to have been held in Westminster, in February and May, 1286;—in fact, it seems to have been Edward's desire to hold, whenever practicable, three or four such meetings in each year. Now, as he very seldom, in the first twenty years of his reign, had any occasion to ask his people for money, his object in thus frequently meeting his parliament must have been that of a frank and unrestrained interchange of thought and feeling as to public affairs. This was a characteristic feature of the king's mind. Weak sovereigns and hesitating statesmen always *fear* a parliament, and are eager for its separation and departure. But Edward knew nothing of fear, and he had one of the most transparent of minds. Even when vehemently thwarted and opposed, as by archbishop Winchelsey and earls Bigod and Bohun, his first thought generally was to send for his opponents to come to him, for that "the king wished to have a private colloquium with them." In the present case there was no quarrel or difference of opinion; but, in all probability, the chief matter for discussion was the king's intended visit to the continent, and the measures to be adopted for carrying on the government in his absence.

Not until the summer of that year was he able to take his departure. On the 24th of June, 1286, he embarked, accompanied by his queen, and attended by a splendid train of bishops, earls, barons, and knights. He was received with due honour by king Philip, and was conducted to St. Germain's, where he remained for several weeks. Many important questions required to be discussed by these two potent sovereigns. There were various claims, some of which had been long undecided, on the part of the crown of England, on Normandy, Limousin, Saintonge, etc.; there was homage to be paid for possessions in France, to king Philip; and there was the difficult question, in which Edward had consented to act as umpire between the houses of Aragon and Anjou, touching the crown of Sicily.

The various questions arising out of the disputed territory in Normandy, Limousin, Saintonge, etc., occupied much time. France, now strong and at peace, felt no disposition to relinquish one foot of territory. On this point Philip was immoveable; and Edward, though equally warlike with his grandson, the victor of Crecy, felt none of the ambitious longings of Edward III. for conquests in France, nor any desire for such barren honours as those of Agincourt or Poictiers. He brought the various topics of discussion to a peaceful settlement; accepting an annual payment in lieu of some territory which Philip was unwilling to relinquish, and gaining, on the other hand, a concession of the right of appeal as regarded Gascony.

Quitting the court of France so soon as these discussions were concluded, Edward passed on to Bourdeaux, where many things required his presence and his decision. But the chief affair which had brought him to the continent remained now to be adjusted; and, like many similar questions referred to the decision of a third party, it opened a nearly interminable controversy. The two chiefs, the king of Aragon and the count of Anjou, were equally unworthy of Edward's solicitude. He found it very difficult to effect any arrangement, and a task still more hopeless to induce them to keep their engagements when made. Like the English barons in 1263, who agreed to refer their dispute with Henry III. to the arbitration of Louis of France, meaning to abide by his decision only so far as suited their own purposes,—the two combatants in the present case could in no way be made to carry out their own pledges, or to submit to the decision which they had professed to desire. Edward succeeded at last in making a treaty which restored the prince of Salerno, Charles's son, to his liberty; but as soon as he had returned home, the two rivals treated the rest of their engagements with mutual disregard.

The king and queen landed at Dover in August, 1289, and Edward's first acts were of a religious nature. He had experienced, while abroad, deliverances of a more than ordinary kind. For several weeks he had suffered from a dangerous illness, from which, however, he had now entirely recovered. And on one occasion, while at Bourdeaux, a flash of lightning entering the room in which he and the queen were sitting, killed two of the attendants, while the king and his consort remained untouched. We have already stated that, after the manner of those times, Edward was a most religious king.' Very naturally, therefore, his first thought on landing was to pay a visit to the abbey of St. Edmund's-bury, there to perform "the vows made while he was in trouble."

But his presence, and his strong right arm, were soon demanded by various public necessities. His absence had naturally tended to give opportunity for lawless practices, both among the higher and the lower classes. The excellent "Statute of Winchester," made not long before his departure to the continent, had been scarcely brought into operation. Bands of outlaws concealed themselves in the forests, and waylaid travellers. Often they proceeded to still greater lengths. During a fair held at Boston in Lincolnshire, Thomas Chamberlain, a man of some note, had set fire to the town, hoping, with his associates, to take advantage of the confusion and to pillage the place. He himself was taken and hanged, but none of his accomplices were discovered. And the root of these disorders lay deep, and in a quarter which ought to have been beyond suspicion. The judges of the land were corrupt, and for bribes would release the robber and the murderer. The archbishop of Canterbury, who probably greeted the king on his landing, acquainted him with these disorders, and made known to him their secret cause. Edward lost no time in acting with his accustomed energy and vigour.

On the 13th of October, the king celebrated the feast of St. Edward, and on the same day obeyed the injunctions of the prophet (Isa. lviii. 6) by issuing a proclamation, that all persons who had been aggrieved or oppressed by the judges or other ministers should come before him at the ensuing parliament, and exhibit their complaints. The result showed that the people put their trust in the king, and felt assured that his promise would be kept. A fearful case was established against the judges; and the chancellor, Burnel, whose whole course commands our respect, "brought forward very serious charges against those high functionaries for taking bribes and altering the records." All except two—John de Metingham and Elias de Bokingham—were convicted. The chief baron Stratton was fined 34,000 marks; the chief justice of the king's bench, 7000 marks; the master of the rolls, 1000 marks; while Weyland, the chief justice of the common pleas, who was the greatest delinquent, fled to the convent of the Friars Minor at Bury St. Edmunds, where he took sanctuary. The king, when informed of this, sent a knight with a guard, not to violate the sanctuary, but to blockade it till the judge should surrender. After holding out for two months, Weyland submitted, and petitioned for leave to abjure the realm. This, which involved the forfeiture of all his goods, was granted to him; and his property, when taken possession of, was found to amount to 100,000 marks —"an almost incredible sum," says Blackstone, being, indeed, equal to about *one million sterling* at the present day. Nothing could more fully establish the guilt of the accused judge, or more strikingly show the enormous extent to which his criminal practices had been carried.

"These sentences," says lord Campbell, "had on the whole a very salutary effect." The example was a terrible one; yet in our own day we have seen heavier sentences, such as transportation or penal servitude, inflicted for lighter offences. The king, however, immediately added a new precaution, by ordering that, in future, every judge on his appointment should take an oath to accept no gift or gratuity from any one.

Another class of offenders was about the same time

brought under the notice of the king and his parliament. Dr. Henry says, "The Jews seem to have taken occasion, from the king's absence and the venality of the judges, to push their exactions to a greater length than ever; and the cry against them was now become so vehement and universal, that the parliament which assembled at Westminster on the 12th of January, 1290, came to a resolution to banish the whole race out of the kingdom."

Rapin adds, "The king was unable any longer to protect them without disobliging the parliament. They had enjoyed various privileges, such as synagogues in London, a sort of high priest, and judges of their own nation to decide on their own differences. These advantages they lost by not being able to curb their insatiable greediness of enriching themselves by unlawful means, such as usury, adulteration of the coin, and the like." Another writer cites a complaint of their exactions, which shows that they were in the habit of requiring from forty to sixty-five per cent. for the use of money; a system which would naturally and very quickly be felt to be intolerable.

Hence their entire expulsion was resolved upon, and ordered. It was not an act of "religious intolerance," but a result of popular indignation. In effecting this, the impatient exultation of the people led them in some cases to actual ill treatment of the Jews. The sailors of a ship in which some of them had embarked placed them upon a sandbank at low water, and left them to be drowned. The king ordered the perpetrators of this crime to be brought to trial, and on their conviction capital punishment followed.

In a parliament held on the 8th of July, 1290, "several important statutes were made;" and gradually, but constantly, the idea of *legislation* by a *parliament* took root, grew, and became fixed in the English mind. The writs for this parliament command the sheriffs to send from their respective counties two or three knights, with full powers, "ad consulendum et consentiendum his quæ comites, barones et proceres, tum duxerint concordanda."* When assembled, it placed upon the statute-book the statutes "de Consultatione," "de Quo Warranto," "Quia Emptores," and those of "Westminster III."

In the spring and summer of this year, 1290, queen Eleanor had the satisfaction of witnessing the marriage of two of her daughters. The princess Joanna, born at Acre, and now in her eighteenth year, was united on the last day of April, in the monastery of St. John, Clerkenwell, to Gilbert de Clare, earl of Gloucester, the most powerful peer in England; and on the 9th of July, in Westminster Abbey, Margaret, the queen's third daughter, was married to John, duke of Brabant. One of the young princesses, Mary, had in the preceding year followed the example of her grandmother, Eleanor of Provence, and had taken the veil in the convent of Ambresbury, where the old queen had long resided.

Of the frank and cordial manners of the court, and of the harmony subsisting between the king and his consort, we catch a few indications from the remaining records. Thus we find that on Easter Monday, 1290, seven of the queen's ladies of honour invaded the king's private chamber to perform the feat customary on that holiday,† of "heaving" or lifting the monarch in his chair; and from their hands he was only released on paying a fine of forty shillings to each, to be set at liberty. On another occasion, while the king and his attendants were saddling and mounting

---

* Parry's History of Parliaments, p. 54.

† This custom still exists, after the lapse of more than five hundred years, in some of the midland counties of England.

for the chase at Fingringhoe in Essex, the king espies Matilda of Waltham, his laundress, among the lookers-on in the court-yard. He merrily proposes a wager of a fleet horse, probably with the queen, that Matilda cannot ride with them, and be in at the death of the stag. The wager is accepted; Matilda starts and wins, and Edward has to ransom his horse for forty shillings.

On the marriage of the king's daughter, Margaret, to the duke of Brabant, as many as four hundred and twenty-six minstrels were present, and the bridegroom distributed among them an hundred pounds. Some entries about this period shows the king's quick irascibility. On one occasion we note an expense incurred in repairing a crown or coronet which he had thrown behind the fire. And on the princess's wedding-day, an esquire, or gentleman of the court, had irritated the king by some supposed neglect or misbehaviour, and received from him a stroke on the head with a wand. But the offender was able to show the king that he had been hasty and, perhaps, unjust. Most princes would probably have been content with an expression of regret; but Edward was warm and hearty, alike in reproof or in retractation. Finding that he had done his attendant a wrong, he at once *fined himself twenty marks*, equal to about two hundred pounds of our present money, which sum was duly paid to the aggrieved party, and charged in the king's wardrobe account. Gifts of various kinds were constantly issuing from Edward's hands. In one year, 1286, the new year's gift to queen Eleanor was a cup of gold, worth £23 6s. 8d.; and in another, a pitcher of gold, enamelled and set with precious stones.

But all this mutual and well-placed affection was now to find the common termination of all earthly enjoyments. That happy and entire union which had subsisted for nearly five-

and-thirty years was drawing to a close. The king and queen, after taking leave of their daughter Margaret, now duchess of Brabant, left their palace in Westminster for the midland counties. Edward had given directions for a parliament to be summoned to meet at Clipston, a royal palace in Sherwood Forest; and in the interim, he hoped to enjoy his favourite recreation of the chase. He also began to receive, about this time, frequent applications from Scotland, and he probably meant to go northward on that business. The queen, as usual, was with him, or near him; but while he was moving about during September, she seems to have remained at Hardby, near Lincoln. We find by mention of her physicians, and of medicine purchased for her at Lincoln, that she had an illness of some duration. It is described as a lingering disease, or slow fever. Hardby was a manor belonging to a family of the name of Weston, and we observe a sir John Weston in the queen's service. The house was probably placed by the family at the queen's disposal, as a quieter place for a sick person than the palace of Clipston, where the parliament was about to assemble.

It is usually said that Edward was on his road to Scotland, the queen slowly following him, and that she was taken ill on the journey, and died before he could return to her. But it has been recently shown that he remained in the vicinity of Hardby during the whole of her illness.* The parliament was held at Clipston—the king being present at the end of October, and it sat until the second week in November, when he returned to the sick room. We find him at Hardby from the 20th to the 28th of November, on which day the queen died.†

For two or three days silence reigns at Hardby. There is an entire cessation of all public business; as if the

* " Archæologia," vol. xxix., p. 169.   † Ibid., p. 174.

powerful mind of the king had been, for the moment, utterly prostrated. But, after this pause, we find the widowed monarch at Lincoln, where he doubtless went to issue his orders for the funeral. And all the measures he took with reference to this object and to the matters which followed, and which were connected with it, give proof of the depth of his feeling for his departed consort. It has been said, with great truth, that "this funeral procession was one of the most striking spectacles that England has ever witnessed." *

About ten days were occupied in the sad and solemn journey from Lincolnshire to Westminster, the king and his relatives following the body the whole way. When the procession approached a town which was to furnish a resting-place, it halted until the ecclesiastics of the place approached with their procession, to bear the body to its temporary abode, before the high altar in the principal church. These halting-places were afterwards made the site of crosses, richly sculptured, and intended to remind passengers in all future times of the good queen's last journey. These crosses were raised at Lincoln, Grantham, Stamford, Geddington, Northampton, Stony Stratford, Woburn, Dunstable, St. Alban's, Waltham, West Cheap, and Charing.

The body of the departed queen, as it entered one of these towns, was met by the monks and clergy of the place, who, receiving and conveying it to its temporary resting-place, kept watch over it all night long, with mournful chants and unceasing prayers. It was thus slowly brought to the neighbourhood of London, and here, apparently, the king left the procession by night and entered the metropolis, in order that he might meet the body at the head of the nobility and of all the dignified clergy of

* "Archæologia," vol. xxix., p. 174.

London and Westminster, on its approach to its last resting-place. Some of those then present would be able to recal to memory the day when, five-and-thirty years before, they had accompanied king Henry and the rejoicing citizens of London to meet the young Eleanor, then for the first time approaching their city as the prince's bride.

We have already alluded to the manner of the disposal of the queen's remains. It is most probable that it was chiefly in accordance with Eleanor's own desire. One portion was deposited in Lincoln cathedral; another in the church of the Black Friars in London; but the body itself was conveyed to Westminster, and placed near to the tomb of king Henry, which was even then hardly completed. It is needless to add that the funeral rites were in accordance with all the rest of this solemnly-magnificent ceremony; "cum summâ omnium reverentiâ et honore."

The king remained at Westminster for about a week after the interment; doubtless he was chiefly occupied in giving directions for the extraordinary honours which were yet to be paid to the memory of his departed consort. He then retired to Ashridge, a house of "Bons Hommes," recently founded by his uncle, the earl of Cornwall, which enjoyed the reputation of possessing "a few drops of the precious blood of Jesus." This may have been a principal reason for the selection of this spot by the king, who himself reckoned among his most valued treasures "two pieces of the rock of Calvary, which had been presented to him by one Robert Ailward, a pilgrim."

Edward remained at Ashridge until the 26th of January, 1291, a long retirement for a man of such active energy. He then went to Evesham, or Eynsham, and from thence to Ambresbury, where his mother resided, and where he would also meet his daughter Mary. The spring opens before we find him actively engaged in public business, and there are many proofs that he never ceased to lament his beloved Eleanor. Assuredly the measures he adopted during the next two years to do honour to her memory, were of a kind which, for munificence and persevering thoughtfulness, have very seldom been equalled.

The twelve crosses, which were apparently the first thought that occurred to him, constituted in themselves a princely monument. There are records still extant of no less than £650 17s. 5d. paid for the work done on that erected at Charing, a sum equal to £10,000 of our money. The cross at West Cheap cost £300; that at Waltham, £95; that at St. Alban's, £113. But it is probable that the statues were supplied by a different artist. We are surely within the mark when we reckon that a sum equal to £30,000 or £40,000 of our present money was expended on these mementoes.

A splendid tomb was placed in the minster at Lincoln; another, in the form of a chapel, was raised in the church of the Black Friars in London. The principal sepulchral monument, however, was naturally allotted to Westminster Abbey. There the best artist that could be procured was employed to form in metal a recumbent effigy of the queen, placed appropriately on a richly-ornamented tomb. The cost of the tomb is not recorded, but we find entries of as much as £113 6s. 8d., equal to about £1700 of our present money, paid to the artist employed on queen Eleanor and king Henry's effigies. A distinct payment also appears of a smaller sum for the erection of a workshop, in which these two statues were fabricated.

But the chief work still remained to be done. Edward had noble and splendid conceptions of princely works and long-enduring memorials, but his sagacious and reflecting mind could not rest satisfied with works in stone or works in metal. The almost universal belief of the church in England in those days, even "holy bishop Robert" not dissenting, was, that prayers and alms especially directed to the welfare of a departed soul had a beneficial effect upon that soul in the intermediate state.

This opinion, when compared with the teaching of Holy Scripture at the time of the Reformation, was found to be delusive; but in the thirteenth century it had not even been questioned. Edward's care, therefore, for the well-being of his beloved Eleanor in the invisible world soon began to manifest itself. While at Ashridge, and himself engaged in continual prayers for his departed consort, he found time to write a very earnest and pathetic letter to the abbot of Clugny, one of the most famous monasteries in Europe, entreating the prayers of that fraternity for her, "whom living he had dearly loved, and whom, though dead, he should never cease to love." And such a request was, doubtless, accompanied by a princely offering. But in his own realm Edward could be more definite and elaborate.

At Hardby a chantry was founded, and another at Elynton; and on the first and second anniversaries of the queen's death we find mention of various religious services and of large distributions of alms. But the principal provision was naturally reserved for Westminster. In his gifts to the abbey church for perpetual prayers and alms on behalf of the departed queen, "the king was quite profuse." He gave to this church the manors of Knoll, Arden's Grafton, and Langdon, Warwickshire, with other lands in the same county; and the manors of Bidbrook in Essex, Westerham in Kent, and Turweston in Bucks, for a perpetual commemoration. Special services of the most solemn kind were provided for, and seven score poor persons were to have charity. The charter for these gifts was dated in October, 1292, showing that neither the lapse of time nor the distractions of the momentous Scottish controversy could withdraw his mind from this earnest and settled purpose.

Edward, however, was well versed in the Old Testament scriptures, and he remembered Isaiah's warnings against religious ceremonies without justice or charity. On the anniversaries of his consort's death, we often remark the occurrence of large distributions of alms. But another thing is also noticeable. The queen had enjoyed from her husband's affection large landed possessions. Her stewards or bailiffs might have wronged or oppressed her tenants. We know not what proclamation may have been made, or invitation given, calling upon all who had any complaint to offer, to come forward; but it seems quite clear, that some such proclamation must have been issued; for the records are very numerous, in the next year or two, of the investigation of such complaints. And a fixed and honest purpose to do justice to all parties is evident in all these transactions.

The sorrow felt for queen Eleanor's death was, apparently, general and sincere. Her name is connected with no political contention or intrigue; and she seems to have made no enemies. Rishanger, writing at the time of her death, styles her "this most saintly woman and queen;" and adds, somewhat hyperbolically, that she was like "a pillar that supported the whole state." Walsingham, who wrote in the next age, described her more intelligibly, as "a woman pious, modest, pitiful, benevolent to all." He adds, that "the sorrowful, everywhere, so far as her dignity allowed, she consoled, and those who were at variance she delighted to reconcile." But her best eulogium is found in her consort's grief. His penetration and sagacity, his native nobleness of soul would have rendered it impossible for him to love a mean and unworthy object. But his affection for her was not a mere youthful passion. It was after a companionship of five-and-thirty years that he gave his testimony to her worth; and that testimony was one which few women indeed in the whole world's history have ever received or have ever merited.

V.

RETROSPECTIVE VIEW.

The autumn of the year 1290 was a solemn epoch in this great king's life. In this autumn died his beloved Eleanor; in this autumn died, also, "the maiden of Norway," the young queen of Scotland, whose death ushered in so many troubles.

Halcyon skies had for a whole quarter of a century gilded Edward's course and prospects; but a few weeks sufficed to end the sunshine of his prosperous career. From the battle of Evesham, in 1265, to the death of his queen, and the opening of the Scottish controversy in 1290, his life had been one of great enjoyment, great harmony, and great usefulness. "Held in universal esteem at home," and "famous throughout the world" for wisdom and valour, his lot might be regarded as one of no common prosperity. But this sad year, 1290, ended all this happiness. Clouds and storms arose, and though brief intervals of calm occurred, we find a king who was "slow to all manner of strife," compelled in his fifty-seventh year to don his armour and mount his horse, and set forth to meet a Scottish inroad, and from that time forth until his death in 1307, almost in every year we find him, in whom the infirmities of age must have begun to make themselves felt, in harness and in the saddle, sleeping at night by his horse's side on the bare heath, working with his men in the laborious siege of a fortress, and encountering, all the time, what to such a man was by far more painful—treachery from professed friends, and from his foes, perpetual simulations of submission, followed by constant treasons and breaches of covenant, the moment the sword was lifted from their throat. We open, in this sad year, the second volume of Edward's reign, but before we close the first, let us glance for a few moments at the past, and try once more to rectify the widespread error, or rather the constant misrepresentation, which shows to us this great king as, by choice, a man of war; when he was, more than most other sovereigns, a man of peace.

One of the ablest, and generally one of the fairest of our modern historians, thus commences his account of Edward's reign:—" Laying aside his disputes with his neighbours as a French prince, his active and splendid reign may be considered as an attempt to subject the whole island of Great Britain to his sway." * And a few pages later we are told that " his ambition tainted all his acts," and again, that " a conqueror is a perpetual plotter against the safety of all nations." And another justly-esteemed writer, Mr. Sharon Turner, tells us that " The reign of Edward was that of a prince whose sedate judgment and active talents advanced the civilization and power of his country. It may be considered under four heads—his incorporation of Wales, his wars in Scotland, his foreign treaties, and his internal reforms."

Thus both these writers, and with them a multitude of smaller note, agree in describing Edward as a man of ambition, a man covetous of his neighbour's possessions, a conqueror, " perpetually plotting" against the safety of others. Now, our quarrel with this view is not merely that it is inaccurate or imperfect, but that it is diametrically

* Sir J. Mackintosh.

opposed to all the principal facts of the case, calling white black and black white, and representing a sovereign as ambitious and unscrupulous, whose real character was that he was scrupulously conscientious ;—" as careful in performing his obligations as in exacting his rights,"* or, again, to cite the old chronicler,

> " Slowe to all manner of strife;
> Discreet and wise, and true of his worde."

Such writers as those we have cited place before their readers a king who, from his very accession, coveted and " plotted against " both Wales and Scotland. To this we oppose the indubitable facts, that when Llewellyn withheld his homage, Edward, instead of proceeding to extremities, was patient and forbearing, sent him summons after summons, offered to go to Shrewsbury or to Chester to meet him, and waited, in all, two whole years before he took up arms. And, again, that when Llewellyn was reduced to extremities, and might have been banished and Wales annexed, Edward granted him peace the moment he asked it, replaced him in his seat, attended his marriage, and did all he could to make him his friend. The war which led to Llewellyn's chance-medley death, and to the annexation, was a war made by Llewellyn and David, not by the English king.

As for Scotland, the conquest of which is placed in the fore-front of Edward's ambitious designs, it is surely enough to say that he ascended the throne in 1272, and that during more than eighteen years he never stirred one step or moved a finger against the honour and independence of Scotland. In 1290 the Scottish throne became vacant, and he was clamorously besought, for years, by all the chief men

* Pearson's Hist. of England, vol. ii., p. 292.

in Scotland to interfere. Yet, instead of seizing the opportunity, he stood aloof, went, at last, cautiously into the question, and in November, 1292, adjudged the throne to Baliol.

Four more years elapsed without the slightest move on Edward's part against Scotland. But in 1296, the twenty-fourth year of Edward's reign, the Scotch joined with his enemy, the king of France, and invaded England. And then, and not before, being in his fifty-seventh year, did the king enter Scotland, a country which, we are now assured, he had been coveting and " plotting against " for a whole quarter of a century. We say, then, once more, that these constant representations of Edward, which we find in a multitude of historians, great and small, exhibiting him as an ambitious man, a conqueror, a " designing man," constantly " plotting against the safety of his neighbours," constitute, on the whole, one of the most extraordinary instances of literary injustice and wrong that is to be found in all British history.

Let us look for a moment at the actual results, the real facts, of these eighteen years. Surely a period of this length, extending from the thirty-third to the fifty-first year of Edward's life, might be expected to show his real character, the true bent of his mind. A conqueror, an ambitious man, is not likely to waste the whole prime of his life in peaceful inactivity, and only to exhibit his cupidity and unscrupulousness when grey hairs were beginning to show themselves. The victors of Crecy and of Agincourt followed no such course. What Edward really was, he showed in these eighteen years. The conquest of Wales, the only interruption of an otherwise peaceful course, was, as we have shown, forced upon him. He had no choice in the matter. The Welsh princes would not have peace. But, with this one exception, what was the character of this protracted period—the whole prime of Edward's life?

It was that of constant, careful, sedulous improvement. No department of the government was exempt from his thoughtful scrutiny. The revenues of the crown were carefully examined, and their economical employment provided for. In place of "seizures" for the king's use, we now find "purchases." The household expenses were placed on a proper footing. The king could exhibit royal splendour when public occasions called for it; but the general rule of his expenditure was that of frugality. A modern writer observes, that "his household as king was both well-regulated and economical. We have a record of his expenses while residing at Langley, Bucks, in Lent, 1290." This, of course, was not a season of festivity; but we find that "in the first week his expenses were £7 10s. 4½d; in the second, £5 19s. 0½d.; and in the third, £5 12s. 2½d.* Now, bearing in mind the habits and usages of that time,† when the regulated price of a lamb was *sixpence*, and of a goose, *fourpence*, we shall see at a glance that this expenditure for a king, in retirement during the season of Lent, was both liberal and economical. It

* Blaauw on " the Barons' war," p. 34.

† The "Chronicle of Lanercost" gives us this anecdote of the manners of that day: "Richard de Clare, earl of Gloucester, paid a visit to Robert Grosstete, bishop of Lincoln, who received him with great honour, and desired his seneschal to provide a fitting dinner. At table the earl was seated at his host's right hand, and it was a day when meat was not permitted by the Church. It was customary to eat choice sea wolves [the dog-fish, still eaten in parts of Normandy], and the servant placed a very fine fish before the bishop, and a smaller one before the earl. The bishop was angry, and said, 'Take away this fish, or else bring the earl one equally fine.' The servant said that there was no other so large. 'Then,' said the bishop, 'take away this first and give it to the poor, and bring me one like the earl's.'"—"Chronicle of Lanercost," p. 44.

contrasts forcibly with the reckless extravagance of his father Henry, and of his still more wasteful son, the second Edward. Henry, after his royal festivities at Bourdeaux and Paris in 1254, returned home burdened with debts, which he himself described as " horrible to think of." And the younger Edward, when just commencing life, seems to have been accustomed to spend as much *daily* as we have just seen his father spend *weekly!* We have a record of his household expenses for three days in 1293, when he was staying in a country residence. On Thursday his expenses amounted to £7 4s. 5d., on Friday, to £6 8s. 1d., and on Saturday, to £6 4s.; being at the rate of about £46 per week. The expenditure of his household in that year amounted to £3,846 7s. 6d., which at the present rate of money would be equal to more than £50,000 per annum. That such habits in youth should lead to a reign of discomfort, closing on dishonour, is not to be wondered at.

Edward I., however, though economical, was no lover of money. On fitting occasions his expenditure was royal. His coronation banquet was one of unusual splendour and liberality. His Round Table celebrations must have been very costly. Fond of hunting, his stables must have occasioned a considerable outlay. His presents were magnificent, his charities were very large. The entries under this head, in his "Wardrobe Accounts," were numerous, and must have reached an aggregate, in each year, of large amount. One of the chronicles of the day makes this brief allusion to his charities:—

"King Edward, turning aside to the northern parts, celebrated Easter at Newcastle, where he distributed great abundance of oblations in the monasteries, and gave large alms to the people; insomuch that many men not poor did not blush to pretend themselves so, being allured by so great a liberality."*

On the first anniversary of his consort's death, besides great and costly solemnities at Westminster, the Black Friars in London, and at Lincoln, we find mention made of many other places—Haverfordwest, Burgh, Haverleigh, Somerton, Lindhurst, Ledes, and Langley—where the day was observed with especial rites, and the distribution of alms. All this was done at the king's expense, and sums varying from £19 to £30 were given to each place. But £30 in those days was nearly equal to £500 at the present day.

On the second anniversary, besides many other celebrations, alms were distributed to the prisoners in Newgate, to the hospitals of St. Giles, St. James, St. Thomas, St. Mary, and St. Bartholomew, in London, and also to the seven houses of Friars' mendicants in the same city.

Edward reformed the coin of the realm. He strove to restore purity to the administration of justice. By many stringent regulations he tried to abolish usury, which had grown to be an enormous evil.

It is in his reign that we first find an annual account of the public revenue and expenditure.† So admirably were the finances of the government administered, that in all these eighteen years, 1272—1290, we find only four applications to the people for an "aid"—a vote of taxes for the expenditure of the crown ; and each of these is for a declared and special purpose.

In his fourth year, the second after his coronation, he asked and obtained a *fifteenth*, to clear off his remaining liabilities on account of his expedition to the Holy Land—a work deemed, in those days, to be a public duty.

* "Chronicle of Lanercost," A.D. 1291.   † See Appendix.

In his fifth year, he asked for a *twelfth*, to provide for the expenses of the anticipated war with Wales.

In his eleventh year, the war in Wales having broken out a second time, he obtained a *thirtieth* from the laity and a *twentieth* from the clergy.

And in his eighteenth year, having returned from a prolonged visit to Gascony and other parts, where he had incurred many expenses, he asked and obtained a *fifteenth*.

These four small levies are all that Edward required during the first eighteen years of his reign. And the termination, for ever, of the destructive warfare on the borders of Wales, which had so long laid waste several counties of England, was far more than an abundant compensation to his people. Had he never been assailed by others, the rest of his reign might have passed over without any further demands upon his subjects. Had not Philip of France endeavoured to deprive him of Gascony, while the Scotch, in reckless violation of their recent oaths, allied themselves to France and invaded England; there is no reason to suppose that any burdens would have been laid upon the people, or that the earls of Norfolk and Hereford would have found any opportunity for their resistance or their " patriotism."

But the chief glory of his reign was, that he saw and appreciated that great public necessity—the want of good laws, and of a constitutional legislature for their consideration and enactment. We have already cited, but must here repeat, his first avowal, made as early as in the year 1267, of what he deemed to be the true office, the first duty of a king. Speaking in his father's name, he said,—

" Our lord the king, providing for the better estate of his realm of England, and for the more speedy administration of justice, as belongeth to the office of a king; the more discreet men of the realm being called together, as well of the higher as of the lower degree; it was provided, agreed, and ordained," etc.

Here we have, before he had ascended the throne, but at a time when he assuredly governed the vessel of the State, a brief but pithy outline of the constitution of England; and that outline it was the effort, the business of his life to fill up. With a vigorous hand he applied himself to the work of establishing a system of wise laws, and of improving the administration of justice. His sagacious and active mind penetrated and pervaded every department. And hence it is, that, in the judgment of all competent historians, the thirteenth century is the starting-point of the history of England. A writer of the Elizabethan age * repeatedly notices with admiration, " his noble industry," his " unceasing labours"; and this praise is justified by the recorded facts. In former reigns, foreign contests, and the suppressions of rebellion, or the enjoyment of hunting, filled up the reigns of the Norman kings. But Edward lived for England. In the former reigns, a brief charter had sometimes been extorted from the king; and in Henry's long reign our Statute-Book commences, with six ordinances, made in the course of fifty-six years. But so soon as Edward ascends the throne, legislation of the highest order at once begins. Crowned in 1274, in 1275 we have the " Statute of Westminster," " a code, rather than an act of parliament." In 1276, the statutes on *Coroners* and on *Bigamy*. Occupied with Wales for one year, in 1278 we have the " Statute of Gloucester;" in 1279, the great " Statute of Mortmain." Once more Wales claimed his attention; but in 1283 was passed " the famous statute" *de Mercatoribus*. In 1284, followed the " Statutes of Wales." In 1285, the second " Statutes of Westminster;" and subsequently, the " Statute

* Castra Regia. Roxburgh Club.

of Winchester,." He was then abroad for three years; but on his return, we have, immediately, the statutes "Quo Warranto," "Quia Emptores," and "Westminster III." Thus it is evident that Edward deemed, most wisely and justly, that the establishment of good and wholesome laws was his primary duty.

A hasty observer might remark that the quantity of this legislation was not large, and that a statute or two in a year might be reckoned a slow rate of production. But the answer to this is obvious. The work of legislation was but newly undertaken, and those who had addressed themselves to it were prudently cautious. Some of these statutes, too, were large and comprehensive measures, well deserving a prolonged and careful consideration. But this brings us to a distinct and separate question—the character and value of Edward's legislation. And this is the most wonderful feature in the whole case; for the quality of this legislation is probably unparalleled. Who is a higher authority on such matters than Sir Edward Coke?—and he, describing Edward's laws, says:—

"All the statutes made in the reign of this king may justly be styled *establishments;* because they are more constant, standing, and durable laws, than have been made ever since. Justly, therefore, may this king be called, our Justinian."

Fifty years after Sir Edward Coke, lived the great and good Sir Matthew Hale, who, in describing the growth of the common law of England, says of this reign:—

"Never did the laws, in any one age, receive so great and sudden an advancement. Nay, I may safely say, that all the ages since his time have not done so much, in reference to the orderly settling and establishing the distributive justice of this kingdom, as he did in the short compass of his single reign." He adds: "Upon the whole, it appears, that the very scheme, mould, and model, of the common law, as it was rectified and set in order by this king, so in a great measure it has continued the same, through all succeeding ages to this day. So that the mark or epocha we are to take for the true starting of the law of England, *what it is*, is to be considered, stated, and estimated, from *what this king left it*. Before his time it was, in a great measure, rude and unpolished; while, on the other hand, as it was thus polished and ordered by him, so it has remained hitherto, without any great or considerable alteration."

It would be easy to enlarge on this subject, but we are limiting ourselves to an outline. Sir William Blackstone thus describes this remarkable period of legislation:—

" Edward established, confirmed, and settled the great charter and the charter of forests.

" He gave a mortal wound to the encroachments of the pope and his clergy, by limiting and establishing the bounds of ecclesiastical jurisdiction; and by obliging the ordinary, to whom the goods of intestates at that time belonged, to discharge the debts of the deceased.

" He defined the limits of the several temporal courts of the highest jurisdiction, the king's-bench, common-pleas, and exchequer, so that they might not interfere with each other's proper business.

" He settled the boundaries of the inferior courts, in counties, hundred, and manors.

" He secured the property of the subject, by abolishing all arbitrary taxes and talliages levied without consent of parliament.

" He guarded the common justice of the kingdom from

abuses, by giving up the royal prerogative of sending mandates to interfere in private causes.

"He settled the forms, solemnities, and effect of fines levied in the court of common-pleas.

"He first established a repository for the public records of the kingdom.

"He improved upon the laws of king Alfred, by that great and orderly method of watch and ward, established by the statute of Winchester.

"He settled and reformed many abuses incident to tenures, by the statute of *Quia emptores*.

"He instituted a speedier way for the recovery of debts, by granting executions, not only upon goods and chattels, but also upon lands, by writ of elegit; a signal benefit to a trading people.

"He effectually provided for the recovery of advowsons as temporal rights.

"He closed the great gulf in which all the landed property of the kingdom was in danger of being swallowed, by his reiterated statutes of Mortmain.

"I might continue," adds Sir William, "this catalogue much further; but, upon the whole, we may observe that the very scheme and model of the administration of common justice, between party and party, was entirely settled by this king."

Legislation, then, and not military aggrandisement, was the work to which Edward gave himself; and to liken him to Justinian does him much less than justice. The Roman emperor lived at the close of a long period, during which Rome had abounded in laws, and in which the laws had grown too complex and voluminous. His merit is, that he collected and arranged them into a code. Edward's position was wholly different. He was born at a period when

England, then rising into the position of a nation, found itself without written laws and without a legislature; and he set himself to work, with clearness of vision and with largeness of heart, to supply both these wants. In the first of these merits he does not stand alone. Other rulers have seen the need of laws, and have set themselves to supply that need. But too often they have wished that the work should be theirs, the power theirs, and the merit theirs also. Now it is Edward's peculiar glory that, from the very opening of his public life, he seemed to have seen and adopted the great truth which lies at the foundation of all "constitutions," that "what concerns all should be by all approved," and that "common perils should be met by remedies prescribed in common." These words fell from him in 1295, but the sentiment contained in them is discernible in every step of his whole career.

It is this, then, and not any supposed "attempt to subject the whole island to his sway," which constitutes the chief feature, the principal merit of Edward's reign. To be a conqueror, although indeed this kind of conquest—the bringing one island under one government—would be the wisest and the best; to be a conqueror would be but an ordinary and very common sort of merit. The organ of "acquisitiveness" is possessed by a great many of the human race. Edward's true glory lay, not in his desire to *take*, but in his willingness to *give*. When he went forth, "mighty in arms," it was, in every case, because his foes left him no choice,—because to remain at peace would have been dishonour. But his peaceful conquests, his legislative victories, were entirely his own. Here we see his own mind and will. From his first accession to power, until the latest hour of his reign, two great objects were constantly present to his mind. He saw that the realm required, and ought to have, a parliament, consisting not only of prelates and lords, but of "all the commonalty of the realm, thither summoned;" and next, that a chief function and office of this parliament should be to deliberate upon proposals laid before it, which should become, when assented to, statutes of the realm.

It is the enunciation of these two principles which constitutes the real glory of king Edward's reign. That enunciation was his own voluntary act, and its sincerity was proved by all the measures of his subsequent career. His life was devoted to the working out of this great theory. His first statute, in its preamble, gives a bold and fearless sketch of a free legislature; and, before he died, he had gathered around him, as elected members of that legislature, the representatives of all the most populous towns of his realm of England.

Justly then does the writer whom we have already cited, a contemporary of Spenser and of Shakespeare, describe this king as one "in whom we see the value of wisdom, kingly powers, and noble industry," one who "was a fatherly king to his people; employing all his life, care, and labour to benefit and nourish the commonwealth"—one, in fine, "in whom the good government and commonwealth of England had their chief foundation." *

* "Castra Regia," Roxburgh Club.

VI.

SCOTTISH AFFAIRS—THE ARBITRATION—THE WAR.
A.D. 1291—1296.

THE year 1290, as we have already observed, was the disastrous one which ended Edward's peaceful career, and involved him, without any purpose or desire of his own, in troubles and strife for the rest of his days. The death of a young princess, at a distance of five hundred miles from Edward's dominions, involved the northern part of the island in troubles which he alone had power to quell. His interposition, earnestly and loudly called for, became, apparently, inevitable. But, when once engaged in the attempt, there seemed no option left him in any of the after-proceedings. Step followed step, by absolute necessity, until the annexation of the Scottish realm became the natural and unavoidable close; and in this way, without having any alternative, he became an object of enmity to almost every Scotchman, and drew down on his memory in after times, the bitter and unjust animadversions of a long series of prejudiced historians.

A controversy had existed between England and Scotland for centuries before Edward was born. Various kings of England had received the homage alike of the princes of Wales and of the kings of Scotland. We have seen that when Edward was to be crowned, his brother-in-law, Alexander of Scotland, came to Westminster and paid his homage; while Llewellyn of Wales, not denying his liability, tried to evade that ceremony by various excuses.

But two different meanings were attached in England and Scotland to this fealty due from the Scottish king. The English lawyers and statesmen always maintained that it was due to the king of England *for the realm of Scotland*. The Scots, on the other hand, insisted on another view— that the king of Scotland owed homage for the honour or earldom of Huntingdon, a possession held by him within the realm of England; but that for Scotland itself he owed no fealty, and ought not to come under any obligation. This quarrel, or difference of opinion, had existed for two or three hundred years. It came to the surface at Edward's coronation, when his brother-in-law, the king of Scotland, appeared at Westminster in great state to pay his homage. He came attended by a hundred knights, and, as we have already narrated, "each knight, as he dismounted from his horse, cast the steed loose, and whosoever could catch them, had them to their own behoof." But still, when the homage was to be paid, the usual question arose. The English lawyers and statesmen demanded an unconditional homage for the realm of Scotland. The Scotch persisted in limiting it to "the lands their king held of king Edward in England." No quarrel ensued; the question seems to have been postponed, for we find that three years after, Edward writes to the bishop of Wells, that "his beloved brother, the king of Scotland, had agreed to perform an unconditional homage at the ensuing feast of Michaelmas." Alexander then appeared before the parliament at Westminster, and offered his homage in these words: "I, Alexander, king of Scotland, do acknowledge myself the liegeman of my lord Edward, king of England, against all his enemies."

This Edward accepted;* and it is abundantly evident that, as the two brothers-in-law had no intention of quarrelling, the real point in dispute—the allegiance claimed "for the realm of Scotland"—was left undecided—Edward not conceding, Alexander not admitting, the alleged rights of the English crown.

This position of postponement, declining to bring the matter to a quarrel, continued during the whole of Alexander's life. Edward and he remained in amity; but Edward in this and all other disputed questions, always used the reservation—"saving the rights of my crown;" *i.e.*, "whatever properly belongs to the king of England, *that* I do not concede."

In 1261 a daughter had been born to Alexander of Scotland in the castle of Windsor, and in due time this daughter was married to Eric, king of Norway. Her brother, the only surviving son of Alexander, was also married, about the same time, to a daughter of the count of Flanders. But the lapse of a few years saw the removal of almost the whole family by death. Margaret, Alexander's wife and Edward's sister, died in 1274, her son in 1282 or 1283, and her daughter, the queen of Norway, in the following year. Alexander himself was killed by a fall from his horse in 1286; and thus the only successor to his house remaining was the young princess, his daughter's child, who was styled "the maiden of Norway."

When Alexander suffered the loss of both his children in 1283—4, a meeting of the estates of the realm was held at Scone, at which meeting the succession was declared to belong to "the maiden of Norway." When, two years later, the unexpected calamity of Alexander's own death occurred, another meeting was held, and recourse was had

* Tytler's History of Scotland, vol. i., p. 61.

to Edward, whose niece, the late queen of Norway, had been the young maiden's mother. He was in Gascony at the time, and he contented himself with counselling the Scotch to choose a regency, and to carry on the government in the young queen's name. The intelligence does not seem to have hastened his return from the continent, which did not take place until two or three years afterward.*

A council or parliament was accordingly held at Scone on the 11th of April, 1286, at which a regency, consisting of six "guardians of the realm," was appointed. The persons chosen were, *the bishop of St. Andrew's*, the earl of Fife, the earl of Buchan, the bishop of Glasgow, the lord of Badenoch, and James, the steward of Scotland.

But in the absence of any visible sovereign, it was not surprising that the Bruces, and Baliols, and other families which claimed to be in the line of succession, should draw together, consult, and form confederacies, having in view the contingency which afterwards did actually arise—that the young "maiden of Norway" might die before she could ascend the throne. These rivalries and confederacies increased, and the parties strove with each other, until, at length, as the historian of Scotland confesses, "open war

* Had Edward shown any forwardness in interfering in the affairs of Scotland, we may be certain that such interference would have been noticed with censure by all the Scotch historians. Yet, for merely abstaining from such interference, he is thus criticized by one of the fairest of the whole, Mr. Tytler:—"Edward contented himself with observing the turn which matters should take in Scotland, certain hat his power and influence would in the end induce the different parties to appeal to him; and confident that the longer time he gave to these factions to quarrel among themselves and embroil the country, the more advantageously would this interference take place." This criticism is a striking instance of the spirit in which every step taken by Edward is regarded by Scottish writers. He cannot even abstain from interference, without being censured for so abstaining! And yet the whole of this censure rests upon the merest conjecture.

broke out between the adherents of Baliol and Bruce; and, for two years after the death of the king, continued its ravages in the country."

Such was the state of affairs during the last portion of Edward's stay on the continent; and assuredly, for this sad predicament of Scotland, he was in no way answerable. But the natural and inevitable consequence was, that so soon as he arrived in England, he was compelled, by appeals directed to him from all sides, to begin to concern himself with the troubles of that kingdom. Sir Francis Palgrave has shown, by a reference to the original documents, that such appeals were addressed to him by the earl of Mar, by Robert Bruce, lord of Annandale, and by a body called "the seven earls of Scotland." These parties all "appealed to the king of England and his royal crown." So invoked, the king invited them to send commissioners to meet him at Salisbury in November, 1289, there to treat of "certain matters of import;" and to which meeting the king of Norway would also send an ambassador of his own. The Scotch readily acceded to his proposal, and they sent to this meeting at Salisbury the bishop of St. Andrew's, the bishop of Glasgow, Robert Bruce, and John Comyn.

The "matters of import" which Edward propounded to this meeting, concerned a plan, the best which human skill could have devised, for restoring and securing the tranquillity of Scotland. The young prince of Wales was now in his sixth year—the maiden of Norway was of nearly the same age. If these two children were betrothed to each other, the kingdom of Scotland would at once be placed under the joint protection of England and Norway. Thus all would be security and order; and, in course of time, on the succession of the young prince to the throne of England, the unity and harmony of the two kingdoms, under one head, would be secured in the best and most unobjectionable manner. Even the Scottish historians, with one consent, admit the wisdom and prudence of this plan, which Hume himself describes as "favourable to the happiness and grandeur of both kingdoms."

They also concede, that the negociation was conducted with the greatest fairness and liberality on Edward's part. Appealed to on all sides, he could not question his own position, as, practically, the superior lord. The king of Norway had instructed his ambassadors to treat with the Scottish commissioners "only *in the presence* of the king of England." And, referring to a claim which he had upon the Scots for a sum of about 3,000 marks, he requests the king " to issue his commands to the guardians of Scotland " to pay him the money. The young queen, also, while she was the daughter of the king of Norway, was also the daughter of Edward's niece. In every way, therefore, the interposition of these two kings was the reverse of officiousness or assumption.

Nevertheless, Edward, with his usual liberality of feeling and practical wisdom, allowed the Scottish commissioners to make almost their own terms. He treated with them, says one Scottish writer, "quite on a footing of equality." " The terms agreed upon," says another, "were strictly honourable to the weaker party." And thus was framed and completed, so far as human beings could accomplish it, "a project," which Hume describes as " so happily formed and so amicably conducted."

But everything human is uncertain, and this wise and prudent plan was wholly subverted in a few short months by the death of the young queen on her voyage from Norway in the autumn of 1290. " This fatal event," says Mr. Tytler, " which may justly be called a great national calamity, struck sorrow and despair into the heart of the kingdom." Obviously, that state of anarchy and civil war which had recently called for the interposition of the two kings, might now be expected to return. The pretensions of the rival candidates so nearly resembled each other, and the difference between them was so slight, that neither could be expected to give way; and a bloody, and perhaps a long-protracted strife, seemed almost inevitable.

It is abundantly clear that the arbitration of some eminent and powerful personage was the only conceivable way by which the Scottish nation could escape from this fearful peril. And to whom, but to Edward, should they appeal in this emergency? To him they had already gone, more than once or twice, in their recent troubles. Bruce, one of the claimants, had been so far connected with Edward in times past, that had any other referee been named, he would probably have refused to acquiesce. But to an appeal to the king of England no objection seems to have been made in any quarter.

The bishop of St. Andrew's, whose name has just been given, as the first on the list of the " guardians of the realm," and the first of the commissioners sent to Salisbury, wrote to Edward on the 7th of October, 1290, " *entreating* him to approach the border, to give consolation to the people of Scotland, to prevent the effusion of blood, and to enable the faithful men of the realm to preserve their oath, by choosing him for their king, *who by right ought to be so.**" For so calling upon Edward, the bishop is severely handled by many Scottish historians. But surely, with a civil war impending, the bishop deserves little blame; especially when we see that the prince to whom he thus applied was after-

* Rymer's Fœdera, vol. ii., p. 741.

wards accepted as the arbitrator by all the competitors, and by the assembled nobles of Scotland.

On the fact, that Edward was called upon by the chief men in Scotland at this juncture, there is no dispute, even among the Scottish historians themselves. Dr. Henry says, " The regents, the states, and even the competitors, agreed to refer this great controversy to the king of England ;" and "the bishop of St. Andrew's was sent into England to inform Edward of this reference, and to entreat him to take upon him the office."* And Mr. Tytler adds, that " there is also reason to suspect, from documents recently discovered, that Bruce and his adherents had not only claimed his (Edward's) protection at this moment, but secretly offered to acknowledge his right of superiority."†

Thus invoked by the leading men in Scotland, who wrote to him—" We shall be involved in blood, unless the Most High provide a remedy by your interposition "—Edward, so soon as he had recovered from the depression occasioned by the loss of his queen, wrote to the chief men in that country, desiring them to meet him at Norham, on the English side of the Tweed, on the 10th of May, 1291. Hume adds that the king, " carrying with him *a great army*, advanced to the frontiers." But this statement is shown by the existing records to be utterly untrue. Edward, knowing that he was about to meet all the nobles and chiefs of Scotland, who, in the existing state of things, would assuredly come armed and well attended, issued writs to about fifty-eight of his military tenants in the northern counties, desiring them to meet him at Norham *in the beginning of June*. This was obviously a measure of precaution. He went to the place of meeting with the

---

* Henry's History, book iv., c. i.
† Tytler's Scotland, vol. i., p. 84.

Scottish chiefs, attended by his ordinary retinue. But, foreseeing that some troubles might arise, and that it would be most inexpedient that the umpire or superior lord should be powerless in the presence of the Scottish barons, he took measures to have in attendance, in about *three weeks after* the commencement of the proceedings, a few thousand men, being merely such a force as two or three counties could easily raise. Hume again speaks of Edward's "powerful army," and represents the Scottish barons as having been "betrayed into a situation, in which it was impossible for them to make any defence." But, of any "powerful army" there is not the slightest trace in history; and if Hume had consulted Rymer, he would have seen, that among the fifty-eight military tenants who were summoned to meet in June, there appeared the names of John Baliol, Alexander Baliol, John Comyn, and Robert Bruce, all of whom held lands of Edward, as English barons. Thus the Scottish leaders, so far from any "betrayal," were fully apprised several weeks before of Edward's plans, and were quite at liberty, if they thought fit, to adopt measures for resistance.*

We reach now, then, the 10th of May, 1291. The military retainers whom the king had summoned to meet in June were scarcely yet assembling at their homes. Edward stood, surrounded by his nobles and lawyers, without any other than his usual retinue. He began, therefore, without

* Sir James Mackintosh, accepting Hume's story without examination, talks of "the circumvention of the estates of Scotland, at Norham, in 1291." But in the records of the period there is not the slightest trace of any "circumvention." Edward met the estates of Scotland at their own request. Army he had none, at that time, with him. He met them on equal terms, for public conference. He told them frankly, and at once, in what capacity he came—*i.e.*, as superior lord They demurred. He then gave them time to deliberate, and appointed a second meeting in the following month. To speak of these proceedings as a "circumvention" is a mere abuse of language.

any thought of force, by proceeding to explain in what capacity he came among them.

Scotchmen now often strive to assume that he had been invited,—had been selected, merely as an umpire, to decide upon a single point, by agreement of all parties. In such arbitrations, however, we generally hear of some document, some contract or treaty; as when Louis of France arbitrated between Henry and his barons in 1264. But of such an agreement or contract there is no trace in the present instance. The lords and great men of Scotland had begged his interposition, and they now simply "appeared,"—as men are usually wont to appear when any court sits in which they have a question depending.

Edward, however, was pre-eminently a man of order and of respect for law. He therefore began by leaving no doubt as to this part of the case. He at once told them, without the least reserve or delay, by the mouth of Roger Brabazon, his chief justiciary, " that the disturbances which had arisen, in consequence of the late king's death, were grievous to him, and that, in consequence thereof, and for the restoration of peace, he had travelled a great distance, in order, as lord paramount, to do justice to all." And first, he asked them, in the most distinct manner, whether they heartily recognized him as lord paramount of the kingdom of Scotland?

This was, unquestionably, the most frank and open way of proceeding, and it was also rendered necessary by the position of the question. It would have been manifestly absurd for the king to have undertaken the decision of the controversy, without first having it distinctly settled and understood in what capacity or character he was acting.

Edward here advanced no new pretensions. The

English claim for centuries had been the same—a claim always advanced when England had a powerful sovereign, though often carelessly abandoned when she had a weak or worthless one. Thus, in 1189, the two kingdoms came into violent collision, and, after a great defeat, William the Lion of Scotland consented to make peace on the following terms:—

"William was to become the liegeman of his lord the king Henry, for Scotland, Galloway, and all his other lands, and to perform fealty to his liege lord in the same way as other vassals. His brother, his barons, his clergy, and all his other vassals, were to become the liegemen of the English crown, acknowledging that they held their lands of the English king, and swearing to support him, their liege lord, against the king of Scotland, if the latter ever failed in his fidelity."*

And yet, not many years after, Richard I. of England, caring much more for Palestine than for Scotland, easily relinquished this fealty. Thus was it always. England, having many records of Scottish homage, always claimed it when she was strong, but easily relinquished it when she was weak, or had some other quarrel on her hands.

Was it, then, noble or generous in Edward to seize this opportunity of Scotland's greatest weakness to assert this obnoxious claim? This is a question which may deserve a moment's consideration.

In affairs of state, questions will sometimes arise which require to be handled with reference not to feelings or sentiments, but to the general utility. Spain might say to England now, "Is it kind or generous in you to retain possession of a corner of Spain, merely because the fortune of war gave it to you a century ago?" But before England

* Robertson's Scotland under her Early Kings, vol. i., p. 373.

evacuated Gibraltar, her sovereign and government would feel bound to consider the matter, not in the light of sentiment, but with a view to the general good of the English realm and people. And so with Edward in that day. He had been called to the banks of the Tweed in May, 1291, not by any occasion or desire of his own, but by the urgent need of Scotland. Placed in that position, he must act, he felt, with a constant eye to England's good. Not aggressively, but firmly maintaining that same position which, nearly twenty years before, like former English kings, he had asserted to be England's right.

The superiority which he claimed, was no vain or ostentatious pre-eminence. It was a thing of vast importance to England; while to Scotland itself, though resisted, it was a positive good. The object sought was, that this island of Britain should be at peace with itself—should be preserved from intestine dissensions. If the king of England was really the lord paramount, then the king of Scotland, paying fealty to him, was bound to be always on his side, and thus war between the two was precluded. But if, as the Scots were fond of maintaining, the two kingdoms were wholly independent of each other, then the smaller might, whenever it pleased, make war upon the larger. And hence it was always found, that whenever France quarrelled with England, she sent to Scotland, and persuaded the Scottish king to take part in the contention. And thus this island of Britain, instead of being, as at present, united and strong, was frequently divided against itself, the northern part attacking the south, and inflicting heavy injuries upon it. It was this state of disunion which Edward tried to terminate, as he had previously tried in Wales. To both he said: " Pay to me that homage which you owe; vow to be my true man against all enemies. Pay this vow and keep it; so will this island know no more internal contention." Had Llewellyn of Wales and Baliol of Scotland, making this vow, "kept their covenant," neither of them would ever have been disturbed in his seat by the covenant-keeping king of England.

Edward met the assembled lords of Scotland, then, and began by plainly avowing the position in which he deemed himself to stand. He had invented no new claim; he asserted no right, now, which he had not asserted many years before. To justify his position he had desired his law-officers to gather from the records of the kingdom, proofs that his claim was neither new nor destitute of foundation. A collection of these proofs was now presented to the Scottish lords, going back to the days of Edward the Elder, the son of Alfred. Many of the instances alleged were merely incidental :—that England's leave was asked before Scotland did this or that. But some more positive testimonies were on record.

Going back as far as to the times of Athelstan, A.D. 926, Roger de Hoveden, and William of Malmesbury, and Henry of Huntingdon, describe the king's victory over Constantine, king of the Scots, and how Constantine submitted and swore fealty to him. In Edred's reign, say William of Malmesbury and Henry of Huntingdon, the Scots were again defeated, and again made to take the oath.

Under Edward the Confessor, say Hoveden and Malmesbury, Siward of Northumberland defeated Macbeth, king of Scotland, and gave the crown to Malcolm, as king Edward had commanded. In 1091, say Hoveden and Huntingdon, William Rufus marched against the Scots; and Malcolm, being afraid, made peace, "paying homage to him as he had done to his father." And in 1097, say the same writers,

William sent Edgar into Scotland, where he defeated an usurper in a great battle, and made the son of Malcolm king.

Of the treaty of 1189, between William the Lion and Henry II., we have already spoken. Still, however, amidst all these proofs, it should never be forgotten, that whenever England was weak or perplexed, Scotland had always been ready to throw off the yoke, and to declare that she was, and always had been, entirely independent.

Edward had now been called, by the general voice of Scotland, to come forward and decide an important question, and so to save the realm from a civil war. Was it to be expected that in doing this he could forget his own position, or the claim which England had asserted for the last three or four hundred years? Would it have been right or commendable if he had done so, seeing that upon the decision of this claim depended the unity and harmony, the internal peace and strength, of the two sister kingdoms in all succeeding ages?

Was it to be expected, either, that he could overlook the circumstances attending the present appeal? What meant the application made by the Scotch to him while in Gascony, or the repeated appeals to him since by the bishop of St. Andrew's, by the seven earls of Scotland, by Robert Bruce, by the earl of Mar, and others, all "*appealing* to the king of England and his royal crown," if Scotland was as independent of England as it was of France or of Norway? Sir Francis Palgrave has well observed, that "We have now full evidence that the interposition of Edward was neither wanton nor aggressive, and that it little deserved the terms by which it has been described. Kings have hard measure meted out to them by historians. Let the English monarch be tried by the test and example of an English gentleman: If, on the death of the copyhold tenant, all the persons claiming the right of admission unite in applying to the lord of the manor for a new grant, will it be easy for him to doubt that he is the lawful owner of the domain?"*

Such, then, was the first question opened at Norham. It was, clearly, a necessary one; for how could Edward commence his duties as judge, or arbiter, until he knew whether, and upon what grounds, he was admitted by the contending parties to occupy that position. Hence he said to them, at the very outset, "I come here as lord paramount; do you receive me in that character?"

Their first reply seems to have been, that they were not prepared to give an answer to such a question; and that they wished for time to deliberate. The king expressed surprise that they should be unprepared to give an answer, *since they were not ignorant of his intentions.* We gather from this expression, that the king had made no secret of his views or purposes; and that there was nothing sudden or unexpected in the demand which he made. Still, as they desired time to deliberate, he adjourned the meeting to the next day; and on their then appearing still undecided, he gave them a further delay of three weeks.†

The lords of Scotland, therefore, had the fullest liberty,

* Palgrave's Documents, vol i., p. 25.

† Mr. Tytler, in his account of these transactions at Norham, introduces two quotations, which convey a false idea of their character. From Fordun, he cites these words: "Now," said Edward to the most confidential of his ministers, "the time is at last arrived when Scotland and its petty kings shall be reduced under my power." But Fordun wrote in Scotland just one hundred years after, and pretends to give a confidential communication of Edward to one of his ministers, made half a century before he, Fordun, was born.

But (2) the "Annals of Waverley," says Mr. Tytler, tell us, in 1291, that " the king of England, having assembled his privy council and chief nobility, told them that he had it in his mind to bring under his dominion the king and the

the most entire freedom to choose their course. Edward, as he told them, had made no secret of his intentions. Called by them to the meeting at Norham, he had never purposed to go there in any doubtful character. The position he assumed was identically the same which he had assumed throughout his whole reign. He was lord paramount of Britain, just as Philip was lord paramount of France. He found in divers ancient records, English kings acting in this character in Scotland, even as far back as the time of Alfred's sons. More recently, he found William of Scotland, just one hundred and three years before, consenting to " become the liegeman" of his great grandfather, Henry II., " for Scotland, Galloway, and all his other lands." His own principle through life had been to maintain the just claims of the crown of England, and " while he was careful in performing his obligations, to be similarly jealous in exacting his rights."* He therefore frankly told them,

realm of Scotland, in the same manner that he had subdued the kingdom of Wales."

This would be something like evidence, though of a loose kind, if Mr. Tytler had quoted it fairly. But he has given *only so much* as suited his purpose. The passage in the " Annals of Waverley " runs thus :—

" The king of England, having assembled his privy council and chief nobility, told them that he had it in his mind to bring under his dominion the king and the realm of Scotland, in the same manner that he had subdued the kingdom of Wales. He therefore moved his army into those parts, where in a short time he gained possession of the said kingdom of Scotland."

Thus we see that this passage is only one instance out of hundreds which might be adduced, showing that the old chroniclers often put down under the date of one year facts which properly belong to another. There was, in 1291, no " king " in Scotland to be subdued. Neither did Edward move an army into Scotland, or gain possession of Scotland, until 1296. It is probable enough, that shortly before this, he stated to his council such views as are described in the " Annals." But then, this all happened, if at all, in 1296, *after Baliol had broken faith with him, not in* 1291, when the conferences as to the succession were still going on.

* Pearson's Hist., vol. ii., 292.

at the very outset, in what character he came there, and he claimed of them an equally frank recognition of his place and dignity. They hesitated, they asked for time. He gave it as soon as asked. He dismissed them, desiring them to return in three weeks with their decision. Had they chosen to resist his claim, this delay gave them ample time to assemble their forces, and to return to Norham in June at the head of an army. The charges, therefore, which Hume and Mackintosh and others have brought, of a "circumvention," or a "surprise," are wholly unfounded, and more than usually unjust. Edward's whole conduct in this part of the transaction was frank, deliberate, and manly.

The lords of Scotland, however, were in no mood for fighting. Several of the chief of them indulged hopes of the crown, and expected a favourable sentence at the hands of Edward. To unite in an indignant rejection of the English claim was, therefore, a thing out of the question. With one consent they submitted to the necessity which seemed inevitable. The three weeks elapsed; no measures for resistance had been taken; they returned to Norham in the beginning of June, unprepared to withstand, and consequently prepared to admit, the English claim.

A second time assembled in full conclave, the king's able minister, chancellor Burnel, opened the business. He reminded them that the king his master had conceded to them a sufficient time to prepare any objections they might have to offer to his claim of superiority; and, as they had produced none, he would now proceed in the capacity of lord paramount, to do justice in the matter.

"The chancellor then turned to Robert Bruce, and demanded whether he was content to acknowledge Edward as lord paramount of Scotland, and willing to receive judgment from him in that character; upon which this baron expressly answered, that he recognized him as such, and would abide by his decision. The same question was then put to the other competitors, all of whom returned the same answer. Sir Thomas Randolph then stood up, and declared that John Baliol, lord of Galloway, had mistaken the day, but would appear on the morrow, which he did, and then solemnly acknowledged the superiority of the English king."*

The king himself then addressed the assembly. He declared his intention to pronounce a speedy decision in the controversy; and, meanwhile, to maintain the laws and re-establish the tranquillity of the country. The several claimants then affixed their signatures to two important instruments—the first declaring their consent to receive judgment from the king as lord paramount; and the second, delivering the land and the castles of Scotland into Edward's hands, he engaging to re-deliver them to the person who should appear to be justly entitled. Then a list of eighty commissioners was formed by the candidates themselves, to which list the king was to add twenty-four names; and these commissioners were to receive the claims of the several candidates, and to report them to the king.

On the 11th of June, the regents of Scotland delivered the kingdom, and the governors of the castles gave up those fortresses, into the hands of king Edward, who immediately re-delivered them to the regents, promising to give full possession to the rightful claimant, so soon as the question as to the succession should be decided. The guardians of the kingdom then swore fealty to Edward, as lord paramount, and were followed in the same oath by Robert

* Tytler's History of Scotland, vol. i., p. 88.

Bruce, by his son, by John Baliol, and by the earls of Buchan, Mar, Athol, Angus, Lennox, Menteith, and many other barons and knights. The peace of king Edward, as lord paramount, was publicly proclaimed, and the assembly was adjourned until the 2nd of August, then to meet at the town of Berwick-upon-Tweed. On that day it again met; and the claimants were invited to present their petitions. These, which were twelve in number, were read; and the king recommended them to the attention of the commissioners; enjoining them to give in their report to him, at Berwick, on the 2nd of June, in the next year. Edward was at that time called to England by the illness of his mother, who was then on her death-bed. He had also the disagreeable task before him of suppressing a violent feud which had broken out between the earls of Hereford and Gloucester. He probably also anticipated that the investigation of the claims of so many as twelve candidates, by a large body of commissioners, would necessarily occupy much time. On these grounds he postponed the decision until the following summer, and soon took his departure for England.*

In June, 1292, the commissioners assembled, the king and all the claimants being present. There can be no doubt that it began to be generally understood by this time that the question must lie between Robert Bruce and John Baliol, both of whom were descended from daughters of David, earl of Huntingdon, who was brother of William the

* Wyntoun and Fordun, the earliest Scottish historians, writing at the end of the fourteenth and beginning of the fifteenth centuries, bring in a fiction at this part of the story, telling us that Edward, during the arbitration, offered to give the crown to Bruce, if he would agree to hold it of him as feudal lord. But the fact is, as sir F. Palgrave has shown, that Bruce had already accepted the king as his feudal lord *long before this meeting at Norham.*

Lion, king of Scotland. The table of affinity is given below.*

Some difficulties arising, the king desired further information to be obtained, and adjourned the further hearing until the 15th of October. On that day all parties again

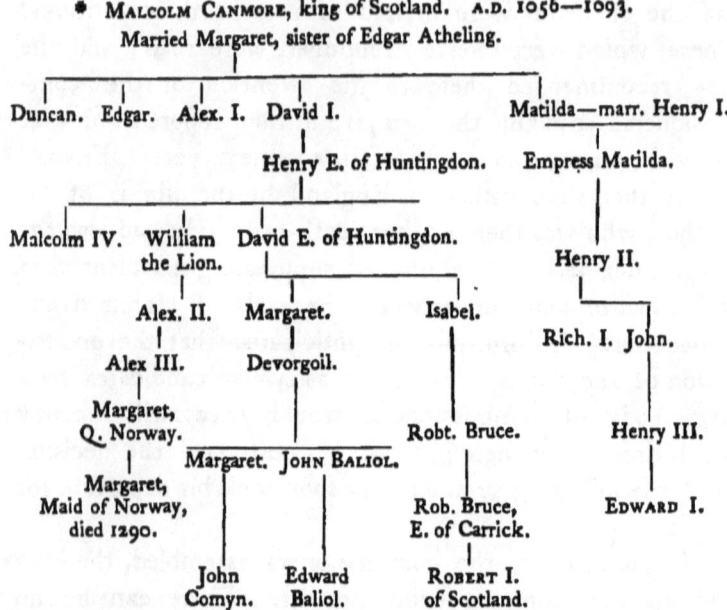

* MALCOLM CANMORE, king of Scotland. A.D. 1056—1093.
Married Margaret, sister of Edgar Atheling.

Macpherson, the editor of Andrew Wyntoun, says, in one of his notes to that author, "It is very surprising that Edward did not claim the crown of Scotland for himself, as heir of Malcolm Canmore, whose grand-daughter Maud was his great-great-grandmother. His great-grandson, Henry IV., got the crown of England without having so good an hereditary title."

The difference between Edward I. and Henry IV. was, that Edward was a thoroughly just man, and knew that his title was wholly inferior to that of Baliol, or Comyn, or Bruce. Hence, while he never overlooked it, he never advanced it. His unquestionable claim, in 1296, lay in the one fact, that Baliol, Bruce, Comyn, and every lord in Scotland, first admitted him as lord paramount, and then made war against him, the undoubted penalty of which was, forfeiture.

met, and the king proposed to the commissioners two questions : first, by what laws or customs the judgment ought to be regulated ? and, secondly, was the kingdom of Scotland to be regarded as a common fief, and the succession to be regulated by the same principles which were applicable to earldoms and baronies? The commissioners replied, that the laws and usages of the two kingdoms must rule the question ; but if none existed to regulate the case, the king must make a new law for a new emergency ; and that the succession must be decided in the same manner as the succession to earldoms, baronies, and other indivisible inheritances.

The claimants were then called upon, and each endeavoured to maintain his own right. The language used by John Baliol, who ultimately obtained the kingdom, is worthy of notice. He urged " that the claimants were in the court of the lord paramount, of whose ancestors, from time immemorial, the realm of Scotland was held by homage ; and that the king of England must give judgment in this case as in the case of other tenements held of the crown, looking to the laws and established usages of his kingdom "*

The king then required of his great council a final answer to this question : " By the laws and customs of both kingdoms, ought the issue of an elder sister, but more remote by one degree, to exclude the issue of a younger sister, although one degree nearer ?" The council replied, that the issue of the elder sister must be preferred. Another adjournment then took place, until the 6th of November. On that day the king declared his judgment, that Bruce's right must yield to the superior claim of Baliol. Whereupon a new question was raised : John de Hastings, descended

* Tytler's History of Scotland, vol. i., p. 96.

from the *third* daughter of David earl of Huntingdon, alleged that the kingdom of Scotland was partible, and ought to be divided among the descendants of the three daughters. Bruce followed, maintaining the same view; and the king referred the question to his council—" Is the kingdom of Scotland divisible; or are its escheats and its revenues divisible?" The council replied, that neither could be divided. One more adjournment then took place, to the 17th of November, when all parties were commanded again to meet in the castle of Berwick-on-Tweed.

" On that great and important day, the council and parliament of England, with the nobility of both countries, being met, and the various competitors appearing, the king solemnly decreed, 'That the kingdom of Scotland, being indivisible, and the king of England being bound to judge of the rights of his subjects according to the laws and usages of the people over whom he reigns, by which laws the more remote in degree of the first line of descent is preferable to the nearer in degree of the second; therefore, John Baliol ought to have seizin of the kingdom of Scotland, with reservation always of the right of the king of England, and of his heirs, when they shall think proper to assert it.'

" After having delivered judgment, Edward exhorted Baliol to be careful in the government of his people, lest, by giving any just cause of complaint, he should call down upon himself an interference of the lord paramount. He then commanded the regents to give him seizin of his kingdom, and directed orders to the governors of the castles throughout Scotland to deliver them into the hands of Baliol. The great seal of Scotland was then broken into four parts, and the pieces ordered to be deposited in the treasury of the king of England."*

* Tytler's History of Scotland, vol. i., p. 100.

On the following day, Baliol, in the castle of Norham, swore fealty to Edward, who gave a commission to John St. John to proceed to the coronation of the new king. This ceremony took place on St. Andrew's day; and towards the end of December the king of Scotland visited Edward in England, and paid homage to him at Newcastle-on-Tyne.

So ended this great transaction, and even Hume is obliged to admit, that " the conduct of Edward, both in the deliberate solemnity of the proceedings, and in the justice of the award, was so far unexceptionable." Other Scotch writers, however, have endeavoured to impeach Edward's honour in this affair on two grounds: They have alleged that he would have decided in Bruce's favour if Bruce would have consented to acknowledge his feudal superiority; and they have surmised, that he gave the preference to Baliol as being mentally the weaker of the two candidates, and therefore the fitter for his purpose.

The first of these fictions is sufficiently refuted by Hume's own statement, that " Bruce was *the first that acknowledged Edward's right of superiority* over Scotland; for even in his petition, in which he set forth his claim to the crown, he applied to him as liege lord of the kingdom, a step which was not taken by any other of the competitors." So far, then, as submission to Edward's claims could merit his favour, Bruce had gone farther than Baliol or any of his other rivals. And the supposition that Edward's preference for Baliol was dictated by selfish motives, is equally opposed to the known facts of the case. Bruce and Baliol were both English barons, as well as lords in Scotland; but Bruce was the more English of the two. He, the competitor, had for many years sat as a judge in Westminster Hall. His son, the earl of Carrick, had accompanied Edward in his expedition to Palestine; and in Rymer, under the date of 1281, we find the following letter:—

"The king, to Bonrunonio de Luk,* et sancto Merc' de Luk, greeting : Whereas our beloved Robert de Brus, earl of Carrick, is in present need of money, we request you that you will cause to be advanced or lent to the said earl or his attorney, for his occasion, forty pounds, and we will cause them to be repaid to you. And when you have lent to him the aforesaid money, you shall take from him his letters patent, testifying his receipt of the same. Witness our hand. Windsor, 10th September, 1281." †

So far, therefore, as we can judge at this distance of time, we should be inclined to think that the king's preference was for Bruce, but that his sense of justice compelled him to give judgment in Baliol's favour. No mental weakness, supposed to exist in Baliol, could be more favourable to Edward's views than the personal friendship of Bruce and his son.

Our English king, then, had preserved his integrity throughout this whole transaction. If any sinister or concealed purposes had been entertained by him, opportunities of furthering them had not been wanting. If the subjugation and annexation of Scotland had been then in his mind, the unwise proposal of some of the competitors—to divide the kingdom into three—offered him a signal opportunity of advancing his plans. Hume admits that "his interests seemed to require the partition of Scotland." Yet he promptly rejected the proposal. Rapin, another historian, who is by no means partial to Edward, admits his purity in

---

* De Luc or De Luke was a Florentine merchant or banker, and collector of the Customs.

† Rymer's Fœdera, vol. ii., p. 597. This, probably, is one of the earliest instances we have of an English king's *cheque upon his banker*.

these transactions. He says, "It appears from Edward's whole conduct, that his intent at first was not to become master of Scotland, but only to render that kingdom dependent on England, in which he did but follow the steps of most of his predecessors." "If he had designed a conquest, he might have found pretences to place English governors and garrisons in the fortresses that were put into his hands; or by acceding to the demand for the partition of the kingdom, he might have so weakened it as to render its wretchedness and ultimate fall inevitable."

The judgment of Mr. Sharon Turner, who is a severe critic of Edward's whole life, is thus given on the transaction which we have just been describing :—

"In justice to one of the greatest sovereigns that has swayed the English sceptre, it is important to remark that, although the incorporation of Scotland with England became at last his determination, there are not sufficient grounds to impeach his probity with this plan before the conduct of the Scotch led him to adopt it. All that he claimed at the outset was the feudal sovereignty of Scotland. But so had the king of France been the feudal sovereign of Normandy and Gascony; and yet the kings of England, who did homage for these possessions, had enjoyed the government of those countries with sufficient independence. There is no evidence that when Baliol was crowned, the king of England projected to abolish the Scottish royalty or parliament. To be the lord paramount, the feudal sovereign of the whole island, as the king of France had been of Normandy, Bretagne, Flanders, and Aquitaine, while these provinces were enjoying their independent hereditary governments, was the honour to which Edward aspired; and the great political object which he would have attained by it would have been, *a termination of the predatory wars*, which had always desolated the borders of the two kingdoms. It was a species of impiety and perjury for the liegeman to make war on his feudal lord; and it exposed him to the loss of life and territory. Scotland becoming a royal fief of the English crown, a new and sacred bond of amity was established between the countries. The facts, that for four years Edward did nothing incompatible with the continuance of the Scottish royalty, and that it was the wilful hostility of Scotland itself which forced him into the field against it, afford reasonable evidence that the line which we have drawn was the limitation of his ambition."*

More recently, Sir Edward Creasy has justly said, that "throughout this memorable transaction there is not the slightest trace of unfairness or rapacity on the part of the king."†

We leave Edward, then, at this important crisis of his history, blameless. No charge can be advanced against him, even by the most vehement of his Scottish assailants, except that of having embraced an opportunity which came without his seeking, to assert what he deemed to be "the rights of the crown of England." This Hume terms "iniquitous." But let it be remembered, that this measure, if successful, involved consequences of the most beneficial kind, alike to both kingdoms. Chiefly, it would have terminated "those predatory wars which had so often desolated the borders of the two kingdoms." And the opportunity offered to Edward of accomplishing this great work, must have seemed one which it would be criminal to neglect. Long before he had approached Scotland, its chief men directed to him many applications, in which they treated him as their superior lord. He was sensible of the prodigious

---

* Turner's History of England, vol. v., p. 75.
† History of England, vol. ii., p. 395.

advantages which would result from any scheme which rendered this state of things permanent. He therefore accepted that which the Scotch seemed eager to offer. At their request he assumed the place and the functions which they tendered. Meeting the assembled barons of Scotland, he frankly and explicitly stated his views. Allowing them an abundant space for deliberation, he again proposed the question. And then, without a dissentient voice, Scotland accepted him as her superior lord. That she, or that some of her barons, afterwards repented of their deed, and wished to retract it, occasioned many calamities to both countries. In fact, this unfaithfulness threw the two realms back into that condition of enmity, from which it had been Edward's aim to rescue them. It led to the sacrifice of hundreds of thousands of lives, and to the long postponement of that union which, after all, was inevitable. But, for all this, it remains indisputable that Edward's aim was a noble and patriotic one; and that the means he employed were direct, straightforward, and suitable to the occasion.

VII.

TROUBLES WITH FRANCE—WAR IN SCOTLAND.

At the close of 1292, Edward returned to England, doubtless with much content and satisfaction, having, apparently, accomplished one great object of his life—the unification of the island of Britain. Its conquest, which is too often described as the end he had in view, was never desired by him; but to bring the whole land into unity, so far as to render internal wars impossible, had been his object from the commencement of his reign. He found Alexander, king of Scotland, and Llewellyn, prince of Wales, and neither country would ever have been disturbed by him had their rulers given their fealty and kept their pledge. But the Welsh were too fond of predatory expeditions into Herefordshire and Cheshire, and the Scotch hoped some day to possess Northumberland, and with this view were always ready to form alliances with France. These Welsh inroads and these Scotch alliances with France, always ending in an invasion of England, Edward determined to check. Therefore his language was, " Pay your homage; give me your fealty; swear, as your fathers have sworn, ' to be my true man.' Vow allegiance, and then keep your vow."

Scotland had at last, without any coercion, been brought into this position; and had Scotland observed Edward's own rule—*Pactum serva*—she would never have seen the fights of Stirling or Falkirk, nor the blood-stained fields of Halidon Hill and Durham, of Dupplin Moor, or Hamildon Hill, or Flodden, or Pinkie. His great desire was peace; for that, not for conquest, he thought and planned, he laboured and contrived. Unhappily, his life was already declining, old age and death overtook him before the work was accomplished. Scotland succeeded, under Bruce, in undoing all his work; but that Scotland was the better for such undoing is, we believe, wherever entertained, a most mistaken notion.

In carrying forward the story of the arbitration without a break, we left unnoticed one or two circumstances which occurred in England during 1291 and 1292. When Edward, in August, 1291, adjourned the Scottish question until the following June, his most urgent reason for such postponement was the serious illness of his mother, queen Eleanor of Provence, who died about the end of that summer at Ambresbury, in Wiltshire, and at whose funeral he was present early in September, attended by a great assembly of prelates and nobles, especially convened for that ceremony.

But there was another matter which still more imperatively demanded the king's attention. Two of the chief nobles of the kingdom—Gilbert earl of Gloucester and Humphrey earl of Hereford—had quarrelled, and had gone to the extremity of open war. The earl of Gloucester was the king's son-in-law. Presuming probably upon this, and confident of his power, he had encroached upon the possessions of the earl of Hereford, and had begun to build a castle on the lands belonging to this earl. Bitter contentions and open violence naturally followed, and the king, hearing of the quarrel, had been obliged to send to the two earls his commands, reserving the hearing of the matter for his own court, but enjoining, meanwhile, an abstinence from all violent proceedings. But the quarrel had gone too far to be so arrested. The followers of the two earls were everywhere at enmity. Houses were burnt, churches demolished, and many persons were killed. Hence, without any delay, on the very morning after the funeral of his mother, the king sat in council at Ambresbury, whither a large assembly of the nobles had come for the religious ceremony, and there called the two earls before him.

The offence they had committed was of the highest gravity. As the king's lieutenants, each in his own district, their first duty was "to keep the king's peace," and to make all other persons keep it. Instead of which, disregarding the authority of the law, they had plunged into open violence, and thus, as far as in them lay, had introduced a state of civil war and utter confusion.

Gloucester, now brought into the presence of law supported by power, put forward some pleas in justification, which required time for their establishment or rejection. The king, therefore, directed the necessary inquiries to be made, and adjourned the further hearing until January 7th, 1292. On that day it was adjudged by the king's council at Westminster—the king himself pronouncing the sentence —that the two earls were both guilty, that the liberties of Glamorgan and Brecknock should be forfeited for their respective lives, and that they themselves should be committed to prison during the king's pleasure. The authority of the law was thus vindicated, and two of the greatest nobles of the realm were shown to be subject to it. After a time the relaxation which was implied in the terms of the sentence took place. The earls were set at liberty, and their forfeitures were commuted for fines proportioned to their respective criminality. Hereford was ordered to pay 1000 marks, which was equal to about £10,000 of our present money; but Gloucester, who doubtless had been the aggressor, and who probably presumed with his connection with the crown, was subjected to a fine of 10,000 marks, which, according to our present value, would be equal to £100,000!

During the summer and autumn of that year, 1292, the affairs of Scotland occupied Edward's attention. Early in 1293 we find him again at home, and soon his attention was imperatively demanded to one of the most disastrous events of his reign—an unnecessary and almost purposeless war with France. Like many similar contentions, it had one of the smallest possible beginnings.

A Norman ship and an English one had sent their boats ashore for water near Bayonne, and a contention arose as to the preference, in which blows were given, and one of the Normans was killed. Vexed at their defeat, the Normans carried a complaint to the French king, who, in a moment of incautious irritation, told them to avenge themselves. So encouraged, the Normans boarded an English ship in the Channel, and hanged up one of the sailors as a reprisal for the loss of their comrade at Bayonne. But the sailors of the Cinque Ports were not likely to submit to such treatment; fresh encounters soon took place, and the Channel became the scene of unauthorized and lawless warfare. Ships were captured and recaptured, and blood was constantly flowing. Edward at once sent the earl of Lincoln to the court of France, to desire that some means might be found to put a stop to these disorders; but Philip was a haughty prince, and disliked to make any admission of his error. But while the earl waited for his answer, the warfare on the coast came to its height. A fleet of about two hundred French ships laden with wine was met with by some sixty or eighty vessels from the Cinque Ports, and a collision taking place, the French fleet was nearly destroyed, and several thousands of the seamen killed or thrown overboard. The news soon found its way to the French court, and Philip was exceedingly enraged; the more so, doubtless, inasmuch as he could not but feel conscious that the whole mischief had sprung from his own hasty and injudicious counsel. But his wounded pride blinded his reason. He sent an angry message to Edward, demanding immediate compensation. Edward sent over the bishop of London to represent, first, that he had his own courts, in which he would see justice done at all times; secondly, that he was ready to agree to an arbitration, which should decide the whole question; or, thirdly, he would meet the king of France himself if any difficulty arose about a settlement. But Philip was too angry to listen to any reasonable proposals. The bishop had to leave the French court without an answer; the English students found it necessary to quit the university of Paris; and generally throughout France the English travellers and residents saw themselves in circumstances of peril. Commerce was entirely interrupted, and all things were falling into confusion. At last Philip cited Edward himself to appear before him in Paris, there to answer sundry charges. The king sent his brother Edmund, who had married the mother of the queen of France. He also took the precaution to send an able commander, St. John, into Gascony, with instructions to put that province into a state of defence.

Edmund was received at Paris with apparent kindness, and the queen and the queen dowager expressed great desire for the restoration of peace. But they represented to him that Philip was chiefly enraged at some insults which he had received from the Gascons; and that, if Edward would give him temporary possession of that province, so as to vindicate his honour in the sight of that people, he would engage to restore it immediately, and would accept a very easy satisfaction for all other injuries. This sort of formal and temporary possession, given to the superior lord, was not an uncommon thing in those days. We have already seen that Edward in the Scottish arbitration, had the kingdom and its castles put into his hands, on his engaging to restore them to the rightful owner; *and he did so restore them.* In the present case he does not seem to have supposed it possible that two crowned queens could be lending themselves to a fraud. "Therefore," says Hume, "he sent his brother orders to sign and execute the treaty with the two queens. Philip solemnly promised to execute his part of it, and the king's citation to appear in the court of France was accordingly recalled. But the French monarch was no sooner put into possession of Gascony than the citation was renewed; Edward was condemned for non-appearance; and the province by a formal sentence was declared to be forfeited and annexed to the crown." *

To a prince like Edward, this must have been a double mortification. He was himself the very soul of honour, and to find his equals and associates capable of fraud and deceit must have been grievous to him. He also prided himself on maintaining to the full all the rights and honours of the crown which he wore; and hence to be robbed of a noble province by mere chicanery and falsehood, would be doubly vexatious. But to this loss he never for a moment submitted, nor did he cease his efforts till he finally regained that territory for the British crown.

* Hume adds, very strangely, "Edward had thus fallen into *a like snare* with that which he himself had spread for the Scots." What "like snare"? Scotland had been placed in his hands on his promise to restore it, which promise he kept. Gascony was placed in the hands of Philip on a similar promise; but that promise was broken. Instead of likeness here is contrast.

In the summer of 1294, he prepared a large armament for the recovery of the province; and appealed to the clergy at Winchester for a liberal aid, which was readily granted him. A parliament held in November gave him *a tenth*, which was voted and paid with more than ordinary readiness; and Edward was preparing to lead his forces in person, when a new peril called for his presence in another direction. The Welsh had felt aggrieved a year or two before, by the levy of a fifteenth, granted by parliament, and collected by English officers in a manner to which they were, as yet, unaccustomed. Hearing now that the king was about to sail for Gascony, they deemed it a favourable juncture for an attempt to throw off the English yoke. It was always their wont to act by a sudden outbreak. Accordingly, taking advantage of a fair at Carnarvon, a rendezvous was appointed, and the leaders succeeded in surprising the castle and in putting all the English to the sword. A small force, under the earls of Lancaster and Lincoln, advancing into Denbighshire, was defeated by the Welsh; and on the whole, Edward felt that it would be unwise to leave England with such a sore unhealed.

He therefore proceeded, in November, into Wales, having placed the expedition for Gascony under the orders of the earl of Richmond, who had with him de Vere, St. John, and other officers of distinction. The king kept his Christmas at Conway; but shortly afterwards, attempting to penetrate further in spite of the season, he was placed for a short time in a position of difficulty and peril. He had led the way, with the vanguard, over a mountain stream, which, rising suddenly, became impassable, and thus divided the few men who were with the king from the rest of the army, while the baggage and provisions were still in the rear. Thus separated from the main body of his forces, the king was blockaded by the Welsh, and found his little party nearly destitute of provisions. There was not bread enough for their wants, and water mixed with honey was the only drink that remained to them. A single keg of wine was discovered, which the soldiers naturally proposed to reserve for the king's use. But Edward rejected the thought, exclaiming, "No, in a case of need all things should be in common; and we will all fare alike till God shall give us release. I, who have led you into this difficulty, will know no preference." Happily the waters soon began to subside; the rest of the army found means to join the king; and the Welsh were quickly put to flight.*

We shall see the king, a few years later, in his sixtieth year, sleeping, the night before the battle of Falkirk, on the open heath, with his shield for his pillow, and his horse for his companion. And doubtless it was this soldierly frankness and hardihood, joined with his knightly fame, and his never-failing success, which gave him such remarkable command over his soldiers, and made a campaign under his leadership so attractive and popular a duty.

This Welsh insurrection did not long detain the king. The leaders of the outbreak, Morgan and Madoc, were soon reduced to difficulties, and threw themselves upon Edward's mercy. Madoc was confined for a time in the Tower of London; of Morgan we only hear that "he received mercy." †

Meanwhile, the hostilities between the Normans and the people of the Cinque Ports raged with augmented fury. The English commanded the Channel, landed where they pleased in Normandy, and ravaged the towns and villages near the coast. They took and burnt Cherbourg. Philip equipped a fleet of three hundred ships, and this large force

* Walter Hemingford. † Matthew of Westminster.

succeeded, for a time, in doing some injury to the Kentish coast. But the French had no great cause for triumph. The "Chronicle of London," now in the British Museum, briefly records, under date of the year 1297, that "the Normauns came to Dovarre, and brent a great part of the towne; *but they were sclayn every moder's son; ther eschaped none.*" One French ship, with three hundred soldiers on board, grounded near Hythe, and fell into the hands of the Kentish men, ship and crew.

One part of Philip's plan failed through the detection of one of his agents. One Thomas de Turberville, a knight of some note in Glamorganshire, being taken prisoner by the French, offered his services to Philip, holding out large expectations of aid he could render to the invaders. He represented that, if released, he could obtain from Edward the command of one of the Cinque Ports; and could thus give the French fleet and forces a secure landing-place. He was accordingly permitted to return, and began to use his best endeavours to carry his plans into effect. But probably his anxiety to be employed on the Kentish coast awakened suspicion; his correspondence was intercepted, and letters, explanatory of his purposes, were seized. He was brought to trial; the evidence was conclusive, and he received sentence of death. And here we see what the real punishment for high treason at that time was. His guilt was more plain and more heinous than that of the Jesuit priests, who, in Elizabeth's reign, conspired against her life and government, in obedience to their spiritual head at Rome. They were, not once or twice, but in considerable numbers, hanged, disembowelled, beheaded, and quartered. But this Turberville, who had conspired, not against his sovereign only, but against his own people, whom he was willing to sell to a foreign invader, received the milder sentence of being drawn to the gallows on a hide or hurdle, there to be hanged and left hanging in chains. In a word, the punishment actually inflicted in Edward's time for the crime of high treason was merely that which, in our own time, has been inflicted for piracy. And yet many writers have represented again and again that the terrible punishment for high treason, which was inflicted for several centuries in England, and which remained on our statute-book until the days of Mackintosh and Romily, was devised and appropriated to that crime in Edward's reign.

Philip's wrath, however, grew with his defeats, and he began to form confederacies with other powers, such as Norway and Scotland, for the invasion and humiliation of England. And this brings us to the commencement of the fearful story of the wars between England and Scotland, which, in the year 1295 began to be contemplated, and in 1296 actually broke out. These wars lasted, in the days of Edward I. and II., for more than twenty years. They again and again broke out in subsequent reigns, until the union of the two kingdoms finally terminated them. The immediate question before us is,—With whom did they at this time originate?

Hume and several other writers unhesitatingly assume that these wars were intentionally provoked by Edward, and formed a part of his plan. Hume says: "His intention plainly was to enrage Baliol by indignities, to engage him in rebellion, and so to assume the dominion of the state as the punishment of his treason and felony."

But upon the very face of the matter, this supposition is manifestly absurd. The war with France had broken out *before* Edward took any hostile measures against Scotland. The Scottish quarrel evidently occurred at the most inconvenient of all periods, and could never have been desired or sought by him at that most inopportune moment.

But in proof that Edward desired to provoke the Scotch to resistance, it is said that " he encouraged all appeals to England ; required king John, by six different summonses, to come to London," and in this way " provoked him to vindicate his liberty."

Strange to say, none of the old Scottish writers thus defend, or account for, Baliol's rebellion. Barbour, the earliest of them, has not a word of this story ; Wyntoun speaks only of one appeal, that of Macduff, the earl of Fife ; Buchanan follows him ; and even Mr. Tytler, the latest and best of all the Scottish historians, rests his case solely upon this appeal of the earl of Fife. No one pretends that Baliol appeared to any other appeal. The citations alluded to must have been mere legal formalities. It was the conduct of Edward on Macduff's appeal which constituted the real grievance. Mr. Sharon Turner, who reviews the whole case with an impartial and a lawyer-like eye, says : " Edward received an appeal against Baliol's judgment preferred by a Scotchman to himself, as lord paramount, and summoned Baliol to his parliament to answer it, and expressed displeasure when he attempted to dispute his homage ; but *this*, between 1292 and 1296, was the extent of his adverse conduct. Two other cases, mentioned by lord Hailes, were, the one, a complaint against Edward's own officers ; the other, an illegal imprisonment of his officers." *

Beyond this contention about appeals, there was no quarrel between Baliol and Edward. Before any judgment was pronounced, Baliol asked for time to consult his parliament. It was granted, adjournment after adjournment

---

* Turner's History of England, vol. v., p. 75.

followed, and, in fact, no judgment ever was pronounced. Meanwhile, Baliol's claim to the honours and lands of Tyndale, Penrith, and Sowerby, with a third part of the manor of Huntingdon, was allowed, and he was generously exempted from a payment of £3,000 due from the estates of his mother.*

The quarrel with Scotland, then, which produced such terrible results, may be said to have taken its rise, formally, from Edward's assertion of the right of receiving appeals. But was this any extravagant or inordinate pretension on his part?

On the contrary, it was an essential point of his prerogatives as lord paramount, and it was known to be so, by all parties from the beginning. For nearly seven years past the Scotch had been appealing to him. They had sent after him to Gascony, in 1286, to know what course they should take on their king's death. In 1290 they had again applied to him, in the most urgent manner, to come and decide between the opposing claims of the competitors for the crown. At their request he met the nobles of Scotland, and at once told them, "I come as lord paramount; do you recognize me as such?" After some delay, and therefore without hurry or precipitation, he was so recognized. And when he had decided the question in Baliol's favour, he again distinctly warned him of their mutual relations, counselling him "to be careful in the government of his people, lest by giving any just cause of complaint, he should call down the interference of the lord paramount." Thus there was never the least concealment or reserve on Edward's part. He stated, from the first, what he conceived to be his rights, and he found nothing but acquiescence on the part of the Scotch. And it was several

* Lingard's Hist., vol. ii., p. 540.

weeks after this explicit declaration, that Baliol came to him at Newcastle, and took the oath of homage, avowing himself Edward's liegeman " for the kingdom of Scotland and all its appurtenances."

All questions being thus decided between the two, how was Edward to act when the earl of Fife, in the very next year, lodged an appeal against one of Baliol's decisions? To refuse to entertain it would be to abdicate his functions as lord paramount. Such appeals were not unusual, or even of rare occurrence. Mr. Tytler himself says : " Edward, who was a vassal of the king of France, for the duchy of Aquitaine, became involved with his lord superior in a quarrel similar to that between himself and Baliol. Philip summoned Edward to appear in his court at Paris, and there to answer, as his vassal, for the injuries which he had committed."*

But it may be replied that Edward, when so summoned, refused to go, and preferred to declare war against the king of France; and that the same right must be conceded to Baliol. Unquestionably the same right, *if the cases were the same;* but all turns, if we are discussing the moral aspects of the question, on the respective grounds of quarrel.

Edward, as all historians agree, had been grievously wronged by Philip, and was entitled—and, in fact, was bound, to demand redress for these wrongs. In his message to the king of France, declaring war against him, he thus states the grounds of his resistance and hostility : " The king of England did you homage conditionally—namely, according to the form of the peace made between your ancestors and his, which peace you have not kept. Moreover, that all differences between your subjects and his might be ended, a treaty was made between you and the

* Tytler's History of Scotland, vol. i., p. 108.

lord Edmund, his brother, containing certain articles *which you have not performed*. And after that, he hath required of you, three several times, to restore his land of Guienne, and to deliver those of his subjects whom you detain in prison: all which you have refused. Wherefore it seems to him that you no longer count him your vassal, and accordingly he refuses to be so for the future."

Now no one disputes that as Philip had sinned against Edward, so it was quite possible that Edward might have sinned against Baliol. But what are the grievances alleged? There is nothing that deserves the name; for the reception of Macduff's appeal was, on Edward's part, both a right and a duty. Yet, this reception constitutes the whole case against him; and upon this ground alone the Scotch threw all their oaths to the winds, and resolved upon war.

In December, 1292, at Newcastle-on-Tyne, John Baliol, after full warning of the intent and meaning of the homage, had taken the following oath:—

"My lord, sir Edward, king of England, *sovereign lord of the realm of Scotland*, I, John Baliol, king of Scotland, become your liegeman for the kingdom of Scotland and all its appurtenances and appendages; which kingdom I hold, and ought, of right and claim, to hold by inheritance, for myself and my heirs, kings of Scotland, of you and your heirs, kings of England. And faith and loyalty I will bear to you and your heirs, kings of England, of life and limb, and earthly honour, against all men that may live and die."[*]

Such was Baliol's oath, deliberately taken, with a full knowledge of its meaning, in December, 1292. The like oath was also taken by all the nobles of Scotland. Yet, in less than three years after, finding Edward involved in a war with France, they eagerly seized the opportunity of

[* Rymer, vol. ii., p. 590.]

freeing themselves from all these obligations. They sent an embassy to France, and entered into a treaty, engaging to assist Philip by invading England. Such was the first step in the long and sanguinary Scottish wars. Mr. Sharon Turner justly places these wars to the account of the Scotch, remarking that—

"For four years Edward did nothing incompatible with the continuance of the Scottish royalty; and it was the wilful hostility of Scotland which forced him into the field. From 1292 to 1296, though he received an appeal against Baliol's judgment, and summoned Baliol to his parliament, to answer it, yet this was the extent of his adverse conduct. And so far was Edward's behaviour from being revolting to Scottish feeling, that Bruce, the competitor of Baliol, having died, his family desired Edward to receive its homage, and willingly performed it."*

Edward, then, had done nothing to call forth the hostility of Scotland; in fact, he had simply carried out his own professions and pretensions, and expected the Scotch to do the same. Being now involved, by no fault of his own, in a war with France, he called upon Baliol and the other Scottish nobles who had sworn fealty to him, to give him their aid against the hostility of the French. This aid every leading man in Scotland had solemnly sworn to render; yet, instead of keeping their oaths, the Scottish barons instantly violated them in the most direct and flagrant manner. They had sworn "to bear faith and loyalty to Edward, against all men that may live or die;" instead of which they deliberately contracted with Philip to raise an army and to fall upon England, so as to assist the French king's designs. What share of this treason and perfidy ought to be allotted to Baliol it is difficult to determine. The whole power in

* Turner's History of England, vol. i., p. 76.

Scotland seems to have been taken out of the king's hands and usurped by a faction of the nobles, who at first dictated to the king, and at last dethroned him. They assembled a council, or parliament, at Scone, at which they resolved to dismiss all Englishmen who were in any public employments; to seize upon all lands in Scotland which belonged to Englishmen; and even to deprive of their estates in Scotland those Scotchmen who remained faithful to Edward. "In this way Robert Bruce lost his lordship of Annandale. It was given to John Comyn, earl of Buchan, who instantly assumed the rights of a proprietor, and took possession of Lochmaben Castle." *

But the ruling faction was not even content with wholesale confiscation. Mr. Tytler continues—"The party who then ruled in the Scottish parliament, dreading a submission on the part of their king, secluded him from all power, confined him in a mountain-fortress, and placed the management of affairs in the hands of twelve of the leading nobles."

Bruce, the competitor, and formerly an English judge, had lately died. His son, the earl of Carrick, whom we recently saw styled in one of Edward's letters, "our beloved Robert Bruce," and who was, throughout his life, faithful to Edward, would naturally keep the king acquainted with all that was going on. He would apprise him of this state of general disorder, usurpation, and confiscation; the king in prison; all power monopolized by a faction, who plundered and banished their rivals, and who were collecting a force avowedly intended for the invasion of England. This state of affairs would satisfy Edward that, before he could sail for Gascony, he must do something for the pacification of Scotland. The treaty with France was no secret; it was made by an embassy consisting of several persons, and it was

* Tytler's History of Scotland, vol. i., p. 110.

discussed in the Scottish council. Its main provisions would thus inevitably become known, and Robert Bruce would be able to warn Edward that an invasion on the side of Scotland was to be anticipated.

The king was thus involved in war at once in two opposite directions. Gascony had been fraudulently seized upon, and he could not, for a moment, contemplate submission to such a wrong. He therefore prepared a fleet of three hundred and fifty-four ships, on board of which about seven thousand men were embarked; but the state of affairs in Scotland rendered it inexpedient that he should himself accompany this force. He therefore placed it under the command of his brother, the earl of Lancaster, who, after gaining some advantages, died at Bayonne, and left the command to the earl of Lincoln.

Meanwhile, the king knew that it was absolutely necessary that he should take effectual measures to protect his northern frontier against the threatened Scottish invasion. But, although his revenues were so well managed as to suffice for all ordinary demands, the extraordinary exigencies of two wars had placed him in a position of financial difficulty. A year or two previously he had despatched one expedition into Gascony, and now another had exhausted his means, and the armament for Scotland was still to be provided for. A larger supply than usual was needed, and how should it be obtained? The consideration of this question in Edward's mind, produced at last what Hume describes as "the real and true epoch of the House of Commons," and the "dawn of popular government in England."

Two earlier dates have been assigned for this great epoch; but that which is now before us may on some grounds claim the preference. Simon de Montfort, in 1265, while he held both Henry and prince Edward in his custody, summoned a kind of parliament or assembly in Westminster, to sanction some of his transactions with the king; and to this parliament he called a portion of the barons—*i.e.*, those of his own party—some knights, and the representatives of certain borough towns. But this whole transaction was regarded, as Hume remarks, as "the act of a violent usurpation;" and no one ever dreamed in after years of treating it as a precedent.

Nearly twenty years had passed away, when Edward himself, in 1283, not wishing to determine arbitrarily the fate of David of Snowdon, called to Shrewsbury not only the barons and the knights, but also representatives from several of the larger towns; and before these representatives he placed not only the case of David, but also the great "Statute of Merchants"—the first English law, probably, to which the assent of any regularly-appointed borough representatives was ever asked or desired.

But, in the present case, a new cause for this appeal to the people was apparent. A national peril, an exigency affecting the whole realm, had shown itself, and Edward, with his characteristic manliness, resolved to place it frankly before his people, and to ask their aid in a matter in which, as he told them, "all were equally concerned." The writs convening this parliament of November, 1295, must be taken to speak the very language of Edward's own noble mind.* Those writs commence as follows: "As the rule of justice teaches us that what concerns all should be by all approved, so, it also indicates that common perils should be met by remedies provided in common." The dangers to which the

* Nor can we, in this instance, attempt to divide the credit between the king and his able chancellor. Robert Burnel had been taken from his side, by death, in October, 1292.

realm was exposed are then set forth, and the writ concludes: "Seeing, therefore, that your welfare, as well as that of the whole realm, is concerned, we charge you, on your loyalty and attachment to us, that on the day after the feast of St. Martin, you do attend," etc.

These writs were addressed not only to the nobles, the prelates, and the knights or lesser barons, but also to the sheriffs or bailiffs of about one hundred and twenty cities and towns. Each sheriff was directed "to cause to be elected of his county, two knights, and of each city in their county, two burgesses." And these were to meet, for the first time in the annals of England, "to provide against the dangers which threatened the kingdom;" and they were to be invested "with power from the communitates to do what the matter should require."

On this 27th of November, 1295, accordingly, the outline sketched at Shrewsbury in 1283 was filled up, and there met, for the first time, a parliament like that of our own day; —a parliament "the archetype of all the representative assemblies which now meet, either in the old world or in the new."* And, not unnaturally, the burgesses, now for the first time consulted on an emergency of the state, met the king's appeals and requests with even more warmth and liberality than either of the other sections of the parliament. The clergy granted to the king a tenth; the barons and knights an eleventh; but the burgesses gave him, without hesitation, a seventh. Such was the cordial response given to Edward by his people, on his frank appeal to them for support, in this, one of the great emergencies of his reign.

These "aids" granted to the king in the last month of 1295, enabled him to prepare with vigour for the important business of the following spring. To Gascony, as we have

* Macaulay, vol. i., p. 17.

seen, he had despatched a considerable force. The coasts of Kent and Sussex had shown themselves, for two years past, able to cope with all the power of Normandy. The chief point of disquietude, therefore, was in the north. Invasions of the northern counties by Scottish armies had been seen in former reigns; and Edward had received full notice that such a step had been resolved upon by the faction which now bore sway in Scotland.

To wait in London until the Scotch had ravaged Cumberland, would not have been the course of a statesman or of a general. Whether as friend or foe, Edward was always prompt, frank, and outspoken. He directed a parliament to be summoned to meet at Newcastle on the 1st of March, 1296, and to this parliament the Comyns, Baliols, Bruces, and other Scottish leaders would, as English barons, naturally receive summonses. Baliol, especially, not only as an English baron, but also as the chief vassal of the crown, was called to this meeting, there to perform his oath, sworn at that same Newcastle only three years and three months before, in which oath he had pledged his "faith and loyalty" to stand by Edward and his successors on the throne of England, "against all men that may live or die." Edward, as his manner was, would take care to proceed with strict regularity. But he could not feel any doubt that it was a campaign rather than a parliament that he was about to open; and he had made his arrangements accordingly.

Mr. Tytler tells us, of 1295, that "to Bruce, son of the competitor for the crown, Edward affected uncommon friendship; regretted his decision in favour of the now rebellious Baliol, and declared his determination to place him on the throne." And, in 1296, that "Bruce reminded him of his promise to place him on the throne." "Have I nothing to do?" said the haughty monarch, "but to conquer kingdoms for you?" Here is an important statement, which represents Edward as false and deceitful. But when did it first see the light? In Fordun, and in Bower's history, which appeared some time after 1440, or *nearly one hundred and fifty years after* the period referred to! It is no wonder, then, that Hume passes it over in silence, or that sir Walter Scott reduces it to this: " Bruce, after the victory of Dunbar, *conceived* his turn of triumph was approaching, and hinted to Edward his hope," etc.

The object of Fordun, as of the other Scottish historians, was to make out some legal right or title for Bruce. In order to do this, they scruple not to invent. Thus, as we have already seen, they tell us that, before the arbitration was decided, Edward offered to decide in favour of Bruce if he would own him as his superior lord, and that *Bruce refused to do so*. Whereas we know, from documents which are still extant, that Bruce had at that very time actually applied to Edward as his superior lord!

The present fiction is refuted by many well-known facts. Had Edward deceived and disappointed this Bruce (the son of the competitor), it must have followed that the party so deceived would have become bitterly hostile. Instead of which, we immediately find this very Bruce employed by Edward, as "his dear and trusty friend," to receive to his peace the inhabitants of Annandale; and three times after this does Mr. Tytler distinctly recognize this Bruce as being always loyal and faithful to Edward; a thing most improbable, if he had been—as represented by Fordun a century after—grossly deceived and wronged by the king.

The king of Scotland, as Mr. Tytler remarks, was at this time "confined in a mountain fortress," and the Scottish barons who had assumed the management of affairs were busily engaged in the collection and organization of an army. All this would be known to Edward, and accordingly, finding that neither the king nor the barons made their appearance at Newcastle, he put his own forces in motion, and began to approach the Tweed.

Before, however, he could reach the frontier, tidings came that the Scotch had already, without any public warning, complaint, or declaration of war, actually invaded England. On the 26th of March, the earls of Buchan, Menteith, Strathern, Lennox, Rosse, Athol, and Mar, with a force of about forty thousand men, broke into Cumberland, and ravaged the whole country with savage ferocity. The "Chronicle of Lanercost," a record written at the time and on the spot, thus describes the invasion: " In this raid the Scotch surpassed the cruelty of the heathen, for, not being able to seize upon the strong, they wreaked their vengeance on the weak, the decrepit, and the young; children of two or three years old they impaled upon lances and threw into the air; consecrated churches they burned; women dedicated to God they ravished and slew."

This exhibition of savage ferocity, however, gained for the Scotch neither honour nor advantage. When they came before Carlisle, a place of some strength, " a handful of the citizens," says Mr. Tytler, "compelled them to retreat with loss." The only real result of this movement was a disastrous one for the Scotch. They had, by taking the initiative, decided Edward's course. He was, throughout his whole career, "slow to strife," but he was not likely to sit in silence while his realm was invaded and his subjects slaughtered. He had reached Berwick on the 30th of March, and there the intelligence reached him of the Scotch invasion of Cumberland, and of the cruelties they were perpetrating. His exclamation on receiving this news is a characteristic one. " Blessed be God!" he exclaimed, "who hath up to this time preserved our hands blameless! But now, since they themselves have entered our realm in hostile array, we, under his guidance, will retaliate what they have done, and will return their mischief upon their own heads."

Surely those who are fond of representing Edward as an ambitious and unscrupulous man, ought to hesitate when they see him, at a crisis like this, so manifestly anxious to be *right*, and feeling such relief of mind when the aggressions of the Scotch made his path perfectly clear.

He forthwith sent to those who held the command in Berwick, a summons for the surrender of the town on honourable terms. It was refused in the language of scorn. Edward accordingly took measures for an assault. He ordered his fleet to enter the harbour, while he would assault the walls. Three of his ships fell into the hands of the garrison, who instantly put every man to the sword.*

But the avenger was at hand. Edward himself led the assault, and was the first to clear the ditch.† The English, animated by such an example, carried everything before them. The castle surrendered upon terms the next day, and thus one of the largest and most important towns in Scotland was gained in the first three days of the campaign.

Some of the Scottish historians have striven to tarnish Edward's fame by representing the storming of Berwick as a massacre. There is not the slightest ground for such an

---

* Wyntoun, the Scottish chronicler, says—
  "Of these they saved never a man,
  For prisoners in such awhile,
  To kepe is dowte and grete perille."
† Peter Langtoft writes—
  "What then did Sir Edward? Peer he had none like;
  Upon his steed Bayard first he won the dike."

imputation. The carrying any town by storm must always be a dreadful operation, whether the town be Badajos or Berwick; but there was nothing to render the storming of Berwick worse than other efforts of the same kind.*

The Scots had themselves already provoked severity. In their invasion of Cumberland a few days previous, they had " killed all they found, sparing neither age nor sex;" and in this very siege, as we have just seen, when some English ships and sailors had fallen into their hands, they showed no mercy.

While Edward was occupied with the repair and restoration of Berwick, the abbot of Arbroath was announced, who brought to him a message or letter from Baliol, renouncing his homage. But, as Mr. Sharon Turner remarks, " if Baliol had not become Edward's liegeman, such a renunciation was unnecessary; and if he were so, no liegeman could cancel his fealty without the consent of his lord. The renunciation was, therefore, evidence of its own absurdity." The Scottish chronicles, written long after, tell us that Edward exclaimed, "Ah! fool and felon! Of what folly is he guilty?" We may easily believe that he would receive such a communication with indignant contempt. He turned his face towards Edinburgh, and began his march towards that city.

Midway between Berwick and the present Scottish capital stood the castle of Dunbar. Its lord, the earl of that name, was with Edward; but the countess, "hating the

---

* Both Tytler and sir W. Scott condescend to borrow an exaggerated statement, that 17,000 persons fell in this storming of Berwick; but the complaint of the regents of Scotland, made a year or two after, states the number at "nearly 8000." Allowing for some exaggeration, and remembering that some of the dead must have been English, we may believe that the Scotch lost some 5000 or 6000 men—a number not at all remarkable.

English," called in, in her lord's absence, some of the Scottish leaders, and put the castle into their hands. So important was the possession of this strong place considered to be, that the earls of Athol, Rosse, and Menteith, with several barons and thirty-one knights, threw themselves into it, with a large force, hoping to maintain it against Edward's strongest efforts. The king, equally aware of its importance, despatched earl Warenne, with 10,000 foot and 1,000 horse, to capture it if possible. The garrison, alarmed at his approach, sent to "the guardians of Scotland" for aid, and the whole Scottish army, of 40,000 foot and 1,500 horse, moved down to its support. The garrison, now confident of victory, insulted the English as if already beaten. But the earl, says Mr. Tytler, "on the appearance of the Scottish army, at once advanced to attack it. On approaching the high ground, it was necessary to deploy through a valley, and the Scotch imagined they observed some confusion in the English ranks when executing this movement. Mistaking this for flight, they precipitately abandoned their position on the hills, and rushed down with shouts upon the enemy. But instead of an enemy in flight, they found an army, under perfect discipline, advancing upon their disordered columns. Having in vain endeavoured to regain their ranks, after a short resistance they were entirely routed. The victory was complete, and for a time it decided the fate of Scotland. Ten thousand men fell on the field or in the pursuit. A great multitude, including the principal Scottish nobility, were taken prisoners, and the next day, the king coming in person before Dunbar, the castle surrendered at discretion. The earls of Rosse, Athol, and Menteith, four barons, and seventy knights, submitted to the mercy of the conquerors."*

* Tytler, vol. i., p. 116.

Edward lost no time in following up his advantage. He sat down before the castle of Roxburgh, which was surrendered to him by James, the steward of Scotland; Dumbarton castle was yielded by Ingelram de Umfraville; Jedburgh castle followed; and a considerable reinforcement arriving from Wales, Edward was enabled to dismiss to their homes part of his English army.

He now advanced to Edinburgh, where the castle surrendered after a siege of eight days; then to Stirling, where a body of Irish auxiliaries joined him. At Perth he kept the feast of St. John the Baptist, creating new knights, with the accustomed festivities. Here messengers from Baliol found him, with letters announcing the Scottish king's submission. As Baliol had long been kept in durance by the rebellious barons, and as these were now, for the most part, prisoners in Edward's camp, we may reasonably suppose that this submission was one of the first spontaneous acts of the Scottish king on finding himself at liberty. Edward sent back, as his answer, a message signifying that he intended, in fifteen days, to proceed to Brechin, whither the now humbled king of Scotland might repair to meet him. Accordingly, on the 10th of July, Baliol presented himself at Brechin, acknowledged his offence, admitted Edward's right, and resigned the kingdom of Scotland into his hands, as a fief justly forfeited. Edward then assigned him the Tower of London for a residence, with the liberty of a circle of twenty miles round it. Here the dethroned king took up his abode, residing in London for the following three years, after which he was allowed to retire to his estates in Normandy.

On the 28th of August, Edward held a parliament at Berwick, where he received the fealty of the clergy, barons, and gentry of Scotland. Multitudes of all ranks resorted to him—earls, barons, knights, and esquires. "The oaths of homage, the renunciation of the French alliance, and the names of the vassals, which fill thirty-five skins of parchment, are still preserved among the English archives."*

Edward next directed his attention to the settlement of his new dominion; and "the measures he adopted," says Mr. Tytler, "were equally politic and just." The jurisdictions of Scotland were suffered to remain with those who possessed them under ancient and hereditary titles; no wanton or unnecessary act of rigour was committed, no capricious changes introduced; yet all proper means were adopted to give security to his conquest. The earl Warenne was made guardian of Scotland, Hugh [de Cressingham treasurer, and William Ormesby justiciary. The four castles of Roxburgh, Berwick, Jedburgh, and Edinburgh, were committed to English captains. A new seal, in place of the ancient seal of Scotland, was given to Walter de Agmondesham, the chancellor; and an exchequer for the receipt of the king's rents and taxes was instituted at Berwick, on the model of that at Westminster. The ancient coronation-stone of Scotland was removed from Scone and placed in Westminster Abbey, where to this hour it still remains.

Such, then, was Edward's first conquest of Scotland. No one disputes the skill and talent displayed by him. The only charge alleged has reference to the moral character of these transactions. Upon this point, therefore, it will be right to add a few words.

That the union of the several divisions of a great country,

---

* Tytler, vol. i., p. 121. But sir Walter Scott says: "Most of the noble and ancient families of Scotland are reduced to the necessity of tracing their ancestors' names in the *fifty-six* sheets of parchment, which constitute the degrading roll of submission to Edward I."

like England or France, into one great power, is a desirable thing for the country itself, is self-evident. No one doubts that the union of Normandy with France, and of Scotland with England, furthered the interests of all these countries ; or that to sever, now, Scotland from England, or Normandy from France, would be disastrous to all the people of all these territories. It was both right and expedient, then, that the sovereigns of England and France should watch for opportunities of effecting such unions, wherever this could be done consistently with justice and honour. For such an end might be attained by lawful means : as when Philip II. took Normandy from John; or it might be attempted by fraud : as when Philip IV. endeavoured to take Gascony from Edward.

Was, then, Edward's conduct, in the acquisition of Scotland, marked by any kind of injustice or wrong? Hume alleges that it was ;—charging him with " numerous acts of fraud and violence." But, instead of *numerous* acts of this kind, has any one act of either fraud or violence been proved?

We are unable to find a scintilla of such proof. Going back to 1286—7, we find that the only charge brought against Edward, up to that time, is that he abstained from interfering! Next, his proposal in 1289 is approved by all historians as wise, and just, and liberally framed. In 1290 he attempted no interference until the chief men in Scotland earnestly besought his interposition. Their approaches to him had all the aspect of appeals to a superior lord ; and he could hardly understand them in any other sense. He accepted them as such, and plainly told the Scottish barons that it was in this character that he came among them. After some hesitation, they accepted him as " lord paramount," and as such they swore fealty to him.

Scotland obtained, then, at last a king, John Baliol, but

now both king and people had paid homage to Edward, and had acknowledged his supremacy. Soon after, a Scottish earl lodges an appeal against one of Baliol's decisions, and calls upon Edward to do him justice. Edward proceeds, in the discharge of his office, to hear this appeal; and for so doing, heavy complaints are brought against him. Yet, in taking this course, he was guilty, in reality, of no offence whatever. Nevertheless, upon no other ground than this, did Baliol and the Scottish barons deliberately break their oaths, ally themselves with Edward's enemies, and raise an army for the invasion of England.

By all the laws of feudal sovereignty at that time known, they had by this act incurred the penalties of perjury and treason; and, by their invasion of Cumberland, they had commenced a war against their acknowledged lord. They rashly appealed to arms, and defied the power of England, wielded by the first captain of the age. They were overthrown, even before the waning of a single moon. But here, as everywhere, Edward's clemency is the most remarkable feature in the case. Not Baliol only, but all those who had forced him into this war, were justly exposed to the loss of property, if not of life. Yet, the contest once ended by Baliol's resignation, all that we hear of, on Edward's part, is a willing amnesty and a ready forgiveness. Up to this point of the story, then, we must deem the king to stand clear of any kind of moral condemnation.

VIII.

THE WAR WITH FRANCE, AND VARIOUS TROUBLES AT HOME, A.D. 1297.

EDWARD had now, apparently, achieved a great and important object, and he returned in the autumn of 1296 to his palace of Westminster, the undisputed sovereign of both islands, and of all the territories contained within them. But his fifty-ninth year, to which he was now approaching, was destined to prove one of the most trying and difficult conjunctures of his life. He had established his dominion over the whole realm; had frustrated one of Philip's main designs, by crushing the Scottish rebellion; and was now at leisure to deal with that monarch on the soil of France itself. But as each month of 1297 passed along, it brought with it some new peril; until, before the year had closed, a series of troubles and perplexities had so accumulated around him, that few men but himself could have forced their way through so many difficulties.

In dealing with France, Edward felt the disadvantages of his position, arising from the distance of Gascony from England. To convey an army to that country, of force sufficient to reconquer the province, would have exhausted both the treasure and the military strength of England; while, at the same time, neither Wales nor Scotland was in so tranquil a state as to encourage him to undertake such an enterprise. With his usual sagacity, therefore, Edward preferred to assail France on its northern frontier, in the hope of so threatening both the capital and Normandy as to force Philip to relinquish his hold upon the Gascon province. On the side of Flanders, too, Edward could obtain several allies; and its nearness to England rendered the conveyance of both men and stores less difficult and less expensive. For all these reasons Edward had determined, in the course of 1296, to endeavour to form a league between himself, the earls of Flanders, Holland, and Luxembourg, and the duke of Austria, for a combined attack upon France, on its north-eastern frontier. A similar policy was adopted, four centuries after, by William III. and by Marlborough.

But all schemes of this kind—and England has seen many of them—inevitably tend to one result: a subsidy. None of these princes were disposed to go to war with such a kingdom as France, except they were assisted in their preparations by a liberal supply of English money.

Having formed the desired confederacy, therefore, Edward was next obliged to call together his parliament, and to appeal to them for a supply. The barons, without difficulty, granted him a twelfth; the burgesses, an eighth. But when the king's representatives made their application to the prelates and clergy, an unexpected difficulty at once presented itself.

Boniface VIII., the reigning pope, and Winchelsey, the primate, were men of vigorous and aspiring minds, and they evidently desired to tread in the steps of Hildebrand and Thomas à Becket. They believed that they saw the king of England in circumstances of difficulty, and that an opportunity was thus afforded for advancing a new claim on behalf of the church.

Edward had undoubtedly begun to press with increasing weight upon the resources of the clergy. Nor was this at all surprising. His own necessities were now great, and the wealth of the church had long been visibly and rapidly augmenting. " The possessions of the clergy," says Dr. Henry, " never diminishing, but daily increasing, were now swelled up to an enormous bulk, and threatened to swallow up the whole lands of the kingdom." It has been remarked, that in the single reign of Henry III., as many as eight or nine of our splendid cathedrals were built or greatly enlarged; and during the same period, no fewer than one hundred and fifty-seven abbeys, priories, and other religious houses were founded.

Of the church's wealth, however, the court of Rome took care to demand and to obtain a large proportion. Sometimes the pope required a tenth, sometimes a fifth, and once as much as one half of all ecclesiastical incomes. In a few years, in the transactions connected with the crown of Sicily, the pope was computed to have drawn from England no less than nine hundred and fifty thousand marks, equal, according to the values of the time, to above nine millions of our present money! In a subsequent reign, in 1376, the commons represented to the king, " that the taxes paid to the pope yearly, amounted to *five times* as much as the taxes paid to the crown." Rome then, depending so largely on the supplies received from England, would naturally look with jealousy on the increasing demands of the crown, which must inevitably come into competition with those which she herself was accustomed to make.

Winchelsey, as we have said, was a man of great ability; and Boniface was distinguished among the popes. It may be difficult at this distance of time, to determine with which of these two the idea originated, but the fact is certain, that just at this moment, when Edward needed and expected a large supply from the church, the primate produced a bull, or mandate from the pope, " forbidding the clergy to grant to laymen any part of the revenues of their benefices, without the permission of the Holy See."

This was a sudden and a startling blow. By a few words the king saw the whole treasures of the church—his main reliance—shut up and sealed from his touch. He had asked of the clergy a supply of "a fifth." His commissioners appeared in the convocation for a reply. The archbishop rose and said, "You know, sirs, that under Almighty God we have two lords—the one spiritual, the other temporal. Obedience is due to both, *but most to the spiritual*. We are willing to do everything in our power, and will send deputies at our own expense to consult the pontiff. We entreat you to carry this reply to the king; for we dare not speak to him ourselves."

It was clear, that to submit to this novel claim to exemption would be to prostrate the royal authority at the feet of the papal. Already had the pope claimed and exercised a co-ordinate power with the crown, in taxing ecclesiastical possessions, now rapidly becoming a large proportion of all the property of the realm; but he here asserted his sole and supreme power over the whole. In future the king was to receive aid from the clerical body, only when, and so far as, the pope should grant his permission.

With either of the two preceding sovereigns such churchmen as Boniface and Winchelsey might have prevailed, and thus a foreign sovereignty of the most disastrous kind might have been established in the realm. But, happily, England had, at this crisis, a ruler equal to the emergency—a sovereign whom even those historians who are prejudiced against him,* admit to have been a "great statesman," "the model of a politic and warlike king." He saw at a glance,

---

* Mackintosh, Hume, etc.

the serious peril which threatened the realm, and he at once nerved himself to grapple with it. Yet he never, for an instant, showed the passion or the violence of a Rufus or a John. Not for a moment was he ever betrayed into any unworthy measures. "Himself the founder of a stately Cistercian abbey, and a man whose oblations and alms were a large sum in his yearly expenses, he displays even as a legislator a genuine anxiety for the real interests of the Church."* But to yield to this new pretension would have been to surrender the unquestionable rights of the crown, and such a surrender as that could never be dreamed of by a king like Edward. With his usual firmness and sagacity, he took without delay the most effectual and straightforward course to suppress this new kind of mutiny. Comprehending at a glance the mutuality of the obligations of the ruler and the subject, he at once decided that those who refused to bear their share of the public burdens could have no right to appeal to the protection of the guardians of the public peace. A deputation of the prelates waited on him at Castle Acre in Norfolk, to acquaint him with their determination, and to explain the reasons for it; to whom he at once declared, that "since the clergy had broken their allegiance to him, by denying him that assistance which by the tenure of their estates they were bound to pay, he would no longer feel any obligation to protect them, or to execute in their favour laws to which they refused to submit." At once, therefore, "he consulted the lay peers, and issued a proclamation of outlawry against the clergy, both regular and secular"—escheating their lay fees, goods, and chattels to the use of the crown. And, as Edward was always frank and outspoken, his chief justice, Sir John Metingham, publicly announced from the bench in Westminster Hall—

* Pearson's History, vol. ii., p. 310.

"You that appear for the archbishops, bishops, or clergy, take notice, that in future no justice is to be done them in the king's court, in any matter of which they may complain; but, nevertheless, justice shall still be done to all manner of persons who have any complaint against them." "So bold a step," says Rapin, "astonished the clergy, who, since the beginning of the monarchy, had never experienced the like resolution in any king of England."

We are now at the opening of the year 1297. The strong measures of the king quickly carried confusion into the ranks of the ecclesiastical confederacy. The archbishop of York, with all his diocese, and the bishops of Durham and Carlisle, soon made their peace with Edward, and paid their "fifth." It was not long before the bishops of Norwich, Ely, Lincoln, and Worcester, followed their example. Winchelsey vainly thundered his sentence of excommunication against all who should disobey the mandate of the pope. The sentence of outlawry proved to have the greater force. Tenants refused to pay rent; horses were seized on the highway; and the law, meanwhile, repudiated all claims of the ecclesiastical mutineers to avail themselves of its protection. The inevitable result of such a state of things soon showed itself. The clergy, and especially the wealthier of them, rapidly fell off from the archbishop, and sought and obtained the king's pardon and protection.

But this ecclesiastical rebellion had been only the beginning of troubles. Suppressed though it was, it led to fresh difficulties of another kind. The large and greatly-needed supply upon which the king had reckoned was withheld, and it now came in only slowly and in fragments. The "aid" granted by parliament required the customary time for its collection. Meanwhile, Edward had pledged himself both to pay large subsidies to his allies in Flanders, and also to bring over a considerable body of troops. These promises he was now endeavouring, as was his wont, strictly to perform.

But now appears in England, for the first time, *a parliamentary opposition*. Hume and Hallam award great praise to the earls of Hereford and Norfolk for their "firmness and patriotism" in daring to withstand the king; but they forget to give any credit to Edward for having introduced that parliamentary system into England which made such an opposition possible.

It is abundantly clear that the earl of Norfolk disliked the French war in 1297, just as the duke of Norfolk of the last century disliked the French war in 1797, and probably each could have assigned very plausible reasons for his dislike. The important fact, however, is, that alike in 1297 and in 1797, both of these noblemen were left at liberty to oppose the war, and both of them did oppose and obstruct it—the one in the thirteenth and the other in the eighteenth century—without incurring any loss of life or of property for so withstanding the king's views.

There is no reason to doubt that the king had the popular feeling with him. Even in the present day, when peace is so greatly valued, and when considerations of utility govern so many, the news that Spain had surprised and taken Gibraltar, or that France had suddenly seized upon the Channel Islands, would light up a flame of indignation, and raise a cry of war throughout the realm. How was it to be expected, then, that in the days of chivalry, the gentry and burgesses of England could hear of the fraudulent seizure of such a province as Gascony, without generally sympathizing with their sovereign's indignation?

Still, wherever men are free, differences of opinion on all

conceivable questions will show themselves, and we find from the records of the time that the earls of Norfolk and Hereford did not heartily concur with the king's views; and, as we have said, Edward had always conducted his affairs in such a frank and open manner, as to give full play to the expression of all such differences of opinion. Whenever any great public question required solution, his first step always was to summon a parliament; and when the dissentient party had thrown all possible obstructions in the way, we next hear of the king's writing to the earl of Hereford or the earl of Norfolk, to invite him to a private interview, that they may freely discuss the matter in hand.

In the present instance Edward resolved to meet his parliament, for the final decision of all questions concerning the war, at Salisbury, on the 25th of February. Meanwhile, however, pressed by the demands of his allies and the requirements of his own armaments, he laid new and heavy imposts upon wool, and called upon the sheriffs of all the counties to provide for him each a certain quota of wheat, etc.* We do not suppose that there was anything in these measures which materially differed from the practice of modern wars, but it is evident that such claims and demands would often occasion inconvenience and excite displeasure. The great men of the realm, as well as the merchants and farmers, would feel these requisitions, and some of them, doubtless, brought their irritated feelings into the discussions in parliament.

The king's justification, however, was doubtless rested on the old adage that "necessity knows no law,"—a rule

---

* Among the writs of that time we find many addressed to the sheriffs of counties, wherein the king "requests you to advise and take order how you can assist him with one thousand quarters of wheat, for which he will pay you punctually at Midsummer next."

which often decides many hard questions in time of war. Shall a general defending a city be compelled by famine to surrender it, if he knows that one of the citizens has a great store of corn? No, he will seize upon that corn, if necessary by the extremest force, rather than lose the city which he is ordered to defend; but he will take care that the citizen shall be paid the value of his property at the earliest possible moment. Such seems to have been Edward's rule of conduct at this very difficult crisis.

The earl of Norfolk was the high marshal, and the earl of Hereford the high constable of England. Edward, purposing himself to go into Flanders, wished to commit the charge of a distinct force for Gascony to these two earls; but they objected to undertake this charge, alleging that their offices only bound them to attend the king's person in his wars. Chafed at this backwardness, the king, always excitable, grew angry, and is reported to have said that they should either go or hang. To which Norfolk rejoined that "he would neither go nor hang." * The constable and marshal after this withdrew, followed by a large body of knights, their retainers.

We know not much of the other proceedings of that parliament. The king was evidently in a position of great difficulty. Opposed by a large body of the clergy, and now opposed also by two of the greatest earls in the realm, he had still the war with France on his hands, and from it he could not in honour withdraw. Surely we might rather expect the sympathies of Englishmen to be with the king, in this critical juncture, than with the two dissentient earls. Edward, in resisting the wrong done to him by Philip, was

* Hemingford says, " Exiratus Rex prorupit in hæc verba, ut dicitur, ' Per deum, comes, aut ibis aut pendebis.' Et ille, ' Per idem juramentum, O Rex, nec ibo nec pendebo.' "—See Appendix.

merely discharging a plain duty. How, then, can it be deemed "patriotism" in these two great nobles to desert their sovereign in this emergency, and even to throw obstacles in his path?

It seems tolerably clear that the discussions at Salisbury were prolonged, and that the secession of Hereford and Norfolk obliged the king to abandon his purpose of sending a fresh expedition to the relief of Gascony. The 7th of March found the king still at Salisbury, and on that day Winchelsey paid him a visit in that city. It was so much the king's habit to have his opponents "face to face," that it seems most probable that the archbishop waited on him there at his own desire.

The king, when the archbishop arrived, was attending the service in the cathedral. When this was over, Winchelsey had a private audience, the king desiring him to say freely what he would. The archbishop spoke at some length, and was heard patiently and without any interruption. The king, in reply, told him that "if the pope himself had any temporal possessions in the realm of England, he believed that he, the king, might lawfully take of them for the defence of his realm and of the church of England." He added that "this was a cause in which he could dare to die; since he felt that he was doing nothing unlawful, but was obeying a dire necessity which lay upon him and the kingdom." Surely in the frankness, the wisdom, and the calm resolution of the king, there is nothing wanting of the characteristics of true nobleness of mind.

No actual reconciliation then took place—the primate being unwilling to abandon his ground, and the king being resolved never to relinquish his; but Winchelsey promised to send messengers of his own to the pope, and the king at his request promised to show leniency to those of the clergy who had committed themselves on the papal side. On the 25th of March a synod was held at St. Paul's, in which no positive resolution was adopted, but the archbishop and those bishops who acted with him agreed to connive at those of the clergy who should make their peace with the king, though in doing so they disobeyed the pope; and Edward, in April, began to show mercy to those of the recusant clergy who had published the bull in defiance of his orders, and who had been imprisoned for that offence. In May and June he was occupied in assembling his troops, and in providing a sufficient naval force. On the 8th of July, the military tenants of the crown were summoned to meet in London to do their accustomed suit and service. The high constable and marshal attended; but as they had objected at Salisbury to go to Gascony, because the king did not propose to accompany that expedition, so now they objected to go with the king to Flanders, because, as they said, they could not find that any of their ancestors had ever performed any service in that country.

The absurdity of this plea was self-evident; it assumed that the king must not make war in any country except those in which his ancestors had made war. Evidently these two earls had no stomach for the war on any terms. Doubtless they were at liberty to form their own opinion of its expediency or inexpediency, and to a certain extent to act upon it; but it is impossible to estimate very highly the patriotism of two great nobles, who, when such a captain as Edward was embarked in a national contest, could leave him to fight it out without their aid. Still so it was; they begged the king to appoint other officers in their room. Edward, therefore, named Thomas de Berkeley as substitute for the earl of Hereford, and Geoffrey de Geneville for the earl of Norfolk. In thus tolerating the conduct of these two earls, the king showed that self-control and practical wisdom which distinguished him through life; but he was about to go much further. He was on the point of quitting home to open a war, the length and the difficulties of which he could not foresee. He desired, therefore, to leave England, as far as possible, an united and peaceful kingdom during his absence. With this view, having broken up the ecclesiastical confederacy, he announced to Winchelsey and his followers an amnesty for the past, with a pardon for all who were suffering any penalties for their recusancy; and to make his desire for peace and harmony as manifest as possible, he convened a large assembly in or at the entrance of Westminster Hall. Here, on the 14th of July, the king presented himself on a raised platform, accompanied by his son, then in his fourteenth year, the archbishop, the earl of Warwick, and other lords. He then addressed the assembly, first alluding to the burdens which, in the preparation of his armament, he had been obliged to lay upon them. "He owned that these burdens were heavy, but declared that it had been as painful for him to impose those burdens as it must have been for them to bear them. He had taken a part in order to secure the remainder. His sole object was to protect the country from its enemies, and from those who sought its ruin." "And now," he added, "I am going once more to face the dangers of war for England's sake. If I return, receive me again as you have received me to-day, and I will make you full amends. If not, here is my son; place him on my throne, and his gratitude will reward your fidelity." Edward could not conclude without visible emotion; the archbishop was equally affected; and the whole assembly, with outstretched hands, vowed unshaken fidelity.*

* Matthew of Westminster.

A fortnight after, a great council was held, at which the king openly received the archbishop to his favour, and nominated him one of the council of the young prince, to whom he then desired all present to take an oath of fidelity as the heir to the kingdom.

There is something in these proceedings which seems to require explanation. How could a warm-hearted, impetuous ruler, in dealing with such opponents as Winchelsey, Bohun, and Bigod, so constantly avoid any actual collision, any resort to force on either side? We read, with some pain, the account of the scene at Salisbury, in which high words arose; but the circumstance stands alone. Edward, though irascible, "had the rule over his own spirit." He was placed, for several weeks, in circumstances of great difficulty; but his skill, and judgment, and discretion carried him through them all. On the 10th of August the prelates made another attempt on his firmness. They requested his permission " to send to the pope for his license to grant the king an aid." The king, however, was neither to be frightened nor persuaded into any step which would imply his assent to the papal claim. He refused to give any such permission, but he continued to treat the clergy with kindness; and shortly after took leave of the primate, and departed for Winchelsea, where his armament was now assembled.

At this place, in the middle of August, he received from the two earls and their adherents, a remonstrance, in which they alleged—" 1. That they conceive that they ought not to be called upon to do service in Flanders (for the reasons which we have already described). 2. That they have been aggrieved and impoverished by the talliages, aids, and requisitions already levied. 3. That Magna Charta has not been properly observed. 4. That the Charter of Forests is also violated by the king's officers. 5. That they are aggrieved by the tax on wool. And, lastly, desiring the honour and safety of our lord the king, it does not seem good unto them that he pass over into Flanders."

This last clause explains the rest. What the actual feeling or opinion of the two earls really was—whether they were prepared to let France defraud England of her fairest foreign possession—we know not; but it is quite clear that, either on principle or from views of expediency, they disliked the war with France; and disliking the war, it was natural that they should still more dislike the heavy requisitions, aids, and talliages which that war rendered necessary. One main feature of the case, however, is the tolerant and reasonable nature of Edward's government, which now, for the first time, allowed questions such as these to be discussed: first in parliament, and then by a public correspondence; for the king, receiving this public manifesto disapproving his policy, expressed no anger at it. On the contrary, he received and treated it with more tolerance than would be shown for a similar document in most European states in the present day. To the messengers who brought him the earls' remonstrance, he answered with calmness, that he had not his council with him, and could not, in their absence, reply to matters of so great importance; that he should have been better pleased if the remonstrants had gone with him; but since they would not, he trusted that they would raise no disturbance in his absence. Before he embarked, however, he took care to reply to this document in the most public and emphatic manner. A royal declaration was drawn up, and sent to the sheriffs of all the counties for publication. In this document the king recounts the various steps of the disobedience of the two earls, and then repeats the apologies and assurances which he had made at Westminster Hall. He declares that "he grieves that he should so burden his people; and promises that, if he should return, he will amend all things as he ought; and if not, he will desire his heir to do so—for he knows well that no man is so much indebted to the people, or so much bound to love them as he himself. But there is great necessity for him to go to the assistance of his ally, the earl of Flanders; and his going over is of immediate consequence, by reason of the danger which his friends are in—whom, if he should lose, the kingdom might be in great jeopardy." He ends with a desire that his people would pray that his voyage might be prosperous, and have a good result, to the honour of God and the good of the realm; and that a durable peace might follow.

A recent writer, who takes no very friendly view of Edward's course, here remarks, that " The king's greatness of nature carried him through every difficulty. He could demand confidence, for his people knew that he did everything for England; he inspired trust, for he never broke his word; and between a king risking captivity or death, and two nobles refusing the service which thousands of meaner men rendered, public opinion pronounced emphatically for the sovereign. He carried the nation with him." *

Having issued this, his public reply to the objections of the two earls, the king, on the 22nd of August, sailed, carrying with him 500 ships, in which were 1,800 knights and a large force of infantry. But he could scarcely have landed in Flanders before great events occurred both in England and in Scotland—events which concurred with disappointments abroad to induce him speedily to prepare for his return home.

* Pearson's History of England, vol. ii., p. 399.

In the course of the summer, various rumours had reached England, of a spirit of insurrection which had shown itself in Scotland, and of various successes in partizan warfare which had been gained by a leader named Walays or Waleis. Twice or thrice had Edward written to Scotland, to desire his representatives there to suppress these disorders without delay. Had it not been for his engagements with the earl of Flanders, there can be no doubt that he would himself have returned into the north, and have stopped the progress of these troubles in the summer of 1297. But his engagements bound him to appear in Flanders; and he was obliged, therefore, to neglect the warnings of the two earls, who told him that the Scotch, having begun to rebel, would do so with the more hardihood when they heard of his departure.

The English must have disembarked in Flanders at the end of August or beginning of September; and it was in the early part of the latter month that the folly of Cressingham, the treasurer of Scotland, gave Walays the victory of Stirling, and thus nearly destroyed, in one hour, all the great results of Edward's campaign of the preceding year. The news must have reached London by the middle of September; and the young prince found it necessary immediately to summon a parliament, to consider what steps it would be expedient to take.

Norfolk and Hereford now saw an opportunity offered them of a more favourable kind than they could have anticipated. The peril of England was manifest, and all men would feel that union—the union of all her leading men—was so desirable, that no slight difficulty could be allowed to stand in the way. The two earls attended the parliament, having first demanded some guarantees of safety. Their claims were not exorbitant; and we are not entitled to lay to their charge more factious purposes or conduct than has often been seen in opposition-leaders in modern times. The chief grievance which they desired to have redressed was the practice to which Edward had latterly been obliged to resort, of levying aids or talliages without consent of parliament. This, however, was no new claim set up by the crown. Mr. Hallam remarks, that " hitherto the king's prerogative of levying money, by name of talliage or prise, from his towns or tenants in demesne, had passed unquestioned." Edward, then, in his hour of need, had merely resorted to an old prerogative of the crown; and the earls, in demanding the surrender of this prerogative, were claiming a large and important concession from the sovereign to the people.

Some writers have awarded a large meed of praise to the two earls, for their courage and patriotism in wresting such a concession from such a king. But it should be remembered that Edward himself was *absent* when the two earls are said to have shown so much courage; that his return was uncertain and improbable, and that the perils of the state from the Scottish rebellion, were such as to render it impossible that any reasonable request should be denied. It should also be added, that the two earls, who are praised for their courage, took care to send over for Edward's signature, along with the charter—an act of grace, securing their own full pardon for what they had done. It would have been a better and a more befitting proof of courage, had they, after preferring their request or demand, proceeded to raise a few thousand men, and to chase Walays out of Cumberland, where all this autumn he was committing the most fearful ravages.

However, the demands of Norfolk and Hereford were immediately conceded. On the 10th of October the parliament at Westminster framed a new confirmation of the charters, with fresh clauses prohibiting the levying of talliages or prises, without the assent of the prelates, barons, knights, and burgesses; and another statute or order, whereby the king granted a full pardon to the two earls, " for all manner of offences which they may have committed." These statutes were sent over to the king, and within three days they were signed by him and returned. Some historians have actually argued, that this short delay in the adoption of a decision, is to be taken as manifesting Edward's great reluctance and his many internal struggles. It rather shows, that which we may observe in many other important junctures in the king's life—that no question of moment was decided by him without protracted and anxious deliberation. On this concession, however, the laity granted the king an aid of an eighth, the clergy of Canterbury a tenth, and the clergy of York a fifth.

But it is time that we turned to the state of affairs in Flanders. This expedition and this war proved one of the most fruitless efforts of the king's life. A regard to his own pledges and obligations carried him there, at a time when it would have been far more desirable for him to march into Scotland: a disregard of their pledges and obligations on the part of his allies, made all his efforts and sacrifices nugatory. "All Edward's measures in Flanders," says Rapin, "were broken by the treachery of his allies, who forsook him after taking his money." "His embarkation," says Hume, "had been so long retarded by the various obstructions thrown in his way, that he lost the proper season for action." He was merely able to stop Philip's career; and Philip, finding his resources exhausted, and dreading a reverse, began to wish for an accommodation, which Edward, disgusted with his faithless allies, and anxious about the state of Scotland, was quite willing to agree to. A reference of all matters of dispute to the arbitration of the pope was proposed and accepted, and on the 23rd of November a truce for five years was signed, immediately after which Edward directed writs to be issued to the earls and barons of England, calling upon them to meet him at York, on the 14th of the following January.

IX.

WILLIAM WALAYS, A.D. 1297, 1298.

WE come now to a passage in this history which is beset with more than ordinary difficulties. Romance has entered the field, and has nearly thrust truth out of it. "Wallace,"* as he is called in modern times, has been elevated to a similar place in Scottish story that Arthur holds in English, and Patrick or Brian Boru in that of Ireland; but with this difference, that while nobody in England takes "the romaunt of Arthur" to be a history,—in Scotland "the romaunt of Wallace" has by degrees occupied and taken possession of the place which history ought to hold.

Nor has this strange error been confined to Scotland.

---

* That the name was, in his own day, *William Walays*, is a fact concerning which there is no room for doubt. The *Scalachronica* (recently printed by the Maitland Club of Glasgow), was written by one who personally knew the Insurgent leader, and he always writes the name *Walays*. Hemingford and Langtoft, two of the best English historians of that day, always write it *Walays*. In the "Wallace Documents," printed by the Maitland Club, a Charter is given, granted by the Insurgent leader himself, and there the name stands *Walays*. A century later, Andrew Wyntoun, one of the earliest and best of the Scottish historians, writing about A.D. 1420, always speaks of *Walays*. Other writers, following the sound only, write of *Walais*, or *Waleis*. But when many other names suffered change— Botteville into Botfield, and De Moleyns into Mullins—Walays also was corrupted into "Wallace." So entirely has this corruption rooted itself in our English literature, that we shall feel compelled to yield to it, and shall use, in the following pages, the customary name of "Wallace."

Into England, by the industry of Scottish historians, it has been largely introduced, so that now the descendants of those who regarded Walays as a mere marauder and cut-throat, have been taught to look upon him as "the renowned Sir William Wallace, his country's deliverer."

To find our way through or over such obstacles as these can be no easy task. Our first duty is to seek for credible testimony; but in the present case this is all on one side. "It is a necessary condition," says Sir G. C. Lewis, "for the credibility of a witness, that he be a contemporary." * Now, of writers who lived in Edward's day, we have in England some ten or twelve,† but in Scotland we search for a single contemporary in vain. Not a line of history written in Scotland in Edward's day can be found.

Yet, if we draw our idea of William Wallace from the English chroniclers of that time, what other belief can we discover but that which was universal in England from the thirteenth century down to the eighteenth? The Scottish leader was, with all those generations of Englishmen, a rebel leader, a marauder, a ruthless homicide, a miscreant. He had ravaged the north of England with relentless fury, "sparing neither sex nor age." How, then, could Englishmen regard him, but as their descendants regarded Nana Sahib of Cawnpore in more recent days? But the horror excited by the name of Wallace was naturally the more intense of the two, because the Scottish leader had committed a thousand times more cruelties than ever were perpetrated by the Indian insurgent.

Whence came, then, the opposite view;—that which in Scotland is both deeply seated and quite universal? It was

* Lewis on "Roman History," p. 16.
† Hemingford, Trivet, Matthew of Westminster, Wykes, Rishanger, Langtoft, Knighton, the Chronicles of Lanercost, Rochester, St. Alban's, Abingdon, etc.

mainly engendered by a wandering minstrel, a village Homer, who lived two centuries after Edward's day, and who, taking Wallace for his Achilles, composed a whole Iliad of rhymes, by which he gained a subsistence during his life, and which, surviving after his death, gradually convinced the people of Scotland that their forefathers had known "one of the greatest of heroes." Major, the Scotch historian, who wrote in the first half of the sixteenth century, thus speaks: "Henry, who was blind from his birth, in the time of my infancy composed the whole 'Book of William Wallace,' containing the things which were commonly related of him. By the recitation of these he obtained food and raiment. For my own part, I give only partial credit to writings of this description."

That Major was quite right in "giving only partial credit" to the itinerant minstrel, will be evident enough to any one who reads a page of "Blind Harry." The book, composed two centuries after the time of which it treats, bears the same relation to real history as did the "Iliad," or king Arthur's "Romaunt." It extends Wallace's military career, which began in A.D. 1297 and ended in 1298, over more than twenty years. It multiplies the two battles which he really fought into seven. It brings a queen of England to his feet—there being no queen of England at that time in existence. It makes him "duke of Guienne," and places him under the patronage of the archbishop of Canterbury; in short, it is a romance, having no more resemblance to real history than is possessed by "The Seven Champions of Christendom."

Yet out of this very unpromising sort of document there have been fabricated, in modern times, a score or two of "historical tales," both in prose and verse. Some of our best female writers—such as Joanna Baillie and

Felicia Hemans, have delighted in extolling "the noblest of Scotia's sons." Yet, a strange subject is this for a female pen! Of Wallace's personal character we have scarcely an outline traceable to any Scottish origin, except we receive as true the legends of "Blind Harry." And this writer's descriptions convey no other idea than that of a being of extraordinary ferocity.

The minstrel thus introduces him to our notice:—

> "He of age was but eighteen year old;
> Weapons he bore, either good sword or knife."

And these weapons were meant for use against the English; of whom—

> "If he found one without another's presence [*i.e.*, alone]
> After, to Scots they did no more grievance;
> To cut his throat, or stick him suddenly
> He cared nought, found he them anerly" [alone].

And so we find at page 8—

> "Without rescue he stickit him to death."

At page 13—

> "Three slew he there, two fled with all their might."

At page 15—

> "It was his life, and most part of his food,
> To see them shed the burning Southron blood."

At page 16—

> "Wallas, with that, upon the back him gave
> Till his back-bone he all in sunder drave."

At page 17—

> "Five slew he there, before he left the town."

At page 18—

> "A cruel knife fast through his heart struck he."

And again—

> "Out through the body stickit him to death."

And again—
"Through buckler, hand, and brainpan also,
To the shoulders, the sharp sword gert he go."

And again—
"Wallas commanded they suld no man save;
Twenty and two they stickit in that steid."

In fact the " Book of Wallace " reads like the chronicle of a slaughter-house. That our lady poets never studied it, we may be sure; they derived their idea of the Scottish insurgent from modern historians, who had magnified the feats of arms, and had said nothing of the deeds of blood.

But let us turn from the mere legend-writer and panegyrist, and endeavour to ascertain, as far as we are able, the real truth of Wallace's acts and of his character. And probably the safest course to take, on the whole, will be to draw our information chiefly from those Scottish historians of our own day who have seen the error of indiscriminate eulogy, and have endeavoured to present a narrative of a more credible and trustworthy kind. The only other course to take would be to accept the account of the English chroniclers, ten or twelve in number, who lived in Wallace's own day. These, however, write under the influence of a strong prejudice. Some of them, like the Chronicler of Lanercost in Cumberland, had actually seen something of the Scottish leader, and they cannot speak of him but as "a man of blood," "a leader of banditti."

Let us try, then, to glean something of this history from the narratives of those more recent Scottish writers, who have shown some degree of moderation. William Walays was the younger son of a small proprietor in Renfrewshire. "Malcolm (the father) got the five-pound land of Elderslie"(Wallace Documents). "The name Walleys or Waleis," says the editor of that collection, "simply designates any native of the ancient kingdom of Wales." Such persons were often met with in England. There was a sheriff of London named Waleys, or Waleis, in 1272, and about the same time a Waleys or Walays in Wilts, and another in Essex, and a third in Somerset. These, like William Walays of Elderslie, were natives of Wales, or sons of natives who had migrated into England or into the northern parts of the island.

"The family," says Mr. Tytler, "was neither rich nor noble."* Allowing for the altered value of money, we may deem the father to be equal to a yeoman of the present day, who holds a copyhold farm of the value of £80 or £100 per annum; and of such a man, William was the second son. He is described as a frequenter of fairs and markets, and as often engaged in brawls. "His make," says Mr. Tytler, "approached the gigantic; his passions were violent; and a strong hatred of the English began to show itself." The vehement irascibility and enduring animosity of the Welsh character had not been much abated by a change of abode.

Wallace had, we can easily perceive, many of the qualities which go to form a guerilla leader. He had great bodily strength and "violent passions;" he had learned, by frequent exercise, expertness in the use of both sword and cudgel; and such a gallant as this was sure to be followed by multitudes of young admirers. So prepared for the fray, he seems to have entered the arena of public life just at that critical period when the conquest of Scotland had been accomplished, and the English rule of Scotland had but just been begun. This English rule was, to one of his feelings, intolerable. We

* Tytler's History of Scotland, vol. i., p. 134.

may look with some degree of allowance on prejudices of this kind; but our indulgence can hardly be extended so far as to justify the young Scotch-Welshman in the course which his eulogist describes him to have adopted;—of killing every Englishman that fell in his way, so soon as he could find an opportunity.

After several homicides of this kind, it was inevitable that Wallace should be under the necessity of disappearing from the neighbourhood of his abode. He had been able, repeatedly, when an Englishman came in his way,

"To cut his throat, or stick him suddenly;"

but to such amusements there is always a natural limit. Mr. Tytler says, " He was driven to seek safety in the wilds and fastnesses. Here he collected, by degrees, a little band of men of desperate fortunes." " In his attacks on straggling parties of the English, he was generally successful. Confidence came with success, and multitudes flocked round the standard of revolt."* "Wallace and his men lived by plunder; retreating, when pursued, to the woods and fastnesses, whence they again issued forth to attack the English convoys. All the soldiers who fell into their hands were instantly put to death." " Great numbers of the English were openly massacred in almost every district beyond the Frith of Forth." † Mr. Tytler adds : " It was not uncommon for them, at these times, to drive before them troops of aged priests and nuns, whose hands were tied behind their backs; and while the brutal soldiery and their hard-hearted leaders sat on the bridges, these unhappy wretches were cast down headlong, or compelled to precipitate them-

---

* History of Scotland, vol. i., pp. 126, 127.
† Tytler's Scottish Worthies, pp. 172, 184.

selves into the stream, while their drowning agonies were the subject of savage derision." * These atrocities are recorded by Knighton and Trivet, two historians who lived at the time; and Knighton adds that he had received the description from the lips of a priest, who himself had been present at, and managed to escape from, one of these massacres.

Thus establishing a reign of terror, Wallace and his followers were rapidly clearing the country of the English; those who could not find safety in some fortified place, naturally taking to flight. News of these troubles reached England in June and July; but Edward had pledged himself to his allies to join them in Flanders; and to turn northwards instead, would have been a dishonourable abandonment of his friends, and a breach of his deliberate engagements. He could, therefore, only write to earl Warenne, urgently and repeatedly, to collect a force, and to put down these disturbances—spending, if needful, the whole revenues of Scotland in this duty. But Cressingham, the treasurer of Scotland, an arrogant and supercilious man, despised the insurgents, and thus brought on a terrible defeat and loss. The forces of Wallace continued to increase, and towards the end of the summer, one name of note was added to his array. Sir William Douglas, who had been governor of Berwick, and who had, on the surrender of that place, been readily admitted to the king's peace—receiving his liberty and a new grant of his estates, and swearing fealty to the king—was the first man in Scotland to set the evil example of a disregard of a solemn oath. This perfidy and treachery subsequently spread, and became so common in Scotland as to drive the king, towards the end of his life, into a state of absolute exasperation; leading him to abandon that mild and

* Tytler's Scottish Worthies, p. 186.

generous policy, which, for the first thirty years of his reign, he had followed.

We have been describing the occurrences of the former half of the year 1297. The insurgent leader must be assumed to have been gradually becoming more obnoxious for weeks and months before his name occurs on any historic records. The date of his public appearance is not a matter of any doubt. One Scottish publication tells us that "he first appears in May, 1297."* Another says that "he first began his operations in May, 1297." † A third states that "he is first mentioned in May, 1297."‡ It is evident, therefore, that after divers market brawls in the opening months of 1297, Wallace had arrived, in the May of that year, at the dignity of a known partizan leader.

Success, in such a quarrel, naturally begets success. All who disliked the English intruders, and had a delight in guerilla warfare, would eagerly gather themselves around this rising champion. He soon found himself at the head of a force to which the English authorities could oppose no similar array. The open country was in his hands; but he had none of the nobility on his side. Still, he had the only visible power in Scotland. The earl Warenne, however, had, in a few weeks, assembled a force of some 40,000 or 50,000 men in the southern counties and on the border, and was marching northwards in quest of Wallace and his followers. The rebel leader had about an equal power. About the beginning of September the two armies approached each other in the neighbourhood of Stirling. An overweening confidence was, as it is often found, a precursor of defeat. Lord Henry Percy brought to the earl a reinforcement of 8,000 men; but Cressingham, the treasurer, deeming

---

* "Wallace Documents," p. 30. † Chalmers' Caledonia, vol. i., p. 659
‡ Macfarlane's History of England, vol. iv., p. 54.

this an unnecessary increase of the expenditure, dismissed them to their homes.

The English army came in sight of that under Wallace on the 11th of September. The Scotch force occupied a good position on the northern bank of the river, awaiting, as policy evidently suggested, the English attack. A narrow bridge spanned the river at that point, and offered the only visible means of crossing to the opposite bank. A Scottish knight, Sir Richard Lundin, who knew the country, and rode by the earl's side, exclaimed to him: "If you attempt to cross the bridge, you throw away your lives! The men can only pass over by twos, and the Scotch command our flank, and will be instantly upon us. I will show you a ford, where you may pass by sixty at a time; give me five hundred horse, and I will secure it."

Nothing else than fatuity could have disregarded such counsel. But Cressingham, contemptuous and overweening, exclaimed to the earl, "Why do we waste time? Let us pass on as becomes us, and do our duty!" The earl, nettled at this imputation of backwardness, gave the order to advance. As might have been expected, the result was disastrous. The Scotch allowed a considerable body of the English to pass, and then, while they were thus separated from the main force, and endeavouring to form, a fierce attack was made, and in an instant all was in confusion. One part of the Scotch army seized the bridge, while another part was engaged in the slaughter of the disordered English. Many of these leaped into the river and were drowned. Cressingham was among those who had crossed. "His body," says Mr. Tytler, "was mangled, the skin torn from the limbs, and in savage triumph cut to pieces." Wallace himself ordered as much to be reserved for him as would make a sword-belt.

The English were thus sacrificed to the folly of one man, who did not survive to bear the blame. One knight only is recorded to have distinguished himself. Sir Marmaduke Twenge, one of those who had crossed the river, was urged by a companion to throw himself into the stream in order to escape. "What!" exclaimed he, "volunteer to drown myself when I can cut my way through them all! Never let such foul slander rest on us!" "But alas for me!" said his friend, who was on foot, and saw no such possibility of escape. "Leap up behind me," said Twenge, and so burdened he gave his horse the spur, drove him through the midst of the enemy, and rejoined his friends in safety.

Earl Warenne, though brave and inured to arms, seems to have been an impulsive man, who under defeat lost all self-control. At Lewes, in A.D. 1264, so soon as the ranks were broken, the earl was one of the first to take to flight; and now, in like manner, horrified at the massacre which he beheld on the opposite bank of the river, and unable to remedy his fault, he gave the command of the retreat to Sir Marmaduke Twenge, and rode off to Berwick. This sort of panic was even more disastrous than his previous rashness, for in those days the flight of the general implied the dissolution of the army.

The English chroniclers state the loss of the English at five thousand infantry and one hundred horse, but in effect, when the earl left it, the army was disbanded; and so soon as the fate of the day was decided, but not before, "the earl of Lennox and the steward of Scotland," says Mr. Tytler, "*threw off the mask*, and led a body of followers to destroy and plunder the flying English."

Sir Walter Scott, with his usual talent and perspicuity, thus describes the battle of Stirling: "The earl, an experienced warrior, hesitated to engage his troops in the defile of a wooden bridge, where scarce two horsemen could ride abreast; but urged by the imprudent vehemence of Cressingham, he advanced, *contrary to common sense*, as well as to his own judgment. The vanguard of the English was attacked before they could get into order, the bridge was broken down, and thousands perished in the river and by the sword." *

Such was the battle of Stirling, the only victory which gives lustre to Wallace's name; and this, it is quite evident, was, it may be said, laid at his feet; there being probably scarcely a man in his army who did not see the English general's blunder, or who would not, if in command, have taken the same advantage of it.

At the head of a victorious army, Wallace was now obviously the ruler of Scotland, and he instantly and without hesitation took this place. No legal or constitutional delegation seemed to him to be necessary. His dictatorship was established, probably by the " acclamation " of his army, as in the days of imperial Rome. We do not feel entitled to blame this step. Moments of exigency, as in France in our own day, often call for unusual remedies; but as no one can point to any public or national choice of Wallace as regent or dictator, we leave it as, in all probability, the act of the army, such as it was; and we shall presently see that between this " regent " and the lords and people of Scotland, there was very little sympathy.

Of this crisis, October, 1297, Mr. Tytler thus speaks :—
" The majority of the nobles being still against him, Wallace found it difficult to procure new levies, and was constrained to adopt severe measures against all who were *refractory*. Gibbets were erected in each barony or county town, and some burgesses of Aberdeen who had disobeyed the summons

* History of Scotland, vol. i., p. 72.

were *hanged*. After this example, he soon found himself at the head of a numerous army." *

A force such as now followed the insurgent leader was obviously well suited for a plundering expedition, or, to use the common phrase, "a border raid." Wallace led his force into England in October, 1297, and for the peculiar character of that inroad he must be held personally responsible. Plunder would doubtless have satisfied most of his followers, but he imparted to the war a character of unusual ferocity. Again we will avoid using the bitter language of the English chroniclers, and will draw our descriptions from Scottish writers only.

Fordun tells us, that " he wasted all the land of Allerdale with fire." Wyntoun adds ;—

> " All Allerdale as man of warre,
> That time he brent with all his powre.
> . . . . .
> Wharever thai overtook the Inglis men,
> Thai spared none, but slewe all down."

Hector Boece says : " He brent and harried all Northumberland and Newcastle." " He took Dunotter and slewe all personnes found in it."

The blind minstrel glories in the details of these deeds, telling us " how Wallace burnt four thousand Englishmen in the kirk of Dunotter :—

> "Some hung on crags right dolefully to die,
> Some leapt, some fell, some fluttered in the sea;
> No Southron was left in all that hold,
> And all within they burnt to powder cold."

And in his eighth book he tells us a similar tale of a castle or mansion in Yorkshire, which Wallace blocked up and set on fire :—

* Hist. of Scotland, vol. i., p. 142.

WILLIAM WALAYS, OR WALLACE.

> "Five hundred men that were into that place,
> Got none away, but died withouten grace."

The numbers of the sufferers in these two cases are doubtless augmented by the license of the bard; but the important fact to be remarked is this, that the narrations of the English chroniclers, and the charges afterwards brought against Wallace by Edward himself, are substantially confirmed and gloried in by these old Scottish traditions.

If we opened the English chronicles of the time, we should find them teeming with horrid details of how Wallace "forced men and women to dance naked before him, pricking them with lances and swords;" of how he "slew infants at their mothers' breasts"; of how he "burnt alive a whole school full of boys." "The Chronicle of Rochester" even displays on its margin pictorial illustrations of these horrors. We allude to them merely to observe that when his sentence, in 1305, ordered "that his bowels should be taken out and burnt, even as he himself had burnt a church full of men and women," the judges only set forth, judicially, a fact which was well known and entirely believed throughout all Scotland and all England.

Nor do modern Scotch historians attempt to deny the ruthless character of this inroad. The "Encyclopædia Britannica" frankly says: "He proceeded as far as Newcastle, wasting with fire and sword, and *sparing neither age nor sex.*" And Sir Walter Scott thus pithily describes this march: "Increasing his forces that he might gratify them with plunder, he led them across the English border, and sweeping it lengthwise from Newcastle to the gates of Carlisle, *he left nothing behind him but blood and ashes.*"

History from the earliest period, through all the ravages of Huns and Vandals, down to the cruelties of a Tamerlane or a Nana Sahib, records few, if any, deeds of greater savageness than this one great exploit of Wallace's life. And it was the main feature of his brief career. The victory of Stirling was thrown into his lap; at Falkirk he was merely beaten and annihilated, but in this march through northern England he showed his whole character. His panegyrist says :—

> " The host
> Began at Tweed and spared nought they found.
> . . . .
> All Durham town they burnt up in a gleed.
> . . . .
> For prisoners they liked not to keep ;
> Whom they o'ertook, they made their friends to weep."

Sir Walter's pithy sentence expresses the whole. The horde of miscreants whom Wallace led, must have come upon many aged, many infants, many sick—upon schools and nunneries. " They left nothing behind them but blood and ashes." And yet English writers, not a few, have been found, who, after reading these facts, have actually expressed surprise and indignation that the leader of this inroad, when at last apprehended, should have been put to death on the scaffold ! *

This terrible inroad occupied Wallace and his followers during several weeks. But the enjoyment was incautiously prolonged. Before any arrangements had been made for a return to Scotland, " winter set in with great severity. The frost was so intense and the scarcity of provision so

---

* A recent writer, Mr. Pearson, expresses a doubt whether these acts of unusual cruelty are sufficiently established by evidence. This incredulity is hardly reasonable. Several English writers who lived at the time assert the facts; all Scottish historians, Fordun, Wyntoun, Boece, and Blind Harry, confirm the statement, —some in general, others in specific terms; and the charges deliberately read to the prisoner in Westminster Hall, with the sentence passed, surely may be regarded as leaving no room for doubt.

grievous, that multitudes of the Scots perished from cold and famine, and Wallace ordered a retreat." *

In useless revenge for this inroad, lord Robert Clifford collected a force in Cumberland and invaded Annandale. A few villages and hamlets were burned, and about three hundred Scots were slain. It was to put an end to this wretched state of things, by making England and Scotland one people, that Edward had been labouring for several years past.

Wallace had now returned to Scotland; and in Scotland, in spite of all "the great lords," he continued to be the ruling spirit for all the first half of the year 1298. Probably it is to the opening months of this year that we must assign a circumstance narrated by Mr. Tytler, who says: "Soon after his return from this expedition into England, Wallace, in an assembly held at the Forest Kirk in Selkirkshire, which was attended by the earl of Lennox, William Douglas, and others of the principal nobility, was elected "governor of Scotland." †

The place chosen was one more adapted to secrecy than to the transaction of any important affair; ‡ the persons present, whose names are produced, *are but two*. The phrase added: "and others of the principal nobility," refutes itself. The support of the principal nobility was what Wallace most needed; and it is quite certain that, if any other of this class had been present, his name would have been carefully recorded. There is no fact on which all the Scottish historians are more entirely agreed than this: that, "through envy, the lords and great men of Scotland kept aloof from Wallace." Could any numerous gathering of

---
* Tytler, Hist. Scotl., vol. i., p. 143. † Ibid, p. 146.

‡ Selkirkshire, at the present, has about 9,800 people in the whole county. In 1298 it probably had not 2,000.

them have taken place at this time, it is quite certain that they would never have chosen the second son of a Renfrewshire yeoman to be " governor of Scotland."

Wallace, however, having an armed force at his back, and a vehement will in his bosom, accepted this alleged " choice " and appointment, and readily assumed and exercised despotic power. The weight of his right arm is fully admitted by all Scottish writers. Fordun, one of the earliest, says : " If any of the great men would not, of his own accord, obey his mandates, him he held and confined until he wholly submitted to his pleasure." Wyntoun writes :

> " The grettest lordes of our lande
> To him he gert them be bowand ;
> Ild thai, wald thai, all gert he
> Bowsum to his bidding be:
> And to his bidding who was not bown,
> He took and put tham in prisoun." *

Nor was imprisonment the sole means of persuasion to which he had recourse. Hector Boece tells us that "he made sic punition on tham whilk war repugnant to his proclamation, that the remanent pepil, for fear thairof, assisted to his purpose." And again—

> "That samin time thair was that made imploy,
> Men in the north that would not him obey;
>
> .   .   .   .   .   .
>
> Thairfore Wallace, without any demand,
>
> .   .   .   .   .   .
>
> Syne for thair treasoun hangit tham ilkane" [every one].

We know not whether words could more plainly express the fact that a tyranny was established in Scotland in this earlier portion of the year 1298. And the most singular

* Cronykyl, viii. 13.

feature of the case is, that a man who, in April, 1297, was utterly• unknown, establishes, before a twelvemonth had passed over, such a despotic power that "the greatest lordes in the land" were forced to bow down to him, or else to go to the prison or the gallows!

But now the end of this extraordinary kind of rule was approaching. It had been, from first to last, an empire of the sword; and when that sword was broken, it instantly collapsed and disappeared. Edward was duly informed, in October, of the disastrous affair of Stirling; and, relying on the speedy termination of the war with France, he sent over, in November, a summons for a military rendezvous at York, on the 14th of the coming January. Such a summons, to be answered at such a period of the year, was no ordinary one. To call men, by tens of thousands, to leave Kent, and Devon, and Warwickshire, in the very middle of the winter, and to march to York, with the declared intention of thence proceeding to Scotland, was of itself a proof of the depth and earnestness of the king's purpose. But the manner in which this call was answered, showed that the people of England sympathized with their sovereign. The story of Wallace's invasion, with all its horrors, had been carried through the length and breadth of the land; and the feeling which it had aroused was shown in the astonishing fact, that, in the short dark days of January, there marched into York no fewer than 100,000 foot-soldiers and 4,000 cavalry. England has now six times the population it had then; but who would expect that, if our government were, in the present day, to call for a voluntary armament, and to issue that call in November, the result would be the appearance at York, on the 14th of January, of a force of 600,000 infantry, and of 24,000 horse? And yet the means of locomotion known in our day would make it far easier to do this now than it was in 1298, to send the smaller number. But could such a mighty gathering be seen, in England's northern metropolis, on the 14th of the coming January, would not the natural, the reasonable exclamation be, " England is stirred to its very depths"?

The king, however, found it impossible to leave the Flemish coast so soon as he had intended. He learned, too, that the Scottish invasion was over, and that Wallace and his followers had returned to Scotland. He would not run the risk of a second " battle of Stirling," and he therefore sent orders to his generals at York to engage in no important action till he returned. Hence, they contented themselves with relieving the castles of Kelso, Roxburgh, and Berwick, which had been threatened by Wallace, and then, keeping a small force in Scotland, dismissed the remainder to their homes. Of the movements of the Scottish leader himself at this period, we hear nothing.

It was not until the spring was opening, that Edward was able to get clear of his continental entanglements. On the 21st of March he landed at Sandwich, where he was received with great acclamations;—all men feeling that on his sagacity, judgment, and military skill, the peace and safety of the realm of England at that moment greatly depended. His first thought on landing, was, to remember his governing principle, *Pactum serva*. He had promised his people, when he left them in the preceding autumn, that for any wrongs done, or goods taken, by his officers or purveyors for the service of the war, he would make them full amends. At once, therefore, immediately on landing, he directed commissions to issue to two knights and two churchmen in each county—one to be named by the crown and the other by the people, who were to inquire in each district what goods had been taken by the royal purveyors for victualling the king's fleet or army. These commissions were issued in the first week in April; that is, in a very few days after the king's landing.

The next step was, to issue summonses, on the 10th of the same month, for a parliament to be held at York in Whitsun week. These summonses were promptly obeyed. A great meeting took place, and thither came the two earls, Hereford and Norfolk, as they had done the year before; not to help forward the great question, of how Scotland should be quieted, but to prefer, as they had preferred in the preceding year, their demands for a fresh confirmation of the charters. Their own personal grievances had precedence in their minds over all the pressing exigencies of the state. The king, after reigning with perfect justice and equity for twenty years, had recently been forced to make "requisitions" for the carrying on of the war. The validity of such demands seemed to these two great lords a matter of more importance than French aggressions or Scottish inroads.

The king refused to enter upon such discussions at that moment, but he authorized the earls of Gloucester, Warenne, and Warwick, and the bishop of Durham, to pledge his honour and their own, that so soon as Scotland had been quieted, he, the king, would do all in his power to give them satisfaction. This sort of mediation succeeded, and the two discontented earls agreed to postpone the charter-question till the rebellion should have been suppressed. It was agreed, therefore, to fix the 25th of June for a military rendezvous, on which day all the earls and barons engaged to bring their forces to Roxburgh, the appointed place of meeting.

Wallace had now been lost sight of in England for nearly half a year. The ravaged districts of the north were beginning to resume their accustomed appearance, and the fierce resentment of the English people had found time to subside. Yet, when Midsummer came, a great army assembled around the king. The infantry were eighty thousand, but the cavalry had augmented its numbers to seven thousand, of whom three thousand were in full armour. Bearing in mind that the approaching harvest would require most of the available hands in the kingdom, this muster of men taken from the field and farmyard was quite as remarkable as that of the previous January.

This powerful army was now in Scotland. But where was Wallace? The Scottish writers all confess that "the great majority of the nobles were against him." * Force of all kinds he had employed—setting up gibbets, and throwing into prisons all "who would not him obey." But even the strongest measures of this kind were not sufficient to gather round him an army with which he could venture to march against the English. He took, therefore, the more prudent course of retiring as Edward advanced, wasting the country in his retreat. The English army was thus forced to rely wholly on its own resources; while, as no living thing crossed its path, its commanders were unable to learn anything of the movements of the insurgent leader. Edward marched on through Berwickshire to Lauder and Temple Liston. The castle of Dirleston was taken, and two smaller forts; but provisions grew scarce, and the Welsh troops seemed about to mutiny. "Let them go over to the enemy if they will," said Edward, with his usual intrepidity. "I hope to see the day when I shall chastise them both." But the prospect darkened; means of subsistence became more and more unattainable, and a retreat began to be seriously contemplated. Just then, however, Wallace's unpopularity

* Tytler, vol. i., p. 142-147.

with his own countrymen saved the English army from an impending failure. The earl of Dunbar and the earl of Angus, hating the so-called "governor of Scotland," but fearing to take an open part against him, sent an emissary to acquaint the king that Wallace and his army were concealed in the forest of Falkirk, and that they were watching his movements, in the hope of surprising the English army by a night attack.

Edward heard these tidings with the utmost joy. "Thanks be to God!" he exclaimed, "who has hitherto extricated me from every danger! They shall not need to follow me; for I will instantly go to meet them!" Without a moment's delay, orders were given for the march. Very soon the whole army was in motion, wondering at the sudden change. It was late before a heath near Linlithgow was reached, on which the army encamped for the night. "Each soldier," says Hemingford, "slept on the ground, using his shield for his pillow; each horseman had his horse beside him; and the horses tasted nothing but cold iron, champing their bridles." The king fared like the rest. In the night a cry was heard. The page who held the king's horse had been sleepy, and the horse, in changing his position, had trodden upon and hurt the king. Some confusion ensued, but Edward had not been fatally injured; and soon, as the morning was near, he gave orders for the march. They passed through Linlithgow a little before sunrise, and on a ridge of a hill, a little before them, they saw a number of men with lances. It was a portion of Wallace's army. He now could no longer adhere to his policy of retreat; the pursuit of the English cavalry would evidently render such a course disastrous. He was thus brought to a stand, and had no choice but to accept the battle. As the English troops ascended the hill, they came in sight of the whole Scottish army, hastily preparing for the expected attack.

Wallace made the best arrangement, perhaps, that was in his power His men were, for the most part, armed with the long Scottish lance; and he drew up the main body of his infantry in four squares, called in those days " schiltrons." Between these squares were posted the archers; while a thousand horse waited in the rear, for any opportunity which might arise for an onset.

The king, equally energetic and prudent, having now made an engagement secure, proposed to give his army time for rest and refreshment; but the cry of the troops, officers, and men, was for an immediate attack. "In God's name, then," said the king, "be it so;" and at once the earl marshal, and the earls of Hereford and Lincoln, led their troops forward. But they soon found that the Scotch had availed themselves of a marsh in their front, and the attacking force was thus forced to diverge to the left. The second line, under Anthony Beck, inclined to the right; he wished to wait for the king, who brought up the third line, but the eagerness of the men could not be restrained. They pressed forward, and soon came to close quarters with one wing of the Scots, while the earl marshal's force confronted the other.

And now a singular event occurred—a fact which can only be explained by that secret dislike which all the Scotch writers admit to have been felt by "the great men" for Wallace. The whole body of the Scottish cavalry rode off the field without striking a blow. All the Scottish historians agree as to this circumstance; and it can only be rendered intelligible by our previous knowledge that Wallace had recruited his army by strong coercive measures.

The main body of the Scottish army, however, had no

such power of flight. Their leader, several histories tell us, exclaimed, " I have brought you to the ring; now dance as ye can!" It was evident as to the thirty thousand or forty thousand of the Scottish infantry, that their only hope was to stand their ground, and fight to the last. And this they did, as for centuries since then they have always done. To break their phalanx, or in any way to overcome them, was, evidently, no easy task. But the king was prepared for all the exigencies of war. He ordered up his bowmen, every one of whom was accustomed to boast that he carried twelve Scottish lives in his quiver. Under their ceaseless and destructive discharge, the Scottish "schiltrons" soon quivered and shook. Their firmness and obstinacy was of no avail; the English arrows filled the air, until their squares were crowded with the dead and dying. Soon all was confusion and distress, and then, when their ranks became unsteady, the terrible onset of the armour-clad horse of Edward's army followed; the squares were broken up, and only a crowd of wretched fugitives remained. Stewart and Macduff had fallen, but Wallace himself had escaped. The Scottish historians confess a loss of fifteen thousand men. The English report, as we find it in a dozen contemporary writers, was, that the Scots lost thirty-two thousand men, while the whole loss of the English was twenty-eight! This, at first sight, appears wholly absurd and incredible; but when we remember that the Scottish cavalry had fled the field; that the "schiltrons" were shaken and broken up by the English bowmen, and then, that in their retreat they were followed, trodden down, and slaughtered by seven thousand English horsemen—it is not difficult to understand, that the loss of the victors must have been very small, while the havoc made among the flying Scots must have been of the most fearful description.

The Scottish army of revolt was, in fact, annihilated. Some of its leaders fled to Stirling, and, adhering to the settled plan of the campaign, they burned the town before they evacuated it. A Dominican convent, however, was left standing, and here Edward remained for more than a fortnight, to recover from the effects of the hurt in his side. Some of the chroniclers aver, that two ribs had been broken by the horse's tread. If this was indeed the case, it would furnish another proof of the ascendancy of a strong will over merely physical hindrances. This period of rest having terminated, the king put his forces in motion, and proceeded to St. Andrew's and Perth. But no enemy was to be found. The power of Wallace had been annihilated. He again betook himself to his "recesses and hiding-places." The king marched onwards, through Fife and Clydesdale, and Lanark, and Galloway, and, finding no enemy to be encountered, he returned in the autumn through Selkirkshire to Carlisle, where he dismissed his army. The earl marshal and the constable were again discontented, because the king had granted the isle of Arran to a Scottish nobleman without consulting them. To meet these complaints, the king held another council or parliament at Durham in the autumn, in which he granted to some of his nobles the estates of those Scottish proprietors who had taken part in the late disturbances. And thus the strife or civil war of 1298 seems to have reached its termination.

As to the chief promoter of these disturbances, it is clear beyond all dispute, that the battle of Falkirk, in July, 1298, put a final end to his brief career. His first appearance on the page of history, was in May, 1297, and he vanishes from it in August, 1298. "Wallace," says Mr. Tytler, "soon after the defeat of Falkirk, resigned the office of guardian of Scotland." "The Comyns threatened to

impeach him for treason, for his conduct during the war; and the Bruces united with their rivals to put him down."*
"His name does not occur in any authentic record, as bearing even a secondary command; nor do we meet with him in any public transaction" until his trial and execution seven years afterwards. So agree "the Wallace Documents" of the Maitland Club, in which we are told that "immediately after the defeat which he sustained at Falkirk in 1298, *he disappears from history*, and no traces of him are found until a very short time before the execution in 1305." It is, therefore, a fact quite beyond any dispute, that the whole history of this greatly-lauded leader is comprised within a period of fourteen months. The representations of Hume and others, that " through a course of many years" † he fought the battle of Scottish independence, are wholly at variance with the known facts.

Still, however, Wallace, though in obscurity, continued to exist in or near to Scotland, for all those seven years. At one time we hear, that he escaped over to France with a following of "five soldiers." Some time after that, Langtoft tells us that "in moors and marshes with robbers he feedes." During a large portion of these seven years, Scotland was in revolt against England. But not once, in all that time, do we hear of so much as a proposal to entrust any command to William Wallace. Nor does he appear to have been able, in all those years, to induce even a score of men to follow him in his fortunes. Never was there a more total collapse of suddenly-acquired power. In modern times, indeed, we are often told of his having been "idolized by the people of Scotland." But such eulogists close their eyes to many unquestionable facts which lead to a very different conclusion.

It is from the pages of the earliest Scottish histories that

* Tytler, vol. i., p. 163. † Hume, chap. xiii.

we learn of the prisons and the gibbets by which his power, at its zenith, was supported. At Falkirk he is first betrayed by two Scottish leaders, who reveal his plans to the king, and then he is deserted by the whole body of his cavalry. And, finally, it was by a Scotchman that he was at last given into his pursuers' hands, and so consigned to the scaffold. But, though these circumstances show, undoubtedly, that many of his countrymen had no fondness for him, we confess that what weighs most with us is this, that after his discomfiture at Falkirk he continued to live the life of an outcast and fugitive for seven long years, in the mountain recesses of Scotland, without ever being asked, so far as history knows, to take the command of so much as a skirmishing party. Assuredly, there is no token to be anywhere discovered, that at this period, at least, there was any "idolatry" of Wallace on the part of the Scottish people; or any consciousness in their minds, that they had one of "the greatest of heroes" among them.

X.

PROLONGATION OF TROUBLES IN SCOTLAND—PARLIAMENTARY DISCUSSIONS IN ENGLAND, A.D. 1299—1302.

THE rebellion commenced by Wallace had now been crushed, and that leader had been consigned to the obscurity from which he only emerged to ascend the scaffold; but the pacification of Scotland did not immediately follow. Edward had lost much of the elasticity of youth; the bloody fields of Stirling and Falkirk, and the ravage of Cumberland, in 1297, were not likely to make either Scotchmen or Englishmen more placable or friendly; and the disturbing elements introduced into the question by France, by the Papacy, and by a few discontented men at home, postponed for several years the final settlement of this now re-opened question. We speak of it as "re-opened," for it was not long before two of the greatest lords in Scotland, who had submitted themselves and done homage to Edward in 1296, actually craved and obtained an audience, that they might entreat him to restore John Baliol to the throne again!—thus resigning, without any cause, all the results of the toils and conflicts of the past four years. Of all men living, Edward was one of the last to whom so irrational a proposal could, with any hope of success, be made.

But although the king's mind could not thus easily be changed, a real obstacle to a restored and settled peace had been created by the late rebellion. It had been shown that by bringing together a few thousand men, all the English found in country parts and in open towns could be slain or driven away, many castles surprised or captured, and thus the hold of England upon Scotland reduced to the occupation of a few strong places. It had been shown also by the campaign of 1298, that even a mighty army, encouraged by a great victory, might find itself unable to re-establish peace in Scotland. Edward had marched through the land, had found no enemy, and yet, as his army was not what in modern times we call a "standing army," he could only, when the autumn appeared, disband his forces, leaving the kingdom still unsubdued.

The "great lords" of Scotland could not fail to discern in all this some hope of yet "preserving their independence." We now know from experience that such an independence as they preserved, leaving room for frequent wars between Scotland and England (in which Scotland gained one victory and suffered seven defeats), was equally injurious to both countries; but the Scottish leaders had no such experience. Nor could the principal leader among them regard the question without being sensible of a deep personal interest in it.* If Scotland remained a separate kingdom, and if the Baliol family, now in exile, were set aside, then the next heir

* All the claimants at the great arbitration of 1292 derived their title from David, earl of Huntingdon, the grandson of David I. His descendants were these—

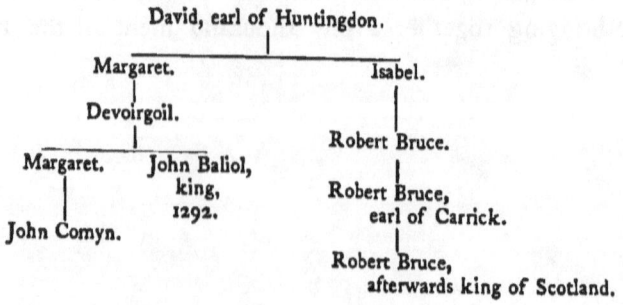

would be John Comyn. It was impossible that this fact could ever be absent from the minds of the Comyn family, then the most potent family in Scotland, or that it could fail to exert an influence on all their movements and decisions. Accordingly we hear, in 1299 and 1300, of a regency set up in Scotland, of which Comyn and Soulis were the principal members, and of embassies sent to both the king of France and the Pope, to ask their aid against the aggressions of the English.

Nor was this the only difficulty in Edward's path. The two great earls, Hereford and Norfolk, still led what we now term " a parliamentary opposition," and Edward could not call his " lords and commons " together, without being certain of meeting them, prepared to advance fresh claims, objections, and propositions. Hume, and, following him, Hallam also, have, somewhat hastily, given to this opposition of the two earls the praise of " patriotism ; " but surely it was patriotism of a very equivocal character.

The earl of Norfolk was the high marshal, and the earl of Hereford the high constable of England. Very naturally, therefore, the king had looked to these two potent peers for support in any just quarrel. Had not Philip of France, by his seizure of Gascony, a great and important province, done to England an unquestionable and grievous injury? Would England in the present day submit to such a fraud and wrong? Would not the nation exclaim with one voice that such an aggression must be repelled? How, then, can we regard with anything like approval the conduct of the two earls in refusing to assist their sovereign in this his dire extremity?

Refuse, however, they did; and not only so, they withstood and obstructed him in every stage of the controversy. And now, when the troubles in Scotland were not yet over, and the dispute with France was still undecided, the two earls attended every parliament, not to assist their sovereign, but to advance and urge against him new demands.

Hume, and, following him, several other historians, have represented Edward as striving to escape from the obligations of Magna Charta, and the two earls as "patriotically" insisting on its maintenance. Scarcely could misrepresentation be carried further than this.

From the very commencement of his reign, Edward, far from manifesting any desire to withdraw from the provisions of "Magna Charta," had shown a willingness and a desire to go far beyond it. De Lolme justly remarks of that great document, that "it had only one article calculated for the interest of that body which was the most numerous in the kingdom." It was, in fact, nothing more than an agreement between the great barons and the crown, for the future regulation of their respective rights and immunities. But Edward's legislation, from the outset, had taken a far wider range. "The whole commonalty of the realm" was never absent from his thoughts. His statutes were made, and made most freely and voluntarily, "for the common weal, and for the remedy of all that were aggrieved." In every statute passed in Edward's reign, the purpose is manifest: not to evade or limit the operation of "Magna Charta," but to go far beyond it.

What was the drift and meaning, then, of these contentions between the two earls and the king, which extended over three or four years, and which perplexed and harassed Edward during a very difficult period of his reign? It may be described in a very few words. Disliking the war with France in 1297, the earls withdrew themselves from any participation in it. But they wished also to withhold all aid either in money or in stores; and therefore they objected to the "prises and talliages" which the king's officers had made. They desired "the charters" to be so confirmed and enlarged, as to deprive the king of the power of making "requisitions," except under the express authority of parliament. Now, this limitation has been, doubtless, one of great value to the people, and for insisting upon it, the earls have been extolled as "patriots." But if we reflect on the matter for a few moments, we shall see that the concession required of Edward was one which it might well seem difficult for him to make.

"Requisitions" and "forced loans" have been heard of in Europe for centuries after Edward's time; nor have they quite ceased even to the present hour. Yet in his day, the power of taking what was imperatively needed for war-purposes was far more necessary than it is now. A nation in the present day, on finding itself involved in war, has recourse to its banks and to its credit, and speedily provides itself with all that it finds needful. And yet, even now, "requisitions" are sometimes heard of. But in the thirteenth century, standing armies, and loans, and national debts were all alike unknown. A king, suddenly deprived, as Edward was, of a noble province, found it necessary to raise and equip and victual an army, as rapidly as possible; and his only resource was, to convene a parliament and to ask an aid, which aid it would require months to collect. Edward, therefore, had been forced to revive and call into exercise certain old rights or prerogatives of the crown, and to "take" what he needed; promising, of course, to pay for all he took, so soon as he should be able. This power the earls now desired to limit, or to abolish; and it cannot be questioned that such a limitation or abolition was a great gain to the people. Edward's ground for hesitation, doubtless, was twofold. He always wished, and claimed, to leave the crown as potent as he found it. "Saving the rights of the crown of England" is a phrase which we often hear from his lips. And besides this, he might justly fear, lest the sovereigns of England, thus fettered, should be unable, in future years, to meet the aggressions of France as they required to be encountered.

The present Regius professor of Modern History in the University of Oxford has well and forcibly remarked, that "this great monarch was not likely to surrender without a struggle the position which he had inherited. For more than twenty years he reigned as Henry II. had done, showing proper respect for constitutional forms, but exercising the reality of despotic power. He loved his people, and therefore did not oppress them; they knew and loved him, and endured the pressure of taxation, which would not have been imposed if it had not been necessary." "Until he is compelled by the action of the barons, he retains the substance of royal power: the right to talliage the towns and demesnes of the crown without a grant. Edward would not have been so great a king as he was, if he had not thought this right worth a struggle, nor if, when that struggle was going against him, he had not seen that it was time to yield; nor if, when he had yielded, he had not determined honestly to abide by his concessions."*

There had been no new claim, or any stretch of the royal prerogative. We have already seen, that Mr. Hallam, who greatly praises the two earls, admits that "hitherto the king's prerogative of levying money by name of 'talliage' or 'prise' from his towns or tenants in demesne had passed unquestoned."† The king, therefore, had done nothing more than

* Professor Stubbs's Select Charters, p. 35.
† Hallam, vol. iii., 3.

bring into use an old right of the crown, which up to this time had never been disputed.

The two earls, however, disliked the war with France, and they disliked, very naturally, the "prises and talliages" —the requisitions of money, corn, and cattle—to which the king found it necessary to resort. They made these levies a matter of complaint in 1297, presenting to the king a remonstrance or complaint just before his embarkation for Flanders. When called to a parliament in Edward's absence in the autumn of that year, they again brought forward this grievance of the king's war requisitions; and in that parliament a new confirmation of the charters was adopted, in which all "prises and talliages" were forbidden, unless levied with the consent of the prelates, barons, knights, and burgesses. And, ever careful of themselves, the two earls added another document, by which the king was to grant a full pardon to them "for all manner of offences which they may have committed." These two documents were accepted by the king while he was in Flanders, and now, in Lent, 1299, he meets his parliament again in Westminster. Again the earls revive the question of the charters, adding now a further demand for a new survey or "perambulation" of the royal forests.

The king granted the required confirmation of the charters, adding, however, the words, "salvo jure coronæ." This proviso displeased the earls, and they quitted the parliament in anger. But Edward really wished for peace and unity at home, and, to content them, he held another parliament after Easter, in which he granted the confirmation of the charters unreservedly.

This "reserving the rights of the crown" has been censured by some writers, as if it betokened some equivocation on Edward's part; but such a device was alien to his whole nature. A more frank or outspoken man is not to be found on any page of history. What he said he always really meant. It had been a ruling principle with him, from the very beginning of his public life, that he would not leave the realm of England, or the crown of England, diminished or lowered through any fault or neglect of his. This principle forced him, " slow as he was to strife," into a war for the recovery of Gascony. He would not have it said of him in future times that he, by hesitation or want of energy, lost England's noblest foreign possession. The same resolve had carried him into Wales and into Scotland. In each case he believed himself to be asserting the ancient rights of the crown of England, and through all his legislation the same thought continually appears. His first great statute closes with these words: " And forasmuch as the king hath ordained these things to the honour of God and holy church, and for the common weal, and for the remedy of such as be aggrieved, he would not that at any other time it should turn to the prejudice of himself or his crown, but that *such rights as appertain to him* should be saved in all points." So also, when deciding the question of the Scottish succession, he does not forget that he himself is descended from Matilda, daughter of Malcolm Canmore, king of Scotland; and he notices this in his judgment, declaring " that John Baliol ought to have seizin of the kingdom of Scotland, *reserving*, however, *the right of the crown of England*, whenever he or his heirs shall see fit to assert it." So also in the parliament of Lincoln, in 1301, we find him desiring those who attended it to settle the perambulation-question, " so that their oaths and the oath of the king as to the rights of the crown may be saved." Thus, at every turn we find him regarding " the rights of the crown " as a sacred trust committed to him, and which he had sworn to defend; and hence, in every concession made to him by the people, he is always ready to use the phrase, " salvo jure coronæ."

The other claim made by the two earls, for a new perambulation (or survey) of the forests, opened a controversy of some duration ; and we shall find it convenient to reserve it for a distinct chapter. But, besides these controversies, one main business of the session was, to receive from the king a statement of the result of the arbitration of pope Boniface, to whom, in the autumn of 1297, both kings had agreed to refer all matters in dispute. The pope's award had been given; and a treaty with the king of France had been signed. Peace was to be restored between the two countries; Gascony was to be given back to England ; and Edward was to marry Margaret, the sister of the king of France ; while his son was to obtain the hand of Philip's daughter, Isabel. In fine, all lands, territories, and goods were to be restored to their owners; compensation being made for waste or damage.

Such was the pacification agreed upon between the two kings, and now made known by Edward to his parliament. But even while that parliament was sitting, Philip made two further demands or applications. The first was, that John Baliol, the late king of Scotland, should be set at liberty. Edward felt no difficulty on this point, only stipulating that the ex-king should not meddle in any way with the realm of Scotland. This proviso could not trouble or annoy Baliol; for he had, not long before, declared his resolution never again to set foot in a country " in which he had experienced so much malice, fraud, treason, and deceit." *

The second point urged by Philip was, that the Scotch should be allowed a truce of seven months—a request to which Edward, having other matters in hand, felt no diffi-

* " Malitiam, fraudem, proditionem, et dolum," Brady, App., N. 37.

culty in acceding. In truth, one affair which he was very desirous of bringing to a conclusion, was his own marriage with the princess Margaret, Philip's sister. He had now been a widower for more than eight years; and a lonely life after a happy wedlock of such long continuance, did not at all suit a man of so ardent and sincere a temperament. Peter tells us how, two or three years before this, while returning from Scotland,—

> "On fell things he thought, and wext heavie as lead,
> How chances 'gainst him foughte, and that his queen was dead;
> His solace all was 'reft, now she from him was gone."

And shortly after this, he began to make inquiries, first as to the princess Blanche of France, and then as to her sister Margaret. The latter princess became, at last, his choice, and she was brought over by the duke of Bourgogne, landing at Dover on the 8th of September. The king, with the courtesy which never forsook him, went to meet her, and at Canterbury, in the cathedral, on the 10th of September, 1299, the marriage was celebrated; the archbishop himself officiating. A large number of foreign as well as of the English nobility were present. Queen Margaret, like her predecessor, seems to have been entirely devoted to her great consort. Like Eleanor, even in war she was always near the king, and his attentions to her were unremitting. Thus, of the Scottish campaign of 1301, Langtoft writes:—

> "The queen Margaret then with childe was she;
> The king bade her not stay, but come to the north countrye;
> To Brotherton on Wharfe, and there she was
> The mother of a son, the child hight Thomas;
> And when the king heard say she had so well faren,
> Thither he went away, to see her and her bairn.
>   .   .   .   .
> The queen, with her son, at Cawood leaves he;
> To them, on the Ouse, full often came he."

A month or two was given to this marriage; but Edward soon remembered that Scotland would need his attention. The seven months' truce claimed for Scotland by Philip would soon expire; and the king had friends in Scotland who needed his aid. He summoned, accordingly, his military tenants to meet him in York on the 10th of November. But when this meeting took place, the king found that his barons disliked the idea of a northern campaign in November and December, and their objections prevailed. The king postponed any active movements in Scotland until the coming spring.

Early in the following year, 1300, the king again met his parliament in Westminster. A new and extensive *Statute on the Charters* was here proposed and adopted. It enacted that the charters should be published by the sheriffs of all counties four times in each year. It ordained that " no prises" should be taken within the realm, save only by the king's takers or purveyors; and that these should be bound to exhibit the king's warrant, and to pay or make agreement with those from whom the things were taken. It also made other good and desirable regulations, all tending to give greater security to property, against violence or illegal conduct on the part of men in office. In this parliament, as well as previously in that of 1299, urgent demands were made for a new perambulation of the forests; and the king promised to take measures for the accomplishment of that object; which promise he faithfully kept.

And now, as the spring advanced, the king prepared for another march into Scotland; reaching the border, this year, at an earlier period of the summer than on most of his former expeditions. The Scotch had now learnt the simple and generally effectual device of retiring on the approach of the English army without offering battle. Edward besieged and took Lochmaben Castle, and then proceeded to Caerlaverock, on the Solway-Frith. This castle also capitulated on the second day. An account of this brief siege, in Norman-French, from the pen of an eye-witness, is among the Cotton MSS. in the British Museum. It is supposed by Sir Harris Nicholas to be the work of Walter of Exeter, a Franciscan friar, who is believed to have written the history of Guy, earl of Warwick, in 1292. The garrison, he tells us, threw themselves on the king's mercy. "They were kept and guarded till the king commanded that life and limb should be given them; and also ordered that each of them should have a new garment."

From Caerlaverock the king marched on to Galloway, where the bishop of that place came to speak of peace. It was not Edward's wont to treat with rebels with arms in their hands; but it seems probable that he gave the bishop a safe-conduct for John Comyn and the earl of Buchan; inasmuch as we find that these nobles, on the part, probably, of the regency, had an interview with him at this period. They rather absurdly proposed that he should let them have John Baliol back again, as king; and should restore the forfeited estates on payment of reasonable fines. Now, Baliol, when he was actually their king, was imprisoned by them in order that they might rule without him; and he, Baliol himself, as we have just seen, had recently declared that he would never again set foot in Scotland. This proposal, too, was made to a sovereign to whom they had taken, more than once, oaths of allegiance; and whose army they feared, at that very time, to meet in the open field. And upon what pretence, on what rational ground, could they make such an application? It was but some three or four years before, that all the nobles and gentry of Scotland had thronged around Edward, to offer him their homage as king of Scotland. And what had he done, since 1296, to forfeit their allegiance? Had his rule been tyrannical? Let the Scottish historians bear witness. "His conduct," says Lord Hailes, "in all things bore the semblance of moderation." "The measures he adopted," says Mr. Tytler, "were equally politic and just. No wanton or unnecessary act of rigour was committed; no capricious changes introduced."* On the whole, this singular request, preferred to a victorious general at the head of his army—that he would quietly relinquish all the fruits of his victories, seems one of the most irrational of the measures of the Scottish leaders.

The king naturally parted from Comyn and the earl in anger, and marched to Irvine, where he waited for the arrival of his supplies by sea. The Scottish army showed itself on the opposite side of the river; but on preparations being made for an attack, it fled to the mountains and morasses. The king then fixed his head-quarters at Dumfries, and employed himself in taking possession of the towns and castles of Galloway, and receiving the submission of the inhabitants of that district.

But now a fresh obstacle arose to an immediate settlement of the affairs of Scotland. The regents, as they were called—Comyn, Soulis, and the bishop of St. Andrew's—had, as we have already remarked, taken measures to solicit the interposition both of the king of France and of the pope. Walsingham, himself a Benedictine monk of St. Alban's, writes, that "about the beginning of this year, 1300, the Scotch, *knowing all things to be saleable at Rome*, sent over rich presents to the pope," praying him to interfere in their behalf, and to stop the king of England in his proceedings against them. Such applications were generally successful at Rome, especially when, as in the present

* Tytler's History of Scotland, vol. i., pp 121, 122.

instance, they gave the papal court an opportunity for the assertion of some new claim. A mandate was, therefore, sent over to England, and consigned to the care of Winchelsey, the primate, who was charged with its delivery to the king in person; which mandate desired the king to abstain from all further proceedings against the realm of Scotland: which realm, said pope Boniface, "*did, and doth still, belong in full right to the church of Rome.*" Such a pretension, now for the first time advanced, might, and doubtless did, appear to all parties to savour of audacity; but Boniface well knew that he might advance it without fear. He had been, and still was, the umpire between Edward and Philip. The questions placed before him had not been finally decided, and Gascony was not yet actually restored. Hence, he knew full well, that however indignant Edward might feel, his practical sagacity would prevent him from actually defying the Roman see. For a certain "consideration," the pope had promised to do the Scotch a certain service, and that compact he thus observed, caring little about the validity of the pleas advanced, which were only intended to serve the purposes of the hour.

In Winchelsey the pope found a prompt and willing agent. This able and artful prelate was always forward in any scheme for exalting the power of the church, and reducing that of the crown. He therefore very naturally undertook the commission assigned to him with evident pleasure; and his letter to the pope, recounting his zealous labours, in obedience to the papal instructions, is a most edifying document. He writes to Boniface, that, immediately on receiving his mandate, he prepared his baggage and carriages, and money for his expenses, and set forth to deliver the pontifical mandate to his lord the king, who was then twenty days' journey from the place where he, Winchelsey, received the papal instructions. He then recounts the difficulties of the journey, and finally states, that he arrived in the presence of the king, who was then in the midst of his army, and at dinner. The king, he adds, was too much occupied with business to receive him that day, but appointed him an audience on the next day at noon.

Winchelsey, in proceeding to give an account of this audience, omits one characteristic incident which is related by Walsingham. The archbishop, on being introduced to the king, according to his appointment, first read, and presented, the papal mandate. But, to manifest his zeal still further, he proceeded to give the king, in addition, some admonitions of his own, garnished with certain flowers of ecclesiastical rhetoric, which, to a clear-sighted and plain-spoken man like Edward, must have been peculiarly nauseous. He counselled the king to yield a prompt and entire obedience to the commands of the Holy Father, inasmuch as "Jerusalem would not fail to protect her citizens, and to cherish, like Mount Zion, those who trusted in the Lord." To which Edward replied, with evident disdain, that "neither 'Mount Zion' nor 'Jerusalem' should prevent him from maintaining what all the world knew to be his right." At the same time, having regard to the peculiar nature of the application, and to the dignity of the pontiff, he first desired the archbishop to retire while he consulted his nobles, and then, recalling him, gave him, by the lips of his chancellor, a more formal reply: "That, since it is the custom of England, that in such matters as relate to the state of that kingdom, advice should be had with all whom they may concern; and since the present business not only affects the state of Scotland, but the rights of England also; and since many prelates, barons, and other principal men are now absent; it is my purpose, as soon as possible, to hold a council with my nobility, and by their joint advice and determination, to transmit an answer to his holiness by messengers of my own."

The archbishop, in his report to the pope, is glad to be able to add some tokens of the success of his mission. He says, "I afterward heard that my lord the king, within four days after my departure, returned with his army into England; and his forces being dispersed, he purposes to stay at a certain abbey called Holme Cultram, on the border. And thus have I reverently executed your commission in every respect, with all the diligence that I was able to use."

We have already stated, that from the peculiar position of his affairs, it would have been most undesirable for Edward to have any serious quarrel with Boniface at this moment. The negociations for peace, which had been carried on for two or three years past, were still unconcluded. Treaties had been signed; but other treaties were still under discussion. The decision of many important points was still in Boniface's hands. Hence to have dealt with the Papal claims in a prompt and peremptory manner, might have driven the pope into Philip's hands, and thrown many important questions into the greatest confusion. Edward, therefore, could only deal with these new pretensions in a respectful and temperate manner. He restored the bishop of Glasgow to his see, on his taking a fresh oath of fealty to him and his successors, kings of England. He complied with a request of Philip's, and granted the Scots a new truce, until the Whitsuntide of 1301; and he issued writs, summoning a parliament to meet at Lincoln on the 20th of January of that year. Before that parliament he proposed to lay the letter or monition of Boniface; and to that parliament he also desired reports to be brought by the commissioners appointed to inquire into the boundaries of the forests. He also sent letters to the two universities, and to the principal religious houses, desiring them to send to Lincoln some of their most learned men, with copies of any archives or other records which might be in their possession, bearing upon the questions agitated in the papal mandate. Having thus taken every proper and expedient measure for meeting this new attack upon his position, the king retired to Northampton, where he spent the Christmas of 1300, surrounded by his queen and family; proposing early in the new year to remove to Lincoln; there to discuss and settle, if possible, both the affairs of Scotland, and also that more domestic question, which had latterly assumed an almost threatening aspect, " the perambulation of the royal forests."

The parliament of Lincoln, A.D. 1301, deserves a high place among the notable events of English history. In it we find the parliamentary system firmly established, in all its dimensions, features, and characters. To its principal act—the reply to pope Boniface—we find appended the names and seals of no fewer than one hundred and four earls and barons; and as the prelates, and the Scottish barons, were, for obvious reasons, excused from taking part in this proceeding, we may safely estimate the attendance of the higher orders, or, what we now term " the house of lords," at more than one hundred and fifty. To this parliament, also, there were summoned representatives from one hundred and thirty-seven cities and boroughs. Probably, in the existing state of society, these merchants and traders,* in the presence of the great barons of the realm, were generally modest and silent; but we cannot imagine so large a body of English-

* Samuel Stanham, a merchant and grocer in Lincoln, was one of the representatives of that city in this parliament of 1301.

men—many of them independent in property and position*—executing a public trust in a spirit of absolute subjection and passiveness.

Lincoln, the scene of this great gathering, must have presented a lively and singular spectacle in the months of January and February, 1301. The royal court itself would have created a throng in any city of the second class. But the splendid trains which always attended the great barons and prelates must have far exceeded, in the aggregate, the officers and attendants on the court. And when to all these were added some two or three hundred borough-representatives, all requiring both lodging and provisions, we may feel sure that this city of the fens must have been the scene of a turmoil, bustle, and commotion, which none of its inhabitants were likely ever to forget. Langtoft tells us that—

> "At the park afterwards his parliament set he,—
> The good king Edward, at Lincoln his citie:
> At St. Katherine's house the earl marshal lay;
> In the Broadgate lay the Bruse, erle was he that day;
> The king lay at Nettleham; it is the bishop's towne:
> And other lords there came, in the countrie up and downe."

It probably would not be easy to ascertain how the victualling of all these hundreds, or rather, thousands, was accomplished; or in what way it became an affair of state. But the existing records show, not only that great provision was made beforehand; but that these matters were thought of by the king himself. From Dumfries, in the previous October, the king, so soon as he had determined on holding this parliament, sent writs to the sheriff of Lincolnshire, enjoining him many weeks beforehand, to provide, for the

* The city of London, about this time, allowed its four representatives for their joint expenses, out of the city cash, twenty shillings per diem; which would be equal to fifteen pounds daily, at the present time.

intended meeting, four hundred quarters of corn, four hundred quarters of barley, one thousand quarters of oats, and hay for four hundred horses for a month. The sheriff was also to provide one hundred cows and oxen, one hundred pigs, and three hundred sheep. And all this was, distinctly, for the parliament; while for the royal household a separate order was given, of four hundred quarters of corn, one hundred beeves, sixty pigs, and four hundred sheep. The king was probably able to procure the provender for his stables, by orders addressed to some of his own tenantry.

As the time of meeting drew near, other necessary matters were thought of. A writ, dated Worksop, December 2, 1300, enjoins the sheriff to procure sixty dozens of good parchment, for records of the matters to be agreed upon. Other orders of the same kind follow. Samuel Stanham, who was himself a representative of the city of Lincoln in this parliament, had at its close a demand against the king's treasurer for £96 14s. 5d. for sugars, figs, etc.; and for £54 10s. for fish. He also claims £6 16s. for herrings and stock-fish supplied to prince Edward, then scarcely seventeen years of age. Multiplying these sums by fifteen for the altered value of money, we shall perceive that they imply a liberal expenditure in the royal establishments.

The parliament being opened in the accustomed form, it appears that the two earls obtained precedence for their favourite questions—the perambulations and the disafforesting. These topics, urged by the constable and the marshal—Winchelsey being their prompter and secret adviser—led to prolonged and vehement debates. As these discussions form part of the great disafforesting controversy, we shall pass them over for the present, only observing that Edward's skill, firmness, and moderation were taxed to the utmost on this occasion. He succeeded, however, after many days of fierce debate, in calming the troubled waters, and bringing the parliament to a practical result. What were termed "the reports of the commissioners of perambulation" were adopted, and orders for extensive disafforesting were given. Thus pacified, the barons consented to a grant of a fifteenth, to be paid by the feast of St. Michael next ensuing.

And now, these internal dissensions being for a time set at rest, the parliament took up the question of pope Boniface's letter. Upon its audacious and baseless claims there seems to have been no difference of opinion. Edward's law-officers, aided by all the documentary evidence that could be discovered, had, there can be no doubt, prepared a complete answer to the papal assumptions; but it was prudently suggested that, in the king's present circumstances, it was not desirable that he should appear as a personal rejector and oppugner of the pontiff's pretensions. Hence, doubtless, arose the idea of the plan which was finally adopted. The whole array of the barons of England stepped between the pope and their king, and told the pontiff that he had asked more than his right; and that they could not permit their sovereign, even were he so inclined, to surrender the rights or the dignity of the crown of England. In this important document—after first denying the historical statements of the papal rescript, and wholly repudiating the idea that the kingdom of Scotland had ever, in any way or manner, belonged to the see of Rome—they go on to deal with the question, whether the king of England shall or may appear before the papal tribunal to defend his right, or in any way to acknowledge the pope as an arbiter or judge in this matter. On this point the hundred and four barons thus express themselves:—

"By a custom which has always been inviolably observed—a privilege arising from the pre-eminence of the regal dignity—the kings of England have never pleaded, or been bound to plead, respecting their rights in the forementioned kingdom, or any other their temporal rights, before any judge, ecclesiastical or secular. Wherefore, after discussion and deliberation respecting the contents of your letters, it was our common and unanimous resolve, and by the grace of God shall for the future remain such, that with respect to the rights of his kingdom of Scotland, or other his temporal rights, our aforesaid lord the king shall not plead before you, nor submit in any manner to your judgment; nor suffer his foresaid right to be brought into question by any inquiry; nor send agents or procurators for that purpose into your presence. For such proceedings would be to the manifest disherison of the rights of the crown of England and the royal dignity, the evident subversion of the state of the kingdom, and the prejudice of the liberties, customs, and laws which we have inherited from our fathers—to the observance and defence of which we are bound by our oaths; and which we will maintain to the best of our power; and by the help of God will defend with all our might. Neither do we, nor will we, permit—as we neither can nor ought—our aforesaid lord the king to do, or attempt to do, even if he wished it, the things before mentioned; things so unwarranted by custom or obligation, so prejudicial, and otherwise so unheard of." *

This was the substantial reply given to pope Boniface, and it was a fitting and worthy reply. That it was counselled and framed by the king's ministers cannot be doubted, and we see in it a fresh proof of that remarkable feature in Edward's character—his desire at every step to act *in concert* with his people, to move with them in every important step

* Rymēr's Fœdera, vol. ii., p. 927.

which required to be taken. But to this, the substantial reply, Edward thought it wise and expedient to add a private and friendly letter of his own. He sent this second communication, as he expressly says, "not in the form or shape of a judicial pleading," but as an entirely unofficial communication from one equal to another. Its object, both professedly and really, was to obviate any possible ground of complaint or aggrieved feeling. In this letter the king touched upon the chief points in the history of the two countries, showing that a superiority had existed, and that homage had been paid from kings of Scotland to kings of England for centuries past, and he ended thus: "As, from the above-named consideration, it is plain and notorious that the said kingdom of Scotland belongs to us in full right, and as we have never done anything which could in any way derogate from our rights over the same, we humbly entreat your holiness that you, weighing the arguments above stated, will deign to decide upon them according to the promptings of your own mind, in no way giving credit to the contrary suggestions of those who are jealous of us in this respect, but preserving and approving of our state and our royal rights, if it so please your paternal affection."

The practical result, then, of the whole was, that Edward, firmly rejecting the papal claim, refused even to send commissioners for the purposes of discussing it. He was a sincerely religious man according to the obscured Christianity of his day, and he probably had never heard the pope's claim to an universal primacy so much as questioned; but his own powerful and sagacious mind often enabled him to detect the unwarrantable pretensions of the ecclesiastics of all degrees, and when "he felt himself to be in the right," as he told Winchelsey at Salisbury, he was "ready to go to the death" in defence of his position.

Having thus parried and averted the blow aimed through the papal power, the king that summer mustered his forces and entered Scotland; but the unsettled state of his affairs, and the negotiations still pending with France and with Rome, seem to have distracted his attention and weakened his efforts. He captured one or two strong places, but the Scotch still adhered to their former system of retiring at his approach, and laying waste everything before him. An early winter set in and cut short the campaign, and the king resolved to fix his residence for the winter at Linlithgow, so as to be ready to commence a spring campaign in 1302; but this plan was defeated by an absurd concession made by his agents in France. In prolonging the truce with Philip until November 30, 1302, they foolishly permitted the French ministers to claim the inclusion of the Scotch in this cessation of arms. Thus one whole year more was lost to Edward in his Scottish operations—a loss which, at his time of life, was of great and permanent importance. The final and entire reduction of Scotland was thus once more postponed until 1303—1304, when, as we shall presently see, it was entirely effected.

In the course of the year 1302 we observe the meeting of three parliaments. The first was held in London in March, and of it we have few particulars; another was held in July; and in September and October a third was held in London, at which there attended seventeen prelates and forty-four abbots, nine earls and eighty-two barons, two knights from each shire, and two citizens or burgesses from each city or borough, with full power to do " quod tunc de communi consilio ordinabitur."

XI.

THE DISAFFORESTING QUESTION—THE COMMISSION OF TRAILBASTON, ETC., ETC., A.D. 1299—1305.

We have purposely omitted one topic of dispute which occupied Edward much during the latter years of his life, reserving it for a distinct consideration. We now return to this subject, intending, if possible, to bring the whole of these transactions into one connected view. In speaking of the parliament of Lincoln a few pages back, we noticed the occurrence of this question, but it occupied much time in several other parliaments besides that of Lincoln. It gave rise to a strife which continued during all the years between 1299 and 1305, the subject of which was the proper execution of the Charter of Forests. We have already remarked, more than once or twice, that most of our historians have confused the question by speaking in general terms of Edward's unwillingness to confirm "the charters;" —a vague way of speaking, which entirely clashes with what we know of Edward's continued efforts, during more than twenty years, to strengthen and enlarge Magna Charta by turning it into statute-law; and we have also explained that the points which were really in dispute were these two: first, the king's right of taking "talliages or prises" without consulting parliament; and, secondly, a reduction of the royal forests, under the name and by the means of what was called "a new perambulation."

In tracing the history and the result of these two struggles, it is of great importance to remark at the outset that Edward had reigned for *a quarter of a century* before any controversy on either of these points broke out. From 1272 to 1297 had the king held the sceptre, usually meeting his parliament twice or thrice in each year, and during all that time not a syllable had been heard either of any burdensome " prise or talliage," or of any desire for " new perambulations." In fact, the real and primary authors of all his troubles, during the last ten years of his life, were Philip of France abroad, and the restless and crafty Winchelsey at home. Until disturbed and molested by these two men, Edward had been able so to conduct his affairs as to leave his subjects almost free from taxation; and during all these five-and-twenty years we hear no complaint, either of any infringement of the charters, or of any mismanagement of the royal demesnes. This long period of peace and contentment was terminated at last by Philip's seizure of Gascony, and by Winchelsey's attempt to gain for the church an exemption from taxation.

No one, surely, will for a moment deny that Edward was wholly blameless in both these quarrels. To have patiently or sluggishly submitted to the treachery and fraud practised by Philip, would at once have removed Edward's name from the highest place among English kings, and would have degraded it to almost the lowest. He had no choice in this matter but between resistance or dishonour. Equally certain is it that the immunity claimed by the pope and the primate for the clergy in the matter of taxation, was a pretension utterly untenable and unjust, and one which the king was bound to resist.

But while Edward thus felt himself " thrice armed " in " having his quarrel just," he often found himself beset by difficulties through the deficiency of his accustomed supplies. Hence he was driven by dire necessity to some of those extreme measures which dictators, in any great peril of the state, often feel themselves compelled to use.

And thus arose that kind of opportunity which often produces " patriots." Two of the great nobles, Hereford and Norfolk, evidently disliked the war. They would not go to Gascony *without* the king; they would not go to Flanders *with* the king. In what way they would have preserved the honour of England under Philip's fraudulent aggression has never been explained. They contented themselves with finding fault and raising difficulties. In their remonstrance presented to the king just before his departure for Flanders, they complain of the burdensome taxation to which they had recently been subjected. They also add in one brief and vague sentence an allegation, " that the charter of forests is also violated by the king's officers;" but no demand for a perambulation or any other remedy is advanced by them. The first of these two complaints was admitted, and the remedy applied that same autumn by a fresh grant or confirmation of Magna Charta, with a new clause prohibiting the arbitrary levy of " prises or talliages " without consent of parliament; and so ended that part of the controversy. But the remaining clause in their petition, which opened in the vaguest way the question of the forests, was left for future discussion. The earls had not preferred any definite request or demand.

Such a question, however, when once mooted was not very likely to sink into forgetfulness, for it concerned the possession of property—the right to large landed estates. The " earl " of a county was, in some sense, the proprietor of that county, or, at least, somewhat more than the nominal lord of it. And a royal forest situate within it was just so much taken from the earl's estates; and hence, if in any way he could reduce the limits of the forest, he added thereby and to the same extent to his own territory.

Hereford and Norfolk had already dared the king's anger once or twice, and had suffered nothing by their audacity; and now, whether prompted merely by their own obvious interests or advised by Winchelsey, who seems to have been always their counsellor, they boldly demanded "a new perambulation."

For five-and-twenty years, as we have already seen, had Edward reigned, without a complaint having been made with reference to the royal forests. It is only in 1297 that the first murmur reaches him, that "the charter of forests is violated by the king's officers." He is then just embarking for Flanders; but so far from slighting or disregarding this complaint, on his return, in 1298, he issues a commission to the earl of Lincoln, the earl Warenne, the bishop of London, the bishop of Lichfield, Robert Fitzwalter and William le Latimer, "to enquire into all prises, trespasses, and oppressions committed by the officers of the forests." No backwardness, then, can be charged against Edward in his mode of dealing with this question.

But a "redress of grievances," though at first put forward as their object, was not the real object at which the two earls were now aiming. In 1299 and in 1300, parliaments were held in London, and in each year the demand put forward is for "a new perambulation" and a "disafforesting." This was a new move in advance—a direct aggression. The only object that a "perambulation" could have, clearly was, to take something from the royal forests. If it did not mean this, it meant nothing.

Now this was assailing the king in a manner most disagreeable to his feelings. As we have already seen, he was jealous of any encroachments on the rights of the crown, and held it to be his duty sedulously to preserve those rights from any diminution. He had never been charged with any attempt to encroach upon others; yet now an attempt was made to encroach upon him. For the principle adopted was, "that all additions made to the forests since the coronation of Henry II., should now be disafforested." Thus domains which had been in the possession of the crown for nearly *one hundred and fifty years* might now be taken away.

"The royal forests were part of demesnes of the crown. They were not included in the territorial divisions of the kingdom, civil or ecclesiastical; nor governed by the ordinary courts of law; but were set apart for the recreation and diversion of the king." And this kind of recreation was the favourite occupation of Edward's leisure hours. He engaged in it with all the ardour of a naturally impetuous mind. On one occasion we read of "the great hunt in Inglewood forest, in which two hundred deer were killed;" on another, of his horse's falling dead under him; and in a variety of ways we are made aware of his especial fondness for this diversion. Hence, on every ground, as an aggression on the domains of the crown, even after a century of quiet possession; and as an attempt to interfere with his own private recreations, Edward felt disposed to dislike and reject this proposal.

But the two earls, doubtless advised by Winchelsey, felt that they had the king at a disadvantage, and they continued to press him closely. The same motives which actuated them, must weigh, they well knew, with almost every baron in parliament. Every landed proprietor who had a royal forest in his neighbourhood, might hope to gain something by an investigation of the king's title, and an inquiry as to the proper boundaries. Nor could Edward peremptorily reject their requests; for Scotland was still in an unquiet state, and the king could only put down those disturbances by the help of his barons and his parliament.

In 1297, as we have seen, the complaint of the two earls was, "that the charter of forests is violated by the king's officers." In 1298, bearing in mind this complaint, the king issues a commission to two earls, two bishops, and two knights, "to inquire into all oppressions committed by the king's officers." But not satisfied with this, in 1299, the charters are again mentioned in parliament, and now the real object—*disafforesting*—peeps out. A new "perambulation" is loudly demanded, and it becomes evident that an important reduction of the domains of the crown is the object aimed at.

So long as the two earls had merely asked for a confirmation of the charters, or for inquiry into the misdoings of the officers of the forests, the king had listened patiently; and had, in fact, conceded all that they desired. But when they urged these new demands, he grew impatient, and, as twilight was coming on, he rose and left the meeting, telling them that he was going out of town.* The sitting consequently broke up, not without some anger. But the king's marriage with Margaret of France took place that autumn; and apparently, being in a good humour, and having reflected on the matter in all its bearings, he resolved to gratify the earls so far as to order a new perambulation to be made. Commissions were issued, as we find in Prynne, either in 1299 or 1300, to a great number of the counties, for inquiries into, and reports upon, the boundaries of the royal forests. And thus, when the parliament met, in the Lent of 1300, in Westminster, the king was able to inform the members that the perambulations which they had

* Matthew of Westminster.

desired were then in progress; and that the reports would be ready early in the next year. At that parliament, also, he passed, as we have mentioned in a former chapter, a new statute "on the charters," which explained and strengthened them on various points—more especially as to illegal " prises and talliages" made by officers of the crown.

Of the great parliament of Lincoln, held in 1301, we have already given some account. It deserves to be ever remembered in England, on various grounds. It was a large and full assembly, containing, in just numbers and proportions, those same elements which are combined in the British parliament of the present day. It had its earls and barons and prelates, in number about one hundred and fifty; its knights of the shire, in full tale; and its borough representatives, in still more numerous array. Its proceedings, too, began to assume that sort of form or order which has been preserved in most representative assemblies from that time to the present. The king sent down to " his faithful lords and commons" a message or speech; to which they, after due deliberation, returned a reply. Motions were made, and an address presented to the king, for a change of ministers;—and the parliament even went so far as to ask to be allowed to name the ministers of the crown. The king, in his turn, gave such a reply as, it may be hoped, a British sovereign of the present day would be advised to give to any such demand. After a while, this heated and personal contest abated; the king made some important concessions; and the parliament granted a supply. Lastly, the pope's audacious claim to the sovereignty of Scotland was taken into consideration; and a resolute and thoroughly English answer was given to the pontiff's arrogant pretensions. On the whole, there have been few assemblies of this kind held in England, which have better deserved to be held in honourable remembrance, than this parliament of Lincoln.

Its mode of dealing with the "Papal aggression" has been described in a former chapter. Its reply to pope Boniface terminated that controversy. But of the discussions which took place on domestic matters we gain only a few glimpses, which show, however, so much of the animation and importance of its debates, as to cause deep regret that we have no detailed record of those discussions. Two facts we learn from allusions to these proceedings made in following years: first, that Winchelsey was a prime though concealed mover in all the attacks made upon the king; and, secondly, that under his advice the earls took another large step in advance; and, seeing that they were likely to obtain the perambulations, now asked, under the crafty primate's instructions, a further concession, which he well knew the king was not likely to grant.

The *Parliamentary Writs* give us some insight into the form and order of public business which had already come into use. Thus, we have a writ dated "Rose Castle, Sept. 25, 1300," addressed to Walter of Gloucester, which recites, "That the said Walter and others had been assigned to make perambulations of the forests: that the king wishes to proceed thereon with the advice of the prelates, earls, barons, and others, without whose counsel the business cannot be duly despatched. That the king wishes to have a *colloquium* with the prelates, earls, barons, and with the rest of the communitas of the kingdom, respecting the perambulations, and on other arduous affairs concerning the king and kingdom. The said Walter is therefore enjoined to be before the king in his parliament at Lincoln, within eight days of Hilary, Jan. 20, 1301, to treat and advise with the prelates and magnates, and others of the communitas of the kingdom, on the said affairs: and he is to bring with him all the perambulations made by him and his fellows, with all documents relating to the same."

There are also other traces of preparations made by the king for this discussion. Thus, in the autumn of 1300, we find a writ dated from "Rose Castle, Sept. 26," by which the sheriff of Cumberland is enjoined to send two knights for his county, and representatives from each city and borough; and to cause them to have their expenses. And also, to see that proclamation is made, that all who had lands or tenements within the boundaries of the forests, and who wished to impeach the perambulation, should appear before the king in his parliament at Lincoln, to show cause against the same. Another writ is addressed to the Justice of the Forests north of the Trent, desiring him "to cause all the foresters in his bailiwick to appear before the king in his parliament at Lincoln, to give counsel in the premises."

Next, parliament being assembled, we have the "Bill," or royal message, sent down from the king to the prelates, earls, and others, on the 20th of January so appointed. It is, probably, the first example of such a document that exists upon our records; and for plainness, directness, and a wise and conciliatory spirit, it has, we apprehend, seldom been exceeded.

"The king wills that the perambulations of the forests shall be shown to the '*bones gentz*' who are come to this parliament. When they shall have examined the same, and shall have considered the evidence which is to be produced, the king wills that the perambulation shall stand, if they advise that it shall be so; and that the king can assent thereunto without violating his coronation-oath and disinheriting the crown. If any matters require to be redressed or changed, let it be done in such convenient way as they may advise and provide; or, if this please them not, let some middle way be provided, so that the business may be settled in a convenient manner; having regard to the dignity of the crown, which shall not thereby be affected; and so that their oaths, and the oath of the king, relating to the rights of the crown, may be saved."

In the *Parliamentary Writs*, the final result, or conclusion, to which this parliament seems to have come, is given immediately after the royal message. In this, however, as in many other similar cases, the formal record of the business transacted affords but a faint and imperfect idea of the character of the debates, or of the real object of the principal movers in the transaction. But, fortunately, two or three chronicles of the period remain, which are entirely in agreement with each other, and which show that the turbulent and ambitious primate had succeeded in forming a powerful and treasonable confederacy, and in bringing matters to the very verge of a civil war.

The " Chronicle of St. Alban's " says :—

" The parliament was protracted by numerous disagreements among the nobles. They had formed a plan to harass the king, and provoke him to anger, by demanding a right to appoint the chancellor, the chief justiciary, and the treasurer." The king is said to have replied, " Would ye deny us a right which every one of you enjoys? Each head of a house among you has power over that house. Why do ye not demand the crown itself?—you might as well do that as make it a shadow. In your own households ye may prefer—ye may pass over—ye may depose this man or that. And would ye deny us the same right? Nay, truly, the king shall appoint his chancellor, his justiciary, his treasurer, during his own pleasure; *or else king we will not be*." He added, " If our justiciary or any officer shall do unjustly, and the offence is not punished, then, indeed, complain if ye will."—"Straightway," continues the chronicler, "those who had urged the demand blushed. Many, however, preferred the *confederacy* and war to peace, and this preference did not escape the king's notice; but when the nobles generally saw how vain their demands were, they humbled themselves before the king, and asked pardon for their presumption."

Of the same transactions Peter Langtoft gives this account :—

"The erles and barons at their first summoning,
For many manner reasons 'plained to the king.
. . . . .
And next they made plaint of his Treasorere;
That evil things attaint he maintained thro' power.
'Of many has it been told; to thee we 'plain us here;
Him for to remove through common assent.
Assign it for more prow (honour) to this parlement;
That can that office give, and do the right usage.'
. . . . .
The king's answer was smart: 'I see ye will,
Thro' pride of heart, revile me with unskille:
And so low me to chace, mine officers to change,
And make them at your grace;—that were me over strange.
There is none of you, but he will at his might
Have sergeants for his prow, withouten other sight.
Shall no man put through skille his lord lower than he;
Ne I nor shall nor will, while I your king shall be.
If any of mine make strife, or taken thing not right,
. . . . .
That wrong I will so mende, if that it be attaint,
That none shall come or send, to make more plaint.
. . . . .
The parties were so felle altercande on ilk side,
That none could easily tell, whether war or peace would tide.
But God that is of might, and may help when He will,
For both the parties dight, and put them in his skille."

We gather, then, from these two contemporary writers that a confederacy had been formed, and that even civil war was contemplated by some of the parties. But what occasion, what provocation had the king given for any such extreme and violent course? For several years past, powerful and courageous as he undoubtedly was, his whole course had been one of concession. First, the two earls, disliking the war in Flanders, begged him to excuse them, and to appoint substitutes in their room. He accepted their excuses, and appointed substitutes. They then sent after him to Flanders a request that he would add a new and important clause to Magna Charta, and also would pardon their offences. He granted both of these requests. Next, remembering that they had complained of offences committed by the officers of the forests, he issues, on his return home, a commission to inquire into this matter.* Their next demand is for a new perambulation of the forests. This, as a direct aggression, excites his anger; but, after a little consideration, he issues writs conceding this point also. And now he meets his parliament with a mass of "reports of perambulations," and desires them, in the most conciliatory manner, to counsel him whether they think that these perambulations should stand and be accepted, or whether they desire any other course to be taken. What, then, in the king's whole conduct had given any ground or provocation for this "confederacy," in which even civil war was contemplated? Clearly, nothing.

Yet the fact, which is thus briefly stated in the "St. Alban's Chronicle," is confirmed by three other documents. In Leland's "Collectanea" we find extracts from "Pakington's Chronicle," one of which runs thus (under the date of 1302): "There was opened to king Edward *a con-*

---

* And not only so; but we find writs of the date of May, 1300, appointing three justices in Leicestershire, and the like in other counties, "to hear and determine, in a summary manner, all complaints of transgressions against the charters."

spiracy, wrought by the archbishop of Canterbury and divers counts and barons against him." Again, *William Thorn*, a monk of Canterbury, narrating Edward's speech to Winchelsey, when he remitted him to the pope, states the king to have reminded the archbishop of "*the treason* which at our parliament at Lincoln you plotted against us." And, in 1305, Edward, in issuing a new "ordinance of the forest," says in it that "he was minded that the perambulation should stand, *albeit that the thing was sued and demanded in an evil point*." Thus, again and again we find traces of the fact which is stated in the "St. Alban's Chronicle," that the archbishop and some of the barons had entered into a "confederacy," in which war (*i.e.*, rebellion) was seriously contemplated as possible.

Edward's firmness, moderation, and skill, however, proved more than a match for Winchelsey, and finally extricated him from this perilous situation. While he utterly rejected the demand that he should give up the nomination of his own ministers, and so make the crown a mere shadow, he himself proposed a middle course. Langtoft described him as saying—

> "Of this I grant this morn, that ye trie this thing
> With six-and-twenty sworn,—if I to your asking
> May accorde right well, the crowne for to save
> Dismembered not a whit,—your asking ye shall have.
>
> "The wisest of the clergie, with erles and barons,
> Together went, to trie of their petitions."

This "select committee" finally brought matters to a practical issue. It must have been judiciously and fairly selected, for while we find on one hand proofs of Winchelsey's presence and influence, in the reservation of the question as to the taxation of the clergy, the demand for a transfer of the regal authority to parliament in the matter of the nomination of ministers dwindles down to a request that "auditours" be appointed, which request the king declines to grant. The final result is given in the "Parliamentary Writs," in the shape of a reply of the parliament to the royal message. In that reply the parliament says that "the 'gentz de la communauté de la terre' show unto the king that they dare not answer which of the two ways should be adopted, on account of the perils which might ensue." But, instead of adopting or rejecting the king's proposal, they submit for his consideration twelve articles or propositions; which, generally, are to the following purport: That the great charters be observed; that all statutes contrary thereto be repealed; that the powers of the justices to be named for the maintenance of the charters be clearly defined; that the perambulations not yet completed be finished by the Michaelmas next ensuing, etc., etc.

To nine of these propositions the king gives his immediate assent. To two he gives qualified and doubtful answers. To one only—that in which the barons say, that they cannot insist on the taxation of the clergy against the will of the pope—the king gives his distinct disapproval. We shall give these three articles in the Appendix,* together with the answers of the king.

These twelve articles, then, with the king's assent to nine of them, seem to have ended the disafforesting question, so far as this parliament was concerned. As a general result, we may say, that the king had piloted the vessel of the state through a difficult and perilous passage. The confederacy was defeated. Winchelsey's purpose of weakening the crown by involving it in war with the barons, was frustrated. Edward succeeded in keeping his parliament

* See Appendix.

together. There were no "withdrawals in anger," as there had been on previous occasions. The barons, including even Hereford and Norfolk, passed on to the next question, the letter of pope Boniface; and they gave that letter a fitting reply. They then voted the king a fifteenth, and agreed to join him, in the summer, for a march into Scotland.

On the other hand Winchelsey had succeeded in doing some mischief. Though it is impossible, at this distance of time, to learn the details, it seems tolerably clear that the king was obliged to yield, in the matter of forest boundaries, more than he felt to be right and just. This clearly appears in the occurrences of the following years. And, whatever wrong of this kind may have been done, the primate strove to render irrevocable, by rising, at the close of the assembly, and pronouncing the greater excommunication against all who should depart from the agreement then made. He also adhered to his former course, of refusing to give the king any "aid" from the funds of the church.

And so ended this great parliament—an assembly of the most remarkable character, whether we look at its patriotic and spirited reply to the pretensions of the pope, or at its large and full exercise of all the proper duties of a representative assembly. With respect to the disafforesting controversy, it seems to have disturbed, rather than settled, that question. It established those new and reduced boundaries which had for some time previous been demanded; but, effecting this in a sudden and abrupt manner, it left occasion for many subsequent alterations.

The next step we perceive to have been taken, is one, which, like many other of Edward's acts, has been grossly misrepresented by some prejudiced historians. It is said, in some of their narratives, that he "persecuted the two earls;"

and it is always implied, that his animosity was excited by their zeal for "the charters."

Now, if we look closely at the king's steps, we shall find him perpetually associating with these two noblemen on friendly terms, long after they had opposed him in the matter of the charters. But the question he had now to deal with, was one of high treason. An offence had been committed, for the like of which many great men, in various periods of the seventeenth and eighteenth centuries, *died on the scaffold*. Yet Edward dealt with it in the most noble and generous way.

"There was opened to king Edward," says Pakington in his "Chronicle," "a conspiracy, wrought by the archbishop of Canterbury, and divers earls and barons, against him, at such time as he was in Flanders. And when the earl marshal was examined of this, and was not well able to clear himself, he made the king his heir, and put him in possession of all his lands. And the king gave him his lands again during his life; and also land of £1000 value in addition."

Several of the chroniclers state, that the earl had no children, and was on bad terms with his brother, who was an ecclesiastic. But whether this were so or not, it is clear that the charge brought against him was one which involved him in great peril. All the writers whom we have already quoted, and Walsingham also, plainly tell us that it had been contemplated to employ *force* against the king. Now any man called before the king's council on such a charge as this, would perceive, that not his estates merely, but his life also, was in danger. Hence his wisest and safest course, especially with such a monarch as Edward, was an immediate and frank submission.

And such a course, with the king, always led to a restoration of good feeling. In the days of the Tudors or the Stuarts, a nobleman who had been guilty of "conspiring against the king," would soon have found his way to the scaffold. With Edward, the usage was very different. A face-to-face encounter—a frank confession and surrender on the earl's part, was soon followed by forgiveness on the part of the king, and so the whole quarrel ended.

The case of the earl of Hereford differed in one important respect from that of Norfolk. The conspiracy spoken of by Pakington was said to have been commenced in the year 1297, when the king was in Flanders; although its last and most strenuous effort was made in 1301. But the earl of Hereford, who had been Norfolk's supporter in 1297, had died in the autumn of the following year, and the present earl was a young man, his son. He had probably merely followed in his father's steps, without any deep concernment in the plot. The king called him to an account, as well as Norfolk; but the young man found a different way of making his peace. He asked for the hand of one of the king's daughters; and, having, like Norfolk, pleaded guilty, he surrendered, like him, his estates to the king, receiving them back again with the hand of the young princess. And so ended this transaction, which some historians have described as a "persecution" of the two earls.

Winchelsey, then, had not only been foiled, but the king had fully succeeded in breaking up his "confederacy." Without severity or vengeance of any kind, Edward had fairly taken the two earls away from the primate; and was now at liberty to deal, at his leisure, with the chief conspirator.

It seems probable, too, from a circumstance which will presently appear, that the young earl of Hereford, on becoming the king's son-in-law, had given Edward full explanations as to the past, and had placed in his hands written evidence against Winchelsey; for shortly after, we find the king resolving to take decisive measures against the archbishop. But with Edward all was orderly and legitimate. Winchelsey had no reason to fear the fate of Thomas à Becket, or of the archbishop whom Henry IV. sent to the scaffold. The king under whom he lived could resolutely withstand either a pope or a primate, when he felt his own cause to be a just one; but his respect for the church, and for the forms of law, was sincere and deeply-rooted. He had the highest kind of complaint to prefer against this intriguing and turbulent prelate; but he resolved to lay it before the pope, and to send the cause to him for judgment. His ambassadors therefore placed the matter in the hands of the pontiff, who immediately cited the archbishop to Rome, to answer for his conduct. William Thorn, a monk of Canterbury, thus describes the next scene: " When the archbishop knew that he was thus cited, he went to the king to ask for permission to cross the sea. And when the king heard of his coming, he ordered the doors of his presence-chamber to be thrown open, that all who wished might enter, and hear the words which he should address to him. And, having heard the archbishop, he thus replied to him: ' The permission to cross the sea which you ask of us we willingly grant you; but permission to return grant we none; bearing in mind your treachery, and the treason which at our parliament at Lincoln you plotted against us; *whereof a letter under your seal is witness,* and plainly testifies against you.' ' We leave it to the pope to avenge our wrongs; and as you have deserved, so shall he recompense you. But from our favour and mercy, which you ask, we utterly exclude you; because merciless you have yourself been, and therefore deserve not to obtain mercy.'"

And so we part with Winchelsey, who disappears from this history; not returning to England until the weak and troubled reign of Edward II. gave him re-entrance, and supplied him with new opportunities for treason and conspiracy; all his plans and objects having one end in view— the prostration of the royal authority at the feet of the pontifical. But, in taking leave of him we feel inclined to contrast, for a few moments, his character with that of another prelate to whom he was, in this parliament of Lincoln, especially opposed. It will be remembered, that one especial demand of the " confederacy" was, the dismissal and disgrace of the king's treasurer; and the concession of the future appointments to that office, to the parliament. Now this treasurer, against whom the conspirators preferred such complaints, was Walter Langton, bishop of Chester. And the guiding spirit of the conspiracy was, as we have seen, Robert Winchelsey, archbishop of Canterbury. Let us, then, briefly sketch the history of these two men; one of whom was Edward's principal domestic foe; the other, his most trusted servant and minister.

Robert Winchelsey, who came to the primacy in 1295, was as restless, arrogant, and intriguing an ecclesiastic as had filled the archiepiscopal chair since the days of Thomas à Becket. In fact, he seems to have been selected by the enterprising Boniface VIII. as a fit agent to carry on the work of Becket and Pandulph; but to do this with any hope of success under such a prince as Edward, it was necessary to affect the tone and language of Stephen Langton.

As an ecclesiastical superior, Winchelsey was arrogant and tyrannical. He had one long contest with the monks of St. Augustine's in Canterbury; another with the earl of Lancaster; one year we find him excommunicating the constable of Dover Castle; the next, the bishop of London; the next, the prior and canons of Gloucester, and so on to the end of the story. But these were merely the amusements of his leisure hours. The grand business of his life, as of Becket's, was to bring, if possible, the crown into subserviency to the papal tiara.

He had no sooner landed from Rome and taken possession of his see, than he convened, says Matthew of Westminster, some of his suffragans in the church of St. Paul, London, "for a special discussion *on the liberties and customs of the church*, reviving and re-establishing certain constitutions which had been approved by the holy fathers, but which, by neglect, had fallen into disuse." The real drift of all this "revival of certain liberties of the church" soon appeared. A very few months had elapsed before the king was compelled, by Philip's seizure of Gascony, to call upon his subjects for aid; and at once the archbishop revealed his real purpose, by producing a papal mandate, which he, probably, had brought with him from Rome, forbidding the clergy any longer to grant "aids" to the king without the special permission of the pope.

This novel assumption, which at once made the pope, and not the king, the ruler over a large part of England, might have succeeded in either of the two preceding or in the succeeding reign; but in Edward the crafty churchman had met with more than his match. By making them practically feel the meaning of the word "outlawry" the king soon brought the clergy to a clearer understanding of their real position.

But, though defeated in his first attempt, Winchelsey was not discouraged. Unable alone to cope with the power of the crown, he immediately began to form "conspiracies" and "confederacies" with any whom he perceived to be discontented; and in this way, by fostering and encouraging the resistance of Norfolk and Hereford, he managed to keep the king in a state of conflict and discomfort from 1296 to

1301, and in this last year he had proceeded to the verge of a civil war. The king at last, irritated and seriously aggrieved, sent him to the pope for judgment, and so in effect cast him out of the realm; but the man, and his plans and purposes, remained unchanged. So soon as this great king, the only person who could control him, was gone, Winchelsey crept back again into England, and we soon find him, under the weak and incapable Edward II., leading the discontented barons, and again attempting to enact the part of Stephen Langton. Such was Winchelsey—a fit agent of the papal court, but to England a troubler and an intestine foe.

Contrast with him the man who, in confederacy with the discontented barons, he essayed, in 1301, to crush— Walter Langton, bishop of Chester, the king's treasurer, and one of his most valued servants. Had we no further knowledge of this prelate than the fact, that the conspirators at Lincoln prayed the king

"Him to remove by common assent,"

we might feel a doubt whether the king had shielded an unworthy favourite, or the barons had conspired against an officer of inconvenient integrity. Happily, we are enabled to discover a few other facts respecting Walter Langton, and those facts all redound greatly to his honour.

Foremost of these must be placed his steady resistance to the excesses of the young prince and his favourite Gaveston. The king was now in the decline of life, and the young Edward had every prospect of being king in a few years. Langton was treasurer, and had the duty assigned to him of providing the young prince with a regular and a liberal income. What could have been a more obvious policy, with any minister of flexible morality, than to cultivate, by any practicable means, the good opinion and the favour of the young prince and of his minion? Yet we find Langton, during all the latter years of this reign, in a state of constant warfare with young Edward and with Gaveston; and as one very natural result—a result which the bishop himself must always have contemplated—we find Edward II., as one of his first acts on ascending the throne, depriving Langton of all his offices, throwing him into prison, and granting to Gaveston all the moveable property of the deprived prelate. This single fact of itself is sufficient to give us a favourable impression of Langton's character. To have withstood the follies of the young prince and his favourite, and to have been persecuted by them for so doing, are surely circumstances which tell much in Langton's favour; but they do not stand alone.

Two or three years pass over, during which the poor ex-treasurer languishes in prison, while his enemies are occupied with the endeavour to find evidence to warrant his condemnation. The discontented barons at Lincoln had brought "many complaints" against him. If he had actually wronged any man, that person would now have the strongest reason for laying the crime to his charge; for in so doing he would not only gratify his own natural desire for vengeance, but would also please those who were now in power. But what do we hear? After being immured in a prison for nearly three years, Langton is at last released, there being no case against him. Under all the circumstances, we doubt if any higher or more triumphant proof of the integrity of the ex-treasurer's character could have been given.

But even this is not all. Winchelsey, the restless intriguer, has now returned, the only man who could keep him in check having been removed; and this factious ecclesiastic at once resumes his former work just where he had been forced to drop it, and begins to conspire against the son as he had been used to do against the father. The "confederacy" of the barons is revived, and Winchelsey is again its inspiring genius. What could have been more natural than for Langton, indignant at the persecution which he had endured, to have joined with eagerness this confederacy, the main object of which was to get rid of Gaveston, the cause of all his sufferings? But the course taken by this honest minister was one of singular integrity. He had been "imprisoned, deprived of his offices, and stripped of all his property;" and yet, after all, his persecutors had been obliged to admit his innocence, and to let him go free; and now " he was the only prelate who refused to join the confederacy against Edward II."* Notwithstanding all the wrongs which he had received at the young king's hands, this noble-minded man remembered his great master, and that master's faithful support of him against his enemies at Lincoln; and he refused to take part in any conspiracy against that master's son. But the proof of Langton's purity and integrity does not even end here. He had been released; the charges against him were now known to be groundless; but one more evidence of the highest kind was yet to be given. Three or four years after he had ignominiously expelled the bishop from his office, and ordered his imprisonment and his prosecution, the young king himself felt compelled to pay a reluctant tribute to Langton's ability and integrity, by actually asking him to resume the treasurership, and to serve him as faithfully as he had served his father! Considering all the past quarrels between these two men, and their frequent collisions and consequent ill-blood, this application must be admitted to be one of the

* "History of Lichfield Cathedral," p. 57.

most striking proofs of integrity that an expelled and disgraced officer ever received; and, taken in connection with the first Edward's other selections, of such men as Burnel, Brabazon, etc., it gives us a deep impression both of that king's skill and judgment in selecting his ministers, and also of his firm and steady support of them in the discharge of their duty.

But we must terminate this digression, and go back to the moment of Winchelsey's disgrace and banishment to Rome. The chief criminal had thus been punished, but, as in many similar cases, the effects of his crime remained. He had fostered the discontent of the earls, and had guided and suggested their course. At Lincoln, though substantially defeated, the "confederacy" evidently obtained from the king some larger concessions, in regard to the forests, than he thought just or right; and the archbishop adroitly struck in at the close of the matter with his denunciation of the greater excommunication, which was calculated and intended to make those concessions unalterable and irrevocable. But this violent way of ending and deciding a great and intricate controversy only led, as violent courses usually do, to further complications. Questions of title and boundary, in the case of territory or landed estates, are those which, beyond most others, require patience and moderation. The king, also, in the present instance was dealt with in a manner which the great barons themselves would not tolerate in their own cases. Twenty years before this period the king had proposed a general investigation of titles, and one of the earls at once drew his sword, exclaiming, "It was by *this* that my forefathers won their lands, and by *this* I mean to maintain them." To thi repugnance the king gave way. But now a different rule was to be applied to the royal domains. The principle asserted was, that whatever could not be shown to have been forest at the accession of Henry II., in 1154, should be disafforested. The adoption of so wide a range must inevitably have introduced great differences of opinion, but there can be no doubt that many of the great barons added largely to their estates at the king's expense by these " disafforestings."

Yet, after all, there was another class, and that not a small one, which had a deep interest in these questions—an interest of a very different, and, indeed, opposite kind to that of the barons. The royal forests were not vast solitudes, or parks occupied solely by animals for the chase. Their borders, especially, were largely peopled by cottagers; who, under the permission of the king or his officers, had reared up dwellings within the privileged limits, and were allowed pasturage and even some kind of tillage therein. This whole class of persons now found their position imperilled. A sudden change of owners had in many places been experienced, and often the poor cottager found reason to regret the alteration. In this way, it soon became evident, that the " disafforesting " question was not one bearing upon the king's personal recreations merely; but was intimately connected with the interests of thousands of his people. We are not imagining a possible or even a probable case. It is upon record, that divers petitions were sent in to the king, at his parliament of 1305, held at Westminster, on the day before the feast of St. Matthew, by " certain people that be put out of the forests by the great men," and who " pray, the king that they may be as they were wont to be heretofore." This is set forth in the preamble to the ordinance. It was, then, in answer to the prayers of many who felt themselves aggrieved and oppressed, that the king passed, in that parliament, an " Ordinance of the Forests;"

in which, with his usual frankness and explicitness, he explains the real position of the question.

He adverts, first, to the origin of the "disafforesting," saying, " Our lord the king (to these petitions) answers, that since he hath granted the perambulation, he is pleased that it should stand, in like manner as it was granted; albeit that the thing was sued and demanded in an evil point."

But next the king proceeds, as far as he was able, to amend the evil complained of, and to give comfort to those who had "cried unto him for succour." He says, that with respect to "them that have lands and tenements disafforested by the late perambulation, and do desire to have common within the bounds of the forests," " the intent and will of our lord the king is," " that if any of them would rather be within the forest as they were before, than out of the forest as they are now, it pleaseth the king very well that they shall be received hereunto; so that they may remain in their ancient estate, and have common and other easement, as they had before. And our lord the king willeth and commandeth, that his justices of the forests, etc., shall take notice of this ordinance."

This was an attempt to undo, so far as might be, some of the ill consequences of the hasty and violent determinations of 1301. But it may easily be perceived, that controversies and collisions would be likely to arise out of this state of things. Upon the strength of the charters and perambulations, and oaths and excommunications of 1301, the "great men" had begun to take portions of the royal forests to themselves, and to add them to their own estates. They also frequently got rid of the cottagers who had long found a home in the forests; and proceeded either to add the land to their farms, or to their own demesnes. To stop these evictions, the king issues a new ordinance. But that ordinance, when produced, would doubtless be met by an appeal to the charter, to the perambulations, and to the archbishop's excommunication of all who departed from them. And, with many churchmen, this terrible anathema would be admitted to have a fearful weight.

It must have been this "conflict of the laws" which drove Edward to a course which, with our light, it is impossible to defend; but which, in those days, was of a kind which was by far too common. The sentence of a primate could only be absolutely nullified by an authority of a still higher kind. Hence, to undo the act of Winchelsey, the king sent to Rome, and asked of the pope a bull, cancelling and setting aside all the obligations of 1301.

This is a step which we shall not attempt to justify, however consistent it might be with the general belief of those days: in truth, we feel it to be the weakest and most indefensible act of Edward's life. Yet still we must not forget, that it was consistent with the current belief of those days. Men knew then, as we know now, that some vows are rash vows; that some oaths, like that of Herod (Mark vi. 26), are unfit to be kept; and they believed also—what we do not believe—that Christ had left authority with the bishop of Rome, to "bind and loose" in all such matters; and that when he had declared any oath or vow to be null and void, it became as though it had never been given. These views, as we have said, were held by all men at that time; * and although we

* Thus Mr. Tytler tells us of Bruce's conduct in 1297;—that "Bruce went to Carlisle with a numerous attendance of his friends, and was compelled to make oath on the consecrated host, that he would continue faithful to Edward. To give a proof of his fidelity, he ravaged the estates of Sir W. Douglas, then with Wallace, seized his wife and children, and carried them to Annandale. 'Having thus defeated suspicion, and saved his lands, he privately assembled his father's retainers, talked lightly of an extorted oath, *from which the pope would absolve him*, and urged them to follow him against the English." (Vol. i., p. 129.)

now reject them, we ought to judge any man's character mainly by his adherence to what he conscientiously believes to be true ; acting honestly on that measure of light which he possesses.

There was also another feature of the case which greatly weighed with the king ; a feature, too, which our courts of equity up to the present hour always take into the account, when examining into the validity of a man's engagements ; we mean, that of coercion and intimidation.

He had left Winchelsey, in 1297, one of the council of the young prince. The council, on Wallace's success, called a parliament in London ; and to that parliament there came Hereford and Norfolk, with a large body of armed retainers, and insisted on a fresh confirmation of the charters, with a new clause. Their demands were remitted to Edward in Flanders, with an earnest request, on the part of the council, that he would concede to the wish of the two earls. So advised, the king assented to these proposals. Since then, it had been shown to him, that all these proceedings in 1297 were the result of a conspiracy between Winchelsey and the two earls ; and he had had a letter put into his hands which proved this fact. At Lincoln, too, in 1301, he had observed the same conspiracy or confederacy at work ; and had again found that civil war was contemplated and prepared for by the conspirators. Thus a sort of treason had been, for three or four years, going on all around him. Any man of a generous and noble mind, and with a just sense of his kingly rights, would naturally feel indignant at such treatment ; and Edward, in his application to the pope, dwells especially on these proceedings, as taking from his engagements that character of freedom which ought to attend them. In our own day, if a woman, in contracting a marriage, or a man, in giving a bond, is found to have been acting under coercion or fear, or to have been the victim of a conspiracy, those obligations can be set aside by our courts of equity. Rome, at that time, claimed to be the court of equity for all the sovereigns of Europe, and the pope professed to act upon principles which are recognized by English lawyers in the present day. The bull was granted, and the extorted concessions declared to be null and void.

Many historians have expressed their wonder that this bull, when obtained, was scarcely acted upon. "The power was not, in fact," says Hume, "made use of." "The king made," says Lingard, "no public use of this document."

This wonder arises from a misconception of the king's real views and objects. Many writers assume, most absurdly, that Edward was hostile to "the charters." Yet one of his first acts, as Hume admits, after receiving the papal absolution, was to grant "a new confirmation of the charters;" thus showing, in the most direct and palpable manner, that it was not against "the charters" that his efforts had been directed.

If we wish to understand the king's actions, and their motives, we have only to study his own words, and there we shall soon discover, that it was to rectify some of the evil consequences of the disafforesting regulations of 1305, and to nullify Winchelsey's sentence of excommunication, that this papal absolution was procured. The bull arrived in Easter 1306, and its publication declared to the people that the archbishop's anathema was made null and void. But the king left them but a short time in doubt as to his intentions; for on the 28th of May came forth that remarkable statute which appears on the hundred and forty-seventh page of the "Statutes of the Realm," and in which the king addresses himself to the hearts and understandings of his subjects, in the following fervent expressions:—

" The king, to all whom, etc.—Greeting :

" While we behold the imperfection of human weakness, and weigh with attentive consideration the burdens that lie upon our shoulders, we are inwardly tormented with divers compunctions, tossed about by the waves of divers thoughts, and are frequently troubled, *passing sleepless nights*, hesitating in our inmost soul *upon what ought to be done*, what to be held, or what to be prosecuted.* Yet, under Him, who, holding in heaven the empire over all things, bringeth everything into existence, and dispenseth the gifts of his grace as it pleaseth Him, while the understandings of men cannot conceive the greatness of his wisdom, We do *resume our power*, trusting that He will perfect our actions in his service ; and in the clemency of his goodness, will mercifully look upon, and supply our deficiency ; that we, relying on his protection, may be directed in the path of our Lord's commandments. Truly, among all the things that rest upon our care, about this chiefly is our mind busied without intermission, that we may provide ease and comfort for our subjects dwelling in our realm, in whose quietness we have rest, and in whose tranquillity we are comforted. We have learned, by the information of our faithful servants, and by the cries of the oppressed, that the people of our

---

* In these remarkable words, occurring in a statute of the realm, and dictated, we cannot doubt, by Edward's own lips, we seem to have a glimpse of his earnest and sincere character. Believing, as all men in his day believed, that there was a Pontiff at Rome who had full power "to bind and to loose," he had applied to that authority, and had been loosed, so he was assured, from an engagement which was mischievous in itself, and which had been improperly extorted from him. Yet, with this dispensation in his possession, what follows? He himself tells us : " sleepless nights." What occasioned them ? Evidently that first principle of all his conduct of which Mr. Pearson takes notice : " He never broke his word." No papal bull, no external decision of any kind, could thoroughly reconcile him to an infraction of the Scriptural rule : " He sweareth to his neighbour, and disappointeth him not, though it were to his own hurt."

realm are, by the officers of our forests, oppressed and troubled with many wrongs, ... Wherefore, being desirous to prevent such oppressions, and grievances, ... and to provide with our most diligent endeavour for the peace and tranquillity of the inhabitants of our realm, We have ordained,

1. (Of presentments of offences.)
2. (Of supplying of officers.)
3. (No officer to be of any jury.)
4. (Punishment of officers surcharging.)
5. (Trespassers in grounds disafforested.)
6. "And moreover we will, that they which had common of pasture in the forest before the perambulation was made, and who were restrained of common by the late perambulation, shall have their common of pasture hereafter in the forest, as freely and largely as they wont to have before the perambulation was made."

This ordinance was sent to the several counties of England, and ordered to be publicly proclaimed. And in it we see the fruit, and the only fruit, of the papal absolution. It is hardly correct to say, as some historians have said, that the king made no use of the bull of absolution: we believe that he made all the use of it that he ever intended or desired to make. In some way or other, he had felt himself in a measure *uncrowned* by some regulation made at Lincoln; and hence he says, on obtaining the papal annulment, "We do *resume* our power." But then, the only use he makes of that power is to relieve those who, by the disafforesting, "were put out of the forests by the great men," and who cried to him for help. As for any infringement or retrenchment, either of Magna Charta, or of the Charter of the Forests, not the least step of the kind is imputed to him, even by the most prejudiced of all the historians. Yet are some of these very ready to ascribe to him a desire or intention of this kind; although they admit that for some undiscoverable reason, it never exhibited itself in action!

Such, then, was the real character, and such the practical results, of those disputes and discussions respecting "the charters," which occurred between 1297 and 1306—*i.e.*, between the twenty-fifth and thirty-fourth years of Edward's reign. On the whole, the people were largely gainers by these discussions; but that they were so, is mainly to be attributed to the constant anxiety shown by the king to meet generously all the demands which were made upon him; and to concede to his people all that it was in his power to grant, "without disinheriting the crown."

One or two other matters of minor, but yet of considerable importance, require to be mentioned at this period of the history; that is, during the last five years of the king's life.

We have already dwelt at some length upon Edward's character as a legislator; and his high rank as a commander requires no proof from us. But England, at this important crisis in her history, needed a man of power in a third capacity—that of a *ruler;* and she found this also in Edward. Two reigns, of sovereigns in various ways unfit to rule, had so far relaxed the bonds of society, and weakened the authority of the law, as to call loudly for the effectual interposition of some one whose power should be sufficient to make the laws not only theoretically just, but also practically useful.

Forty or fifty years before this period, Henry III. had been obliged to sit in person on the bench of justice at Winchester, in order to secure the punishment of offenders who had rendered even the roads of Hampshire dangerous. Some years later we have seen earl Warenne assailing, sword in hand, one of the king's judges in Westminster Hall. Edward had himself suppressed this mutiny; and, persevering in his determination to make the law respected, he next brought the judges themselves to trial, for corrupting that which it was their especial duty to preserve. His correction of the two earls, Hereford and Gloucester, who, in his twentieth year, had broken out into a vehement personal warfare; and his Statute of Winchester "for preserving the public peace and preventing robberies," were further proofs of his sedulous and firm resolve to give his people the benefit of a government of law and order. But, about the thirty-second year of his reign, he found a new evil uprearing itself; and, without any delay, he applied to it the most suitable remedy—a Special Commission.

The mischief itself, which this new authority was intended to suppress, was described in the writs which gave the commission its existence. Bodies of men had associated themselves together in various parts of the country, who, "for certain rewards, bargained to beat, wound, or evil-intreat persons named to them, at fairs, markets, or other places;" and, by the fear which they inspired, these ruffians deterred the sufferers from preferring indictments against them. Such an evil required instant and strong-handed suppression, and this it received at Edward's hands.

Peter Langtoft, after describing the siege and fall of Stirling, and the death of earl Warenne, proceeds to describe this evil, and the king's plan for its suppression. He says—

> "After the interment the king took his way;
> To the south he went, through Lindesay;
> He inquired, as he went, who did such trespass;
> Brake his peace with deed, while he in Scotland was?
> Of such should be spoken, if men of them plaint,

Those that the peace had broken, if they might be attaint.
Wise men of God gave answer to the king,
That such folks were, it was a certain thing;
Through the land is done such great grievance,
That if not mended soon, a war may rise of chance.
These contenders where'er they assigned a place that is,
There they come together, and made a sikerness (engagement)
That they shall all go, to whom or where they will,
To rob, beat, or slay, against all manner skill.
They offer a man to beat, for two shillings or three;
With piked staves great, beaten shall he be:
In fair or market they shall seek him out;
All the land is set with such folks stout.

. . . . . .

For men of such manners, unless there be some justice,
In some few years, perchance, a war shall rise.
The king heard all they said—the plaint of each town;
And gave them a new name, and called them 'Trailbastoun.'

. . . . . .

The king through the land did seek men of renown,
And with the justices them bound, to sit on Trailbastoun;
Some on quest they 'demned to be bounden in prisons;
And those that fled they banisht as the king's felons."

The phrase *trail-baston* is, in old French, "draw the staff." The use and intent of it in the present case has been learnedly discussed by various writers; but it appears to be beyond a doubt that, as Sir Francis Palgrave remarks, "it designates the *offender* and the *offence*, not the court or tribunal." In the "Chronicle of Rochester," already referred to—on the margin of which we find various pictorial illustrations—the representation here given is of two men fighting with bludgeons. And it is evident that the real object of this special commission was to put down, in a resolute and summary manner, what in modern phrase would be styled "club-law." These commissions seem to have been so useful and efficient, as to be continued for about eighty years, or until the middle of the reign of Richard II. Stowe speaks of them as holding special sessions, occasionally, in the metropolis; mentioning particularly "at the stone-cross near the Strand, over against the bishop of Coventry's house;" and sometimes within that prelate's mansion.

Calling to mind the terrible example made of the judges in the seventeenth year of Edward's reign, and combining with it this special and vigorous suppression of provincial disorders, we cannot fail to be reminded of the portrait sketched by the laureate in his recent Idylls; or avoid a question, whether the poet had not this sovereign in his memory when he drew such a portrait:—

> "The blameless king went forth and cast his eyes
> On whom his father Uther left in charge
> Long since to guard the justice of the king.
> He looked, and found them wanting; and as now
> Men weed the white horse on the Berkshire hills,
> To keep him bright and clean as heretofore,
> He rooted out the slothful officer
> Or guilty, which for bribe had winked at wrong;
> And in their chairs set up a stronger race,
> With hearts and hands . . .
> . . . . . and moving everywhere,
> Cleared the dark places and let in the law,
> And broke the bandit-holds, and cleansed the land."

One or two other incidents, bearing upon the same point in the king's character, fall in our way at this period; —that is, in the last three or four years of Edward's life. Sir Nicholas de Segrave was a knight of distinction, probably a brother of John de Segrave, who commanded the English forces at Roslyn. Sir John de Cromwell accused him of treason. Segrave, disliking the formalities of a legal investigation, challenged his accuser to decide the question by wager of battle. But Edward, whose discerning mind always revolted from the absurd idea of deciding a question of *right* or *wrong* by mere physical force, and who had, twenty years before, protested against such a proposal when made by two foreign princes, very naturally refused his consent. The combatants, apparently, thought that they might evade his decision, by crossing the sea, to fight the duel in France. Segrave returned, and was immediately arrested for disregarding the king's prohibition. The case, doubtless, was a novel one, and when the offender was brought to trial, the judges remained three days in deliberation; and at last declared the offender to be liable to the punishment of death, and the forfeiture of his property; but added, gratuitously, that "it was in the king's power to pardon him." Edward's indignant exclamation seems to reveal one point in his character. "Foolish men," he cried out, "after so long a deliberation, to tell me that it is in my power to have mercy! Why, I will do that for a dog who casts himself on my grace!—of what value, then, is such a recommendation? However, put your sentence into writing, that it may remain law for the future." Segrave was then remanded to prison; but after a few days, thirty knights petitioned for his pardon, and offered to be sureties for his future good behaviour. So entreated, Edward gave him a free pardon, and released his property from forfeiture.

In the "Placita Roll" of 1304 there occurs the following entry:—

"Roger de Heefham complained to the king, that whereas he was the justice appointed to hear and determine a dispute between Mary, the wife of William de Braose, plaintiff, and William de Brewes, defendant, respecting a sum of eight hundred marks which she claimed from him, and had decided in favour of the former; the said William, immediately after judgment was pronounced, contemptuously approached the bar, and asked the said Roger, in gross and upbraiding language, if he would defend that judgment; and he afterwards insulted him, in bitter and taunting terms, as he was going through the exchequer-chamber, saying, 'Roger, Roger, thou hast now obtained thy will of that thou hast long desired.'

"For this offence, William de Brewes, being arraigned before the king and his council, acknowledged his guilt; and because contempt and disrespect, as well towards the king's ministers as towards the king himself or his court, are very odious to the king, as hath of late expressly appeared when his majesty expelled from his household, for nearly half a year, his dearly-beloved son, Edward prince of Wales, on account of certain improper words which he had addressed to one of his ministers, and suffered him not to enter his presence until he had rendered satisfaction to the said officer for his offence—it was agreed by the king and his council that the aforesaid William should proceed unattired, bareheaded, and holding a torch in his hand, from the king's bench in Westminster Hall, in full court, to the exchequer, and there ask pardon from the aforesaid Roger, and make an apology for his trespass, and shall be afterwards committed to the Tower, during the king's pleasure."

The pointed reference here made to the king's anger and stern rebukes of his son, naturally directs our thoughts to this passage in Edward's life. His prescient consciousness of the young prince's weakness, and his strong dislike to Gaveston, his chief seducer, are already well known. We have alluded to one distinguished man, who is indicated in the above extract, as the minister with whom the young prince had been brought into collision. Walter Langton, bishop of Chester (sometimes called bishop of Lichfield or

Coventry), was the king's treasurer; and the prince had a stated income payable out of the royal exchequer. Under such guidance as that of Gaveston, it was inevitable that this income would prove insufficient; and that urgent demands for larger supplies would naturally follow. Hence the quarrels and the violent language, alluded to in the sentence on William de Brewes. Another glimpse of light on this subject is afforded by a letter from the prince to the earl of Lincoln, which has recently been discovered in the chapter-house at Westminster. In that letter the prince thus describes these circumstances :—

"On Sunday, the 13th of June, we came to Midhurst, where we found our lord the king, our father. On the Monday following, on account of certain words which, it had been reported to the king, had taken place between us and the bishop of Chester, he was so enraged with us that he has forbidden us, or any of our retinue, to dare to enter his house; and he has forbidden all the people of his household and of the exchequer to give or lend us anything for the support of our household. We are staying at Midhurst to wait his pleasure and favour, and we shall follow after him, as well as we are able, at a distance of ten or twelve miles from his house, until we have been able to recover his good will; which we very much desire. Wherefore we especially entreat you, that on your return from Canterbury, you would come towards us; for we have great need of your aid and your counsel."

The firmness and severity of the king, in this instance, was of no ordinary kind, and we know from the after-life of the younger Edward, that extreme severity was absolutely necessary. The royal prohibition was so effectual, that the young prince encountered real difficulties, and the king was induced, in the course of July to recal his prohibition, and to allow things to revert to their ordinary course. But so long as Gaveston was the prince's companion, it was inevitable that his course should be a vicious and a wretched one. The quarrels with the king's treasurer recurred continually, and in 1305 we read that—

"This year king Edward put his son, prince Edward, in prison, because that he had riotously broken into the park of Walter Langton, bishop of Chester, and destroyed the deer. And because the prince had done this deed by the procurement of a lewd and wanton person, one Piers Gaveston, an esquire of Gascony, the king banished him (Gaveston) out of the realm; lest the prince, who delighted much in his company, might, by his evil and wanton conduct, fall into evil and naughty rule."*

We now know, by the sad fate of Edward II., how well-founded were his father's apprehensions. We see, too, how great was Gaveston's ascendancy, and his consequent audacity, in that he appears very quickly to have stolen back again into the prince's society. For we find an ordinance for his banishment, dated "Lanercost, Feb. 26, 1307," in which he is commanded to swear that he will not return; and the prince, that he will not recal him. And so strong was the conviction which had fastened on the king's mind, of the fatal tendency of this friendship, that one of his last injunctions to the prince, just before his death, was, *never to recal Gaveston*. That injunction, however, like all others, was disregarded; and the loss of his throne, and of his life, was young Edward's well-merited punishment.

* Caxton's Chronicle, Matthew of Westminster, Fabyan, Holinshed.

XII.

THE SETTLEMENT OF SCOTLAND, A.D. 1303—1305.

SOME historians, in recounting the events of Edward's reign, have spoken of three, or even of four conquests of Scotland. But, strictly speaking, the term can only be applied to his first march through the kingdom, in 1296; and his last great expedition, in 1303—4. On both of these occasions the land was thoroughly possessed and quieted; and when Edward returned to England, he left not behind him, in all Scotland, in the open field, one declared foe. Our present chapter will be given to the description of the second of these two progresses.

In the spring of the year 1303 it began to be apparent that both the pope and the king of France, having no real care or concern for the Scots, would at last withdraw that support which they had hitherto given to the discontented in that country. Philip was anxious to be at liberty to devote his whole attention to the affairs of Flanders; and he readily agreed to a treaty which was made in the course of this spring, by which Edward was restored to the possession of Gascony, without any proviso or stipulation on behalf of the Scotch. No such treaty was required in the case of the pope. Boniface had already done all that he had promised or intended to do in behalf of that people. He had interfered in their favour, and had gained them a respite of one or two years—but permanently to quarrel with such a prince as Edward, in favour of a poor and distant nation like Scotland, was altogether foreign to his interest, as well as to his inclination.

The pope, then, having manifested his views, by addressing a letter to the Scotch bishops, enjoining on them a peaceful and dutiful demeanour towards the king of England, and the treaty with Philip having been fully agreed upon, Edward felt himself, at last, at liberty to turn his undivided attention to the affairs of Scotland; and, with his wonted decision of character, he resolved to bring all questions, in that country, to a termination by one sufficient and well-considered effort. On the 20th of January he wrote from his castle at Guildford, to more than twenty of his chief barons, desiring them to proceed, with their whole power, to the aid of John de Segrave, the governor of Scotland, who was about to march from Berwick to Edinburgh, and whom he, the king, intended shortly to join.

Before Edward, however, could reach Scotland, Segrave, like earl Warenne at Stirling, had allowed himself, by carelessness and over-confidence, to be surprised and defeated. He had commenced his march towards Edinburgh with a force of about 20,000 men. But these he had formed into three divisions; and these divisions marched on at a considerable distance from each other, and without keeping up any proper communication. Comyn, one of the so-called "regents," and Sir Simon Fraser, lay between Segrave's force and Edinburgh, with about 8,000 men. They doubtless had good intelligence of Segrave's movements, and of the disposition of his forces. Very naturally, and very judiciously, they made a night-march, and took the first division of Segrave's force by surprise, at the dawn of day; routing and dispersing it, and taking many prisoners. Shortly afterwards the second division came in sight, and the Scotch, still superior in numbers, and exulting in success, attacked and defeated it also. The third division, under Sir Robert Neville, had met with the fugitives from the first two engagements, and were thus warned in time; and they repulsed the Scotch, and recovered some of the prisoners.* Still, on the whole, "the battle of Roslyn" was a serious defeat for the English, and hastened Edward's journey into Scotland, which he reached soon after Easter.

In this engagement at Roslyn, one of the king's officers, called "Ralph the Cofferer," was taken prisoner by Sir Simon Fraser. He offered a large ransom; but Fraser himself " first struck off the hands of the unhappy priest, and then severed his head from his body."†

This same Fraser afterwards craved Edward's mercy, and received it, on condition of leaving the country. This promise, like almost every other engagement made at that time by Scotchmen, was unblushingly violated, and Fraser was again found in arms against that sovereign who had already granted him his life. He was taken and executed as a traitor, and his execution is one of those which are said to "brand Edward's memory with the charge of cruelty." The position, in fact, which is taken by most Scottish writers, seems to be this: that these men, because they were in arms for "independence," were entitled to commit any atrocity that they pleased; but that, when the fortune of war went against them, it was Edward's duty to grant them, at least, a free pardon, and in some cases a reward!

* The Scottish historians, who wrote *a century after*, claim the victory in all three engagements; but Hemingford and Trivet, who wrote *at the time*, distinctly declare that Neville repulsed the Scotch, and recovered many of the prisoners. Hume and Tytler, as Scotchmen, give credit to their own chroniclers; and yet they are uncandid enough to profess to take their accounts from Hemingford and Trivet. But these latter writers, who are the only contemporary witnesses, plainly assert that the advantage, in the third engagement, rested with the English.

† Tytler's History of Scotland, vol. i., p. 186.

The momentary advantage gained by the Scotch at Roslyn had no influence on the fate of the campaign. Edward arrived in Scotland soon after Easter, having summoned his military tenants to meet him at Roxburgh by Whitsuntide. He then passed on to Edinburgh "without challenge or interruption," in the early part of June. He himself marched up the eastern side of the kingdom, having given his son the command of a division which proceeded along the western coast. Having been warned, by the experience of the last four years, of the difficulties created by the devastating system, the king had now made ample provision, and his fleets accompanied his march with abundant supplies. From Edinburgh he proceeded, by Linlithgow and Clackmannan, to Perth. But this march involved the passage of the Forth—the attempt to pass which river had occasioned earl Warenne's defeat at Stirling. Lord Hailes and Mr. Tytler differ as to Edward's plans. Hailes says—" The Scotch fondly imagined that Edward would attempt to force the passage " of the narrow bridge, as Cressingham had done. " But the prudence of Edward frustrated their expectations. Having discovered a ford at some distance, he crossed the river at the head of his whole cavalry."* This ford, it will be remembered, had been mentioned to earl Warenne in 1297, by Sir Richard Lundin. Mr. Tytler, however, thinks that " Edward did intend to pass the river by the bridge; which, on his arrival, he found had been destroyed by the Scots." He observes that, " had the leaders profited by the lesson taught them by Wallace, they would have kept up the bridge, and attacked the English when defiling over it."†

A singular notion Mr. Tytler must have had of the sagacity of a commander of whose military skill he often

* Hailes' Annals, vol. i., p. 304. † Tytler, vol. i., p. 191.

speaks with admiration, to suppose it possible that he could have repeated the folly and misconduct of Cressingham and Warenne, with the lamentable results of which he was so well acquainted. It is true, indeed, that Edward, prepared for all contingencies, would have passed the river by *a* bridge, if the fords had been found impracticable. Peter Langtoft explains the whole transaction:—

> "Counsel he had of one, a bridge he should wrihte (erect),
> Boats and barges ilkon, with flukes to make them tighte,
> The Scottish sea to pass, *if that be had neede;*
> That passage never was, he rode over on his steede.
> The Scots they saw him coming, and fleeand fast they did,
> Moors and mountains over, away they drive for dread."

This plan of a pontoon-bridge was not new to the king. The strong rings and bolts by which he proposed to make fast a bridge over the Menai Strait, twenty years before this period, are even now to be traced on the banks of that water.* He doubtless, therefore, was prepared to take a similar course again, if it should be needful; but he could scarcely have been left in ignorance of Sir Richard Lundin's suggestion. And a ford having been pointed out, "the king," says Mr. Tytler, "forded the river in person, at the head of his cavalry, and routed or dispersed the last remnant of a Scottish army." Langtoft's description, however, is the more picturesque of the two; it was written at the time, and it corresponds exactly with the flight—admitted on all hands —of the Scottish cavalry at Falkirk. To repeat his words:—

> "The Scots they saw him coming, and fleeand fast they did,
> Moors and mountains over, away they drive for dread."

This was the last attempt at opposition in the open field. From Perth the king proceeded to Dundee, and Brechin, and

* Archæological Journal, No. 27.

Aberdeen. The castle of Brechin delayed him three weeks. It was naturally strong, and it had a stout commander—Sir Thomas Maule. But he was struck down by a stone from one of the king's engines; and on his death the garrison at once capitulated.

From Aberdeen Edward marched on to Kinloss in Moray. Some English writers of the time assert him to have even reached Caithness. He may have embarked in some vessel of his fleet, and in that way have visited the coast; but lord Hailes' remark seems a rational one, that in those days the country to the north of Ross-shire was of small account, and it seems improbable that the king should have carried an army into those remote districts. But having thus traversed the land, and found no enemy to abide the push of lance, Edward returned, in the autumn, to Dunfermline, where he took up his quarters for the winter. The Scots were now pretty generally satisfied of the hopelessness of any further resistance. Wallace, indeed, was somewhere hidden; but we hear nothing of a single valorous deed done by him; and none of the Scotch appear to have expected anything from his sword. The barons and other proprietors were now rapidly making their submissions, and being "received to the king's grace;" and, in the course of his residence at Dunfermline, this pacification became almost universal. Peter Langtoft says—

> "The towns, and the counties, and the people all aboute,
> To the king fell on knees, his power did them loute.
> Unto his peace they yield; fealty to him did sweare;
> Truly with him to hold; no arms against him beare."

Matthew of Westminster says—" The nobles of Scotland, their error having met with stern defeat, submitted themselves to the will of the king of England, and he admitted them to his favour, treating them with great mercy, inflicting merely certain fines, and allowing them time for payment."

Christmas arrived, and Edward, as his manner was, gathered his family round him. Langtoft says—

> "To Dunfermline he went; for rest will he there:
> For the queen he sent, and she did dight her chare: (cheerfully.)
> From Cawood she glent (passed) to Dunfermline to fare."

Two or three of the rebel leaders, besides Wallace, still held out, but they were now reduced to great extremities. Langtoft says—

> "The lord of Badenoch, Fraser, and Waleis,
> Lived at theeves' law, and robband always.
> They had no sustenance, the war to maintaine;
> But skulked upon chance, and robbed all betwene."

The few nobles, however, who yet stood out, could not allow themselves to sink to the level to which Wallace had fallen. They saw the necessity for an absolute and final termination of this great struggle. Accordingly, on the 9th of February, 1304, "the earls of Pembroke and Ulster, with Sir Henry Percy, met Comyn at Strathorde, in Fife, and a negotiation took place, in which the late regent and his followers, after stipulating for the preservation of their lives, liberties, and lands, delivered themselves up, and agreed to the infliction of any pecuniary fine which the conqueror should think right. The castles and the strengths of Scotland were to remain in the hands of Edward, and the government was to be administered at his pleasure."*

Those who thus made their peace with the king, saving both their lives and their estates, probably performed their

* Tytler's History of Scotland, vol. i., p. 191.

part, of entire submission, honestly. But there was a single instance of obstinate resistance, which, in its result, places in a strong light Edward's patient forbearance and his clemency: and yet, like many other actions of his life, it is perverted by some writers into a proof of his want of generosity.

The treaty made by Comyn and his coadjutors was the final submission of that which assumed to be the Scottish government. Peace was to be restored; and the castles and all the powers of government were in future to be Edward's. It followed of necessity, that any one who chose, after this, to maintain war against the king, took the position of a rebel. This has been an admitted law, in all nations, and in all times. We can easily call to mind the period, when it was suspected that Soult had fought the battle of Toulouse after receiving the intelligence of Napoleon's abdication; and when it was generally felt, that if such were really the case, death would be his fate, or, at least, his desert. And, unquestionably, after Napoleon's departure, and the establishment of Louis XVIII., any one of Napoleon's commanders who had chosen to hold a fortress against the king, would have found the punishment of a rebel awaiting him.

But in Scotland, although the late regent and his coadjutors had agreed to deliver up the castles to the king, there was one commander who resolutely refused so to surrender his charge.

The castle of Stirling, during one of Edward's absences in England, had been invested by the Scottish forces, and starved into a surrender. The regents had garrisoned it with three hundred men, and had placed it under the command of Sir William Oliphant.

By the treaty recently made, this castle became Edward's, and any man holding it against him was as justly liable to suffer the death of a rebel, as if he had held against the king the Tower of London. In fact, all men who continued a fruitless resistance, had been formally declared outlaws in a Scottish parliament held at St. Andrew's.*

Yet Oliphant refused to submit. He at first tried the device of asking for time to send to Sir John Soulis, one of the late regents, who had fled to France. But the castle was not Soulis's, nor had Oliphant received the charge of it from Soulis in his private capacity, but as one of the regents; and the regents and all the lords of Scotland had now abandoned their resistance. This transparent device, therefore, could not deceive Edward, who indignantly exclaimed, "Am *I* to wait for *his* pleasure? No; if you will not surrender the castle, defend it if you will, and abide the consequences."

There surely cannot be the smallest question, that if the king, with the treaty in his hand which promised him quiet possession of all the castles of Scotland, and with the declaration of the parliament of St. Andrew's before him, had given the garrison of Stirling notice, that unless the castle was surrendered within three days, he would hang every one of them as rebels, he would have been fully justified. Yet, instead of this, he patiently submitted to the toils and perils of a long siege, in which many of his men were killed, and in which his own life was repeatedly endangered.

The castle was exceedingly strong, and the battering artillery of modern days was entirely unknown. It is probable that Oliphant, confident in the natural strength of the place, hoped that he might weary out Edward and his army, and so win for himself a lasting fame. "The siege,"

* Tytler, vol. i., p. 192.

says Mr. Tytler, "had continued from the 22nd of April to the 20th of May, without much impression having been made. But determination was a marked feature in the powerful character of the king. He wrote to the sheriffs of York, Lincoln, and London, commanding them to purchase and send instantly to him, at Stirling, all the balistæ, quarrells, and bows and arrows, which they could collect; and to the governor of the Tower, requiring a similar supply."*

Two months more elapsed before these engines could be collected and brought to bear upon the castle. Meanwhile the king exposed himself in the siege as freely as any of his men. On one occasion a javelin struck him on the breast, and lodged itself between the steel plates of his armour. The king plucked it out, and shaking it in the air, called out to the besieged, that he would hang the man who had aimed it. On another day, a great stone, discharged from one of the engines in the castle, struck his horse such a blow, that he backed and fell. His soldiers rushed forward, and carried the king off—crying out against his rashness; to which he only replied, "We have undertaken a just war in the name of the Lord, and we will not fear what man can do unto us."†

At last, in July, a considerable breach was effected, and the ditch was nearly filled up with the rubbish and faggots thrown into it. A general assault would now have carried the castle; but, seeing their imminent peril, the besieged sent to beg for terms of surrender. They asked for " security of life and limb,"—a request which the king would, doubtless, have granted readily, if preferred at the beginning of the siege, instead of at the end of it. But it was now too late. They had forfeited their lives, by all the

* Tytler, vol. i., p. 196.   † Matthew of Westminster, 1304.

military laws that ever were known. They had been making war for three months past, not in behalf of the king of Scotland, for there was no king except Edward; nor yet in behalf of the regency of Scotland, for the regents had submitted, and made their peace with the king. They had made war with their lawful sovereign, simply to gratify their own feelings of animosity; in a word, they were rebels, taken in the act. Hence Edward's stern reply was a just and proper one : " I will not receive you to my *grace*, but only to my *will*."

" Sir John de Mowbray and Sir Eustace le Poer accordingly proceeded to the castle-gate, and summoned the governor. Oliphant, with his kinsman Dupplin and a squire, met the English knights, and proceeded with them to an interview with the earls of Gloucester and Ulster. At this meeting they consented, for themselves and their companions, to surrender unconditionally to the king of England; and they earnestly requested that he would permit them to make this surrender in his own presence, and would himself witness their contrition."*

It is quite evident that, like David of Snowdon, who, in 1283, prayed to be allowed to see the king, they understood Edward's character; and that their best or only hope lay in the real kindness of his heart. They came, accordingly, before the king, in the attitude and garb of criminals. Doubtless, if in the present century, such an act had been done, the doers of it, either by martial or criminal law, would have been declared rebels, and would have been condemned to die. They said, " My lord, we submit ourselves to your will" The king answered, " My will is to hang you all; and if you dislike that, you may return to the castle." But they still had faith in his mercy; and they persisted in leaving

* Tytler, vol. i., p. 197.

themselves wholly at his disposal; kneeling before him in the attitude of criminals. At last, after a pause, "the king being moved, turned away his face for a time; and those who stood round broke into tears." He then ordered them to be sent to certain English castles, adding, " Do not chain them."* Not a man suffered any punishment beyond a temporary confinement; except one Englishman, who had aided the Scots in getting possession of the castle. He, dragged forth and hanged, died for his treason.

Yet Edward's noble acknowledgment of their soldierly bearing, even in a cause in itself wholly unjustifiable, which was implied in his orders to put no fetters on them, is thus ungraciously noticed by Lord Hailes: " This was the only hope of pardon indulged to men whose valour would have been revered by *a more generous conqueror.*"

Why, such a conqueror as Wallace, of whom the Scots are so proud, would have butchered every man upon the spot! This, indeed, as his own eulogists admit, was his constant practice. A monarch of the ordinary kind, after having been put to so much trouble and loss by a defence which was wholly contrary to the law of nations, would have hanged up the commander, as the chief offender, and have thrown the rest of the garrison into a dungeon. The third Edward, provoked by the long but far more justifiable defence of Calais, actually ordered six of its defenders to execution; only recalling that order at the earnest entreaty of his queen. But the king now before us, after seeing many of his men killed before his eyes, and after having had his own life twice endangered, in a warfare which he knew to be wholly unjustifiable, still so far honours soldierly firmness and tenacity, that he spares all their lives, and commands that no fetters shall be put on them. And yet, after this, he is reproached as

† Matthew of Westminster, 1304.

"ungenerous!" Such is the sort of justice which this great king commonly receives at the hands of Scotchmen.

Scotland was now once more quieted and at rest. The entire surrender made by Baliol in 1296, to a superior lord who justly claimed a fief forfeited by rebellion, had now been a second time confirmed by the voluntary homage and oath of fealty of every baron, knight, or landed proprietor in Scotland. There remained but one man still contumacious, the once terrible, but now despised William Wallace. And he, at last, wearied of the vagrant, outlaw life of the last six years, " prayed his friends that they would beseech Edward that he might yield himself on terms." *

The rebel leader, as we have already observed, was, for some reason or other, entirely deserted by the whole Scottish nation. We have already cited Mr. Tytler's admission— that during all the years which elapsed between his defeat at Falkirk in 1298, and his apprehension in 1305, " his name does not occur as bearing *even a secondary command* in the wars against Edward." Sir James Mackintosh endeavours to account for this, by saying that " the jealousy of the nobles, or the unpopularity of a signal reverse, *hide Wallace from our search* for several years." But " the jealousy of the nobles " had not hindered Wallace from gathering an army in 1297, and another in 1298; nor did " the unpopularity of ' several ' signal reverses," in 1306, prevent Bruce from bringing fresh forces into the field in 1307. How it happened that, after 1298, not even a score of " men of desperate fortunes " could be got to follow Wallace, must remain a mystery. One suspicion has occurred to us, grounded upon the known facts, of his delight in cruelty, a trait which is seldom found in the truly brave; and of the absence of the slightest record of any deed of daring, either at

* Langtoft.

Stirling or at Falkirk. These two circumstances seem to point to the conclusion—that Wallace was taken to be, by his countrymen, during all these years, something very much the reverse of "a hero." One trifling incident in his life is briefly mentioned as occurring during this period. Blind Harry, in his romance, sends Wallace to France, where Philip makes him "Duke of Guyenne." But the real truth of this part of his story is briefly told us in the "Chronicle of St. Albans" (Cotton MSS.), in the following terms:—

"About this time William Waleis, with five soldiers, went to the French country, to ask aid from the king of France. And when he had arrived at Amiens, it was told to the king, who gave orders that he should be apprehended. The king then wrote to the king of England, offering to send Waleis to him."

Apparently, however, Philip, on further consideration, felt that it might not redound much to his honour to give up a man who had voluntarily taken refuge with him; and he therefore devised a middle course, by which he might get rid of the Scotch leader without putting him into the hands of his pursuers. He gave to Wallace a brief note, addressed to his representatives at Rome, recommending the rebel chief to their good offices, and through them to the pope. This note, strange to say, is now preserved among the ancient records in our national collection. A copy of it is given in the "Wallace Documents" (Edinb. 1841); and it is argued by the learned editor of that collection, that this note proves that Wallace went to Rome, and saw the pope. But surely it rather leads to an opposite conclusion. Had Wallace travelled into Italy, and seen the pope, we should probably have found some traces of him by the way, or in Rome itself. But no such foot-marks have ever been found. And again—had Wallace actually reached Rome, and delivered that note to Philip's agents, how should ever it have found its way to the Tower of London? Obviously, the more rational conclusion is, that the said note was a mere pretext on Philip's part—a device for getting rid of Wallace; and that the Scotch leader, having no money, and knowing it to be useless to go to Rome without money, took the note, put it into his pouch, escaped back into Scotland, and was, at last, taken with the paper in his possession. So found, the document would naturally be sent to Edward, and thus it would find its way into the usual receptacle for the state-papers of the time.

At all events, Wallace soon returned from France, and again betook himself to his forest-haunts in Scotland. And now, seeing all Scotland once more quietly at rest under Edward's authority, the obduracy of this violent man began to give way. For more than five years he had lived the life of an outlaw, " having no sustenance " but " robbing always." He now approaches as near to the king as he may venture—still hiding in the forest, and he begs his friends to apply to the king on his behalf. But the application was made in a wrong spirit. Langtoft thus describes it:—

> " Turn we now other ways, unto our own geste; (affairs)
> And speke of the Waleys, that lies in the foreste;
> In the forest he lendes, of Dumfermelyn:
> He prayed all his frendes, and other of his kin,—
> After that Yole (Christmas) they will beseke Edward;
> That he might yield till him, in a forward (covenant)
> That were honorable to kepe wod or beste;
> And with his scrit full stable, and seled at the lest;
> To him and all his, to have in heritage;
> And non otherwise, als terme, tyme and stage.
> But als a propise thing, that were conquest tille him."

This assuredly was one of the most audacious demands ever made. The outlaw knew full well that he had sinned in no ordinary manner and degree, and that, not against Edward only, or chiefly, but against all England. His name was heard throughout the realm with rage and horror. Mr. Tytler justly describes his position in a few plain words :—" Wallace was too well aware of the *unpardonable injuries* which he had inflicted *on the English* " to conceive it possible for Edward to spare his life. And it is with wonder, therefore, that we read, in the treaty made with Comyn in 1304, the distinct inclusion of Wallace :—" As to William Walleys, if he thinks fit to surrender himself, it must be unconditionally, to the will and mercy of our lord the king."* In another place it is said, that " William Walleys might put himself on the grace and mercy of the king, if he thought proper."† Now, as to the meaning of such language in Edward's mouth, there can be no doubt whatever. We have just seen one instance in the case of the garrison of Stirling; to whom he had refused the least promise of grace or mercy. In fact, to be allowed to surrender, was tantamount to a grant of life at least. As we have recently seen, when his judges reminded him that " he might show mercy " to a certain criminal, his exclamation was, " *May* show mercy ! why I will do that for a dog, if he seeks my grace !" On the other hand, when any one had sinned past forgiveness, like Bruce in 1306, *then* he was " not to be received ;" and the young prince was rebuked for holding any communication with him. As to Wallace, it is evident that the king viewed him in the same light as he had viewed the garrison of Stirling. He would enter into no engagement with them : if they chose to surrender, it must be unconditionally, to the king's absolute will.

* " Endroit de Will. de Walleys, le Roi entent, qu il soit receu a sa volute 't a son ordainement." (Palgrave.)
† Rymer's " Placita," p. 370.

Wallace, as Mr. Tytler tells us, "was too well aware of the unpardonable injuries which he had inflicted on the English" to be able to believe it possible for the king to show him mercy; and thus he threw away the only chance that remained to him. His demand, which we have just given in Langtoft's words—that he should have, under the king's hand, not only assurance of his life, but also an estate secured to him and to his heirs for ever,—was just the surest way of raising the king's indignation. Obviously no pretension could have been more preposterous. He was an outlaw, liable to be taken and brought to justice; he was poor and wretched; and his offences, as he well knew, were such as it must be difficult for the king to pardon. Yet, instead of grasping at the single chance which was now offered him, he must needs give the king fresh provocation. And thus his doom was sealed. His demand was made known to the king, and Langtoft tells us the result:—

> "When they brought that tiding, Edward was fulle grim:
> He belauht him the fiende; als his traitore in lond.
> And ever ilkon his frende, that him susteynd or fonde.
> Three hundred marke he hette unto his warison; (reward)
> That with him so mette, or bring his hedde to town.
> Now flies William Waleis, of pese nouht he spedis:
> In moores and mareis with robberie him fedis."

Obviously no other course could be taken. Edward had already stretched his prerogative of mercy to an extraordinary extent, by expressing his willingness to "receive" the outlaw if he made an immediate and unconditional submission. Had he so submitted and received mercy, it cannot be doubted that such lenity would have caused great dissatisfaction among the English people. But Wallace preferred to remain still in his hiding-places, and justice was not long in overtaking him. As two Scottish earls had guided the king to his camp at Falkirk, so now a Scottish knight soon claimed the reward offered for the outlaw's apprehension. Sir John Menteith surprised him in bed, bound him, and delivered him to the English authorities.*

He was carried through England a chained prisoner to his doom. He arrived in London on the 22nd of August, 1305, " great numbers of men and women," says Stowe, " wondering upon him." He was not lodged in any prison, nor was any lengthened proceeding entered into. His chief crime—the savage desolation of the northern counties, was a matter of universal notoriety; nor did he for a moment deny it. He was therefore lodged for one night " at the house of William Dilect, a citizen of London, in Fenchurch-street;" and " on the morrow he was brought on horseback to Westminster,—Segrave and Geoffrey, knights, and the mayor and sheriffs of the city, escorting him. He was placed on a bench in Westminster Hall," and his indictment was read by Sir Percy Malorie, chief justice. It charged him —not, as the Scottish historians would represent—chiefly or solely with rebellion, or with levying war, but with those special barbarities which under the name of war, he had perpetrated.

Some writers lay great stress upon the circumstance, which appears in only one chronicle, that the criminal repudiated the charge of treason—saying, " Traitor was I never, for I never gave my allegiance to the king of England." The fact may have been so, but it is wholly immaterial. No doubt more than half the persons who have died for treason since Wallace's days might have pleaded the same excuse. It is most probable that none of the Jesuit priests

* Langtoft says,—
   " Sir John of Menetest followed William so nigh,
   He toke him when he feared least, one night his leman by."

executed in Elizabeth's days had ever sworn allegiance; and we may be sure that Thistlewood and his gang, who died in 1820, had never taken any such oath. But no one ever imagined that such a fact made the slightest difference in their guilt, or in their position.

Treason, however, or mere rebellion, would never have bronght Wallace from Scotland to Westminster Hall. Comyn, Fraser, and scores of other distinguished men in Scotland, had been guilty of treason and rebellion, and had received the king's pardon. The great difference between their case and that of Wallace consisted in those " unpardonable injuries" which, as Mr. Tytler admits, " he had inflicted on the English," and which Edward, as the king and defender of the English, found it to be now his duty to punish. And, accordingly, his indictment justly describes him as " Willelmus Waleis, captus pro seditione, homicidiis, deprædacionibus, incendiis, et aliis diversis feloniis."

And so it runs throughout. It says little of his treason and rebellion—it dwells more on his murders and his other cruelties. It speaks of his murder of the sheriff of Lanark, " whose body he cut in pieces," reminding us of the fate of Cressingham at Stirling. Passing on to his invasion of the northern counties, it charges, that "with certain of his accomplices, he invaded the realm of England, and all whom he there found, subjects of the king of England, he slew by various kinds of deaths—men of religion, and monks devoted to God, he feloniously massacred; sparing none who spake the English tongue; but all, old men and young, brides and widows, infants and children at the breast, he murdered in a manner more terrible than could have been imagined." No denial was given to these charges; in fact, none could be given: "He pleaded no defence," says Mr. Tytler, "*the facts were notorious.*" His ravage of Northumberland and

Cumberland, "leaving nothing behind him but *blood and ashes,*" was as well known and as certain a fact as the comparatively insignificant "massacre of Cawnpore" in our own day.

His sentence was therefore read. It was precisely such a sentence as would have been passed upon any doer of the like acts in the reign of William III., or in that of George III. It pronounced—

"That for the robberies, murders, and felonies, of which he had been guilty, he should be hanged by the neck: That, as being an outlaw, and not having come to the king's peace, he should be cut down and beheaded as a traitor: That, for the profanations and sacrileges committed by him, he should be disembowelled and his entrails burnt: And that as a warning to others, his head should be affixed to London Bridge, and his quarters in the towns of Berwick, Newcastle, Stirling, and Perth." This judgment was carried into effect immediately.

This "barbarous sentence" is exclaimed against by most of the Scotch historians; but their protests are strangely inconsistent and forgetful. In Edward's day, and for centuries afterwards, it was thought right and necessary to visit great crimes with great punishments. These complex sentences did not begin—we have already remarked—in Edward's day, but long before; and they were continued for many centuries afterward. In Elizabeth's day, when Walsingham and Burleigh, Jewell and Hooker, flourished, many Jesuit priests were sentenced to the same death which Wallace suffered, for merely conspiring against the queen. Later still, we find Montrose sentenced, by a very religious government in Scotland, to nearly the same death. And in England we find William, lord Russell, the Christian patriot, in 1680, *protesting against the omission* of the hanging and quartering in the case of lord Stafford. In fact, the refinement of feeling which, in our day, revolts against these disgusting details, had *no existence* in the fourteenth century, nor for several hundred years after it; and to censure Edward for the cruelty of this sentence, is as irrational as if we were to blame him for wearing armour, or for not using gunpowder. For more than four hundred years after Wallace's death, no Englishman ever dreamed that there had been any peculiar cruelty in the mode of his execution. But since Hume's days it has been the fashion to regard Wallace as a martyr, and to charge Edward with cruelty, for permitting his execution. And even some of our best and most recent historians continue to write in this strain. Thus, Sharon Turner says, " Edward obtained the wretched gratification of destroying his noble enemy; but his cruelty has only increased the celebrity of Wallace, and indelibly blotted his own."* And Mr. Pearson, still more recently, talks of "a new refinement of cruelty," and of "this atrocious sentence," and of Edward's " barbarity."†

But might not a very opposite view be taken with quite as much reason? Might we not blame the king, not so much for undue severity as for a blameable lenity. He offered Wallace his life, if he chose " to put himself on the grace and mercy of the king." So confesses Mr. Pearson, who says, " The words, I think, clearly imply that the king will admit Wallace to mercy, though he will not promise him terms."‡ In fact, if the king's words do not mean this, they mean nothing. Any criminal, at any time or place, may give himself up to punishment, without any royal proclamation allowing him to do so. But could Edward, in

---

* History of England, vol. v., p. 97.
† History of England, vol. ii., p. 428.
‡ History of England, vol. ii., p. 424.

this case, with any propriety, show mercy? That may at least be questioned.

Try it by a similar case in our own day:—A massacre of English women and children was committed, a dozen years ago, at Cawnpore. Would the Indian government have dared to grant a pardon, on any conditions whatever, to the perpetrator of that crime? Assuredly not.

The same question might arise next year in Ireland. There are many men in that country who feel precisely as Wallace felt, and who detest the English rule as heartily as he did. One of these, if he could obtain a success or two, might gather round him a few thousands of men, and might begin a civil war. If he conducted this war in the usual manner, and failed in it, he might surrender and be pardoned. This lenity was experienced by Comyn and many others in Scotland; and the same lenity might Wallace have found, supposing, we repeat, that he had carried on the war in the usual manner.

But supposing the Fenian chief to prefer a kind of warfare resembling that of Wallace in 1297, and that of the Irish rebels in 1798; how would the case stand then? Suppose him to adopt Wallace's system of "no quarter";* to burn schools and churches with all the people in them;† to "spare neither age nor sex;"‡ to leave behind him, in his march, "nothing but blood and ashes" §—would it be easy to pardon him then? Even in this day of universal lenity, would not the general feeling be, "No, if this ruthless destroyer of men, women, and children is not brought to the scaffold, it will be quite impossible hereafter to hang any human being!

* "They spared none, but slew all down."—WYNTOUN.
† Blind Harry.   ‡ Encyclo. Britan.
§ Sir Walter Scott.

One victim, then, and one only, had fallen on the scaffold; and even that one, had he thrown himself on Edward's mercy, would have been spared. But when, especially in those hard and iron days, was so great a change effected at so small a cost? When was a kingdom in insurrection restored to peace with so little of bloodshed, or even of minor punishment?

And now, there being "neither adversary nor evil occurrent," the king determined once more to attempt a thoroughly friendly and conciliatory settlement of affairs in Scotland. In his usual frank and manly way, he resolved to throw himself into the hands of the Scotch, and to allow them to advise him as to the best plan for the government of the country. He called upon Wishart, the bishop of Glasgow, who had already been twice or thrice in arms against him; upon Robert Bruce, who, though an Englishman, was earl of Carrick; and upon John Mowbray—to consult together, and to agree among themselves as to time, place, and other arrangements, for holding a parliament specially about the state and affairs of Scotland; so that all things should be settled to the full content of the whole Scottish people. At their suggestion a parliament was held at Perth, in which ten commissioners were appointed to confer with the king in London upon Scottish affairs. To these Edward added ten Englishmen, with several of the judges. All these were sworn to give the best advice in their power, without suffering themselves to be biassed by friendship or interest. The result of their deliberations was, that John of Bretagne, the king's nephew, should be appointed governor of Scotland, with the assistance of the present chancellor and chamberlain: that for the administration of justice, Scotland should be divided into four districts—Lothian, Galloway, the country between the Forth and the mountains, and the highlands; to each of which districts two justiciaries, an Englishman and a Scotchman, should be appointed: that sheriffs and escheators should be named for the several counties: and that the laws of David king of Scots should be read in an assembly of the people of Scotland, for revision and amendment.

On the 16th of September, 1305, a great council met on the affairs of Scotland, at the New Temple in London. There were present the bishops of Glasgow and St. Andrew's, two Scotch earls, and several barons; and the sitting lasted for about twenty days. A variety of points were discussed and settled, and at last the commissioners came before the king, at his manor of Sheen in Surrey, and read the ordinances which they had made; which he then approved and confirmed. They then all swore upon the Holy Gospels, "Robert Bruce," says Mr. Tytler, "acting a principal part," for themselves and their heirs, and for the whole people of Scotland, that they would faithfully keep and observe the said ordinances. "They then took leave of the king, and returned home, with great appearance of joy and satisfaction."

In a few days after this, the king issued *Forma pacis Scotiæ*—the Form of the peace of Scotland, in which he recounts—

"That the people of Scotland, after they were bound to us by oath of fealty, and by their written engagements, did by evil advice make war upon us, committing murders, robberies, burnings, etc., not only in Scotland, but in parts of England also; but that afterwards many of them returned and were received into our peace and favour; and now John Comyn of Badenoch, and others of his party, desire to be so received: now we, willing to do them special grace, have granted, and do hereby grant, that their lives and liberties shall be safe, and that they shall not be disinherited. And we also pardon the crimes aforesaid, and remit the anger we had against them, they being bound to pay the fines hereinafter mentioned." Then follows a schedule of one, two, or three years' fines, on the principal persons concerned in the rebellion.

And so, apparently, was Scotland a second time pacified and brought under regular government. Not a voice was now heard to disturb the general tranquillity. One execution only, as in the case of Wales, had been found necessary. One man in each of the two countries had gone beyond the bounds of legitimate warfare, and had by special crimes called down upon himself a special punishment. But towards Scotland itself, as towards Wales, the conduct of Edward, both in 1296 and in 1305, was generous, wise, and thoroughly noble. Still, these excellences could not protect him from treachery, perjury, and a third rebellion. These closing troubles, however, of the king's life must be reserved for our concluding chapter.

XIII.

BRUCE'S REBELLION: THE WAR WHICH FOLLOWED.— THE DEATH OF EDWARD: HIS CHARACTER.

PROPERLY to understand the portion of history to which we are now coming, it is necessary to bear in mind that the Bruces with whom Edward had dealings, were three—the father, the son, and the grandson. The first was the competitor for the crown in 1291, 1292. This Robert de Brus, or Bruce, died in 1295; leaving a son, also Robert de Brus, who was through life Edward's faithful and familiar friend. This, the second of the three, died in 1304, and was followed by his son, the third of the same name, who raised the standard of rebellion in 1306, and finally became king of Scotland.*

---

* Many of our popular histories of England, disregarding this distinction, fall into a variety of errors. Thus Oliver Goldsmith, in his larger history, says, that in 1306, the competitor, " being old and infirm, was obliged to give up the ambition of being the deliverer of his people to his son." The fact being that the competitor had died eleven years before, and his son two years before the time of which Goldsmith was speaking. In his abridged history, which for many years was the lesson-book in all our great schools, the statement was thus altered:— " Bruce, who had been one of the competitors for the crown, but was long kept a prisoner in London, escaping from his guards, resolved to strike for his country's freedom." The fact being, that neither of the Bruces had ever been "a prisoner in London," and that the competitor, here spoken of, had died in 1295—eleven years before the period at which we have now arrived. Even Sir Walter Scott falls into a like inaccuracy, saying, "Bruce, the competitor, after Dunbar, 1296, hinted to Edward his hope of being preferred to the kingdom." Whereas, "the competitor" had died a year or two previous.

Of the Brus, or Bruce, family, we may adopt lord Campbell's account. He tells us, that—

"Robert de Brus, or Bruis (in modern times spelt Bruce), was one of the companions of the conqueror, and having distinguished himself in the battle of Hastings, his prowess was rewarded with no fewer than ninety-four lordships, of which Skelton, in Yorkshire, was the principal." "Robert, the son of the first Robert de Brus, became a widower while a young man, and to assuage his grief, paid a visit to Alexander I., king of Scotland, who was keeping his court at Stirling. There the heiress of Annandale fell in love with him, and in due time he led her to the altar." "The fourth in succession married Isabel, the second daughter of David, earl of Huntingdon, grandson of David I. Robert de Brus, afterwards the competitor, was their eldest son." This de Brus "practised in Westminster Hall from 1245 to 1250. In the latter year he took his seat as a puisne judge; and in the 46th year of Henry III. he had a grant of forty pounds a year salary." He married a daughter of the earl of Gloucester, and his son (the second of the three), was, in all probability, born in or near Westminster; where the judge must have dwelt. In 1268 he was appointed chief justice, and remained in that post until the end of Henry's reign. Not being re-appointed, he retired to his castle of Lochmaben. Here (in 1289) he became one of the commissioners for negociating the marriage of the heiress of Scotland with the young prince of Wales. On the death of the youthful Margaret, he advanced his own claim, as the son of David of Huntingdon's second daughter; but the superior claim of John Baliol was preferred, he being the grandson of David's *eldest* daughter. De Brus, disappointed, and resolving not to pay homage to Baliol, " retired," says Sir Walter Scott, " to his great Yorkshire estates," where he died in 1295, the year preceding Edward's first entrance into Scotland. He had been, through life, ranked among the barons of England, and had been always a steady supporter of the crown. We find him on Henry's side at the battle of Lewes in 1264. We find him also acting as sheriff of Cumberland; and he was buried in 1295, at Guisborough in Yorkshire, where his tomb still remains.

His son, the second Robert de Brus of these three, was an intimate friend of Edward's. He accompanied him in his visit to Palestine; he was on such terms of familiarity with him (as we have seen in a former page) as to apply to him for a loan of money; and we observe that in 1300, when the king returned from Scotland, he took up his abode "at Holme Cultram, on the border." Now Holme Cultram is the place where *this* Robert de Brus lies buried. He was governor of Carlisle, and we have no doubt that it was by his invitation that Edward determined to spend some time in this home on the border. This de Brus married the countess of Carrick, and thus added another Scottish estate to his large English inheritance. He was always loyal to the English crown; and, accordingly, when the Scottish parliament of 1294-5 occupied itself in confiscating the estates of all who adhered to Edward, the lordship of Annandale was taken from de Brus. "During the contest of 1295-6, this Bruce, son to the competitor, possessed of large estates in England, continued faithful to Edward."*
And when Baliol resigned the crown, and Edward took possession of Scotland, he nominated "his dear and faithful Robert de Brus, earl of Carrick, *and his son*, to receive to his peace the inhabitants of Annandale." A year or two later, we find him fighting in the English army, against

* Tytler's History of Scotland, vol ., p. 204.

Wallace, at Falkirk.* This, the second Robert de Brus of the three, seems to have lived and died governor of Carlisle, and sheriff of Cumberland, sitting in the English parliaments; and his grave, like his father's, was made on English soil.

His son, the grandson of the competitor, was born, there seems no room to doubt, in or near Westminster, on the 11th of July, 1274.† This date, of itself, indicates the place of his birth, for at that time his father and mother must have been in the metropolis, waiting for Edward's arrival and his coronation. The king was known to be approaching the coast, and, a few days after, he landed. The preparations for the ceremony and the feast had been going on for many weeks previous, and the king of Scotland, the duke of Bretagne, the archbishop, and all the barons of England, were gathered together to greet his arrival. His own personal friend, Bruce, who had accompanied him to Palestine, and who returned the year previous, could not, we may be sure, be absent. Nor was it at all probable that his vivacious lady, whose promptitude and decision had been shown, the previous year, in " taking to herself a husband,"‡ would prefer to remain in silence and solitude in her Scottish home, while one of the greatest ceremonies of the time was proceeding, in which her husband had a right to take a prominent part. Assuredly this Bruce, the second of the three, and his wife, the countess of Carrick, were in Westminster in July, 1274, and hence in that city, about three weeks before the king's arrival, the son, who afterwards became king of Scotland, was born.

* Fordun, p. 981. He also sat, as an English baron, in the parliament of Lincoln. (See p. 220.)

† Fordun, p. 778. Wyntoun, vol. ii., p. 498.

‡ "The countess herself, riding up, and with gentle violence taking hold of his horse's reins, Bruce suffered himself to be led away in a kind of triumph to Turnberry."—Tytler's Scottish Worthies, p. 292.

When rising out of boyhood into man's estate, we find young Bruce in Edward's court. His father, who was intimate enough with the king to ask him to lend him forty pounds,* would find no difficulty in introducing, as we are told he did, his son, when growing up, to a post in the royal household.† That the young Bruce often spent a summer at Turnberry, or at Holme Cultram, we can easily imagine; but his education he gained, we doubt not, as he received his birth, in or near Westminster; with occasional visits to others of the royal palaces.

But the events of 1290—1292 cannot have passed unheeded by the young scion of a Norman house. His grandfather, the inheritor of ninety-four lordships in Yorkshire, had preferred a claim to be declared king of Scotland, and in that claim the young son of the earl of Carrick must have felt the deepest interest. It created a desire which seems never to have left the young de Brus. "The ideal perfection of the knight-errant," says Sir Walter Scott, "was to wander from land to land in quest of renown; to gain earldoms, nay, kingdoms, by the sword." This idea must have been often present in the young de Brus's mind.‡ He was empowered, as we have just seen, with his father, "to receive into the king's peace the inhabitants of Annandale." And from this date, 1296, until 1306, he continued to profess a loyal adherence to the crown of England. But there was an evident vacillation and hesitation in his course. He is claimed, more than once or twice, as a favourer of the insurgents who kept Scotland in commotion from 1297 to 1304. In truth, his position differed some-

---

* See p. 124. This sum would be equal to £600 in the present day.
† "Scala Chronica," Leland, vol. i., p. 540.
‡ "The vision of a crown could not but haunt him."—Burton's History of Scotland, vol. ii., p. 286.

what from that of his father and grandfather. In 1292 it was formally and solemnly adjudged that the right of John Baliol was superior to that of Robert de Brus. But in 1296 Baliol resigned the crown, and the king of England became king of Scotland also. The thought, therefore, could scarcely be absent from young de Brus's mind, that if the two realms were again severed, and if Scotland became once more an independent kingdom, *he*, Robert de Brus, would surely be one of those who might advance the strongest title,—Baliol being now a refugee in France.

This thought seems to reveal itself at several stages of this history. Thus, when in 1297 Wallace raised the standard of rebellion, de Brus was called on to take his side. " His conduct," says Mr. Tytler, " was vacillating and inconsistent." The wardens of the marches called upon him to take his place under the king's standard. He went, therefore, to Carlisle, and took a solemn oath to be faithful to the king. To prove his fidelity, he ravaged the estates of Sir William Douglas, who was then with Wallace; seized his wife and children, and carried them to Annandale. Having thus defeated suspicion, and saved his estates, he privately assembled his father's retainers, talked lightly of "a foolish oath" he had taken, from which he hoped the pope would absolve him, and urged them to follow him, and join the insurgent forces.* During the next seven years we remark the same hesitating and doubtful course.

De Brus was an English baron; his father and his grandfather died on their English estates, and were buried in English graves. In Scotland they were men of note, men of power; but there were greater men in Scotland than they. Accordingly, when Wallace had driven the English out of Scotland, and a sort of " regency " was established,

* Tytler's History, vol. i., pp. 129, 206.

we hear of Comyn, and the earl of Buchan, and the bishop of St. Andrew's acting as "regents," and treating with Edward; but never do we meet with de Brus, either in the field or in the cabinet—either leading an armed force or placing himself at the head of a regency. His name, we believe, is once or twice used, but no proof is given that his concurrence had been obtained. From all open collision with the English government de Brus appears to have shrunk. And hence, when the strife of 1300—1304 came to an end, this cautious politician appeared to have saved himself from damage. Mr. Tytler observes that "Bruce, whose conduct had been *consistent only upon selfish principles*, found himself, when compared with other Scottish barons, in an enviable situation. He had preserved his great estates; his rivals were overpowered; and, on any new emergency occurring, the way was partly cleared for his own claim to the crown."* Writers of a later date—writers whose object was to represent Bruce as a patriot—have put forward his name as concerned, with Comyn, Soulis, and others, in fighting the battle of Scottish independence; but it is very clear that Bruce himself contrived to make Edward regard him as a stedfast and sincere friend. On his father's death, in 1304, he succeeded to the estates, and took the usual oaths of fealty; being released, by the favour of Edward, from the scutage payable to the feudal lord. And in that same year a letter was addressed to him by the king, in the following terms:—

"To our faithful and loyal Robert de Brus, earl of Carrick, and to all other our good people who are in his company, greeting:—We have heard that it is agreed between you and John de Segrave, and our other good people of his company, to follow the enemy; and that you desire we

* Tytler's History, vol. i., p. 209.

should hold you excused if you come not to us on the day appointed : know that for the great diligence and care which you have used in our affairs, and because you are thus agreed to follow the enemy, we thank you as heartily as we can ; and we pray and require especially, as we confide in you, that ye put an end to this affair before ye leave these parts."*

Thus, for a series of years, from 1296 to 1304, did de Brus succeed in making the king believe that, like his father and his grandfather, he was a faithful adherent of the English crown. And accordingly, when 1305 came, and all Scotland, from the Solway to the Orkneys, surrendered to the English king, he, desiring above all things peace and contentment, " placed himself chiefly in the hands of the bishop of St. Andrew's, of John de Moubray, and of Robert de Brus."† The last of the three was an Englishman, and also a Scottish baron. He was in the same position as our dukes of Sutherland of the present day, who are great lords in Staffordshire and other English counties, but one of whom, marrying a Scotch countess, added to his large English possessions almost a whole Scottish county.

That this Robert de Brus, on coming to man's estate, and pondering the prospect before him, did often think upon his position with reference to the Scottish crown, is probable enough, and is suggested by several passages in his history. But so thinking, he would immediately discern three obstacles :—
1. The declared superiority of Baliol's claim, which had been recognized at the time of the arbitration. 2. Next, springing from the same root,—Margaret, the eldest daughter of David, earl of Huntingdon,—there stood John Comyn, a more potent baron in Scotland than he, and one who had, for five or six years past, acted as regent of the kingdom. How

* Halliwell's Royal Letters, vol. i., p. 22.   † Chalmers' Caledonia, vol. i., p. 671.

could de Brus expect that a Comyn would permit a descendant of David's *second* daughter to take the Scottish crown in his presence?* But, 3, there stood in his way the *de facto* king of Scotland, Edward, to whom he, de Brus, and every lord in Scotland, had sworn fealty; and whose strong right arm showed, as yet, no signs of relinquishing so important an acquisition. De Brus could not forget that any appearance of treason on his part, in Scotland, would at once endanger his ninety-four English lordships; and in spite of all that some Scottish historians have said, we feel satisfied, by Edward's letter just cited, and by Bruce's employment to settle "the pacification of Scotland," that the king regarded him, up to the close of 1305, as "our dear and faithful Robert de Brus."

But in October or November of that year, "having sworn upon the Holy Gospels" that he "would faithfully keep and observe the ordinances of the pacification of Scotland, Bruce took leave of the king, and returned home, with great appearance of joy and satisfaction." No one pretends that the king had given him any cause for discontent or alienation. Yet every Scottish historian that has ever written on the subject has avowed his conviction that this swearing on the gospels was a deliberate perjury, and that the show of "joy and satisfaction" was wholly hypocritical. They all assure us that at this very time Bruce was planning and conspiring, with various persons, to obtain for himself the crown of Scotland.

In this temper of mind he began his journey homewards. He would direct his course, naturally, first to Holme Cultram, in Cumberland, where his father had, but

---

* Chambers, in his "Lives of Eminent Scotsmen," says: "John Comyn was the son of Margery, the sister of Baliol, and, setting Baliol aside, was the heir of the pretensions of their common ancestor."

a year or two before, been buried. From Holme Cultram a vessel would carry him in two or three hours to Dumfries, from whence an hour's ride would bring him to his Scottish home at Lochmaben. During his long ride from Sheen and from London, his thoughts would inevitably turn to those three obstacles, of which we have spoken, which stood between him and the crown of Scotland; and we know now what must have been his thoughts. It is easy to describe them, without any risk of error.

Baliol, he knew, had pledged himself, three or four years before, not to meddle any further in the affairs of Scotland; nor had he any concealed intentions of another kind. Voluntarily, and expressing his own feelings, he had declared that he would never again set foot in a country which had treated him so unjustly. Baliol, therefore, who had been an obstacle in times past, might now be dismissed from view; he could obstruct the path no longer.

A more serious question was that which concerned Edward himself; but Bruce had latterly been spending much time in the king's company, and he had learnt enough to satisfy him that the great warrior had seen the last of his battle-fields. Edward was now in his sixty-seventh year. The length of his lower limbs had always been the one fault in his otherwise perfect symmetry, and those limbs now began to fail him. In a public ceremonial, a few months after this, the king's strength gave way before his task had been performed. Bruce might confidently assure himself that, whatever might happen, the victor of Falkirk would never again be found at the head of an army on the soil of Scotland. As for the young prince, he was not worth a thought.

Two principal obstacles, then, were vanishing out of his way, and the crisis, the present moment, was all-important. A plan of a new English government had just been agreed upon, but it had still to be constructed and established. If that government should be allowed to develope itself, to assume the reins, and to take the rule of Scotland into its hands, a new rebellion might be almost a hopeless task. Now, if ever—*now*, with ten times more hope than two years later—*now*, must the effort be made.

But, though two obstacles had almost vanished, the third still remained. Comyn was " the first noble in the realm."* His power in Scotland was far greater than that of Bruce. He had acted, too, as regent of Scotland for some five years past. Upon the course he should now take, the success of any new attempt must mainly depend. He had but recently applied for the king's pardon, and had received it. He had, at the same time, given a new oath of fealty to the king. What would he now do? Should he adhere to his oath, and give his help to put down a new insurrection, what reasonable prospect of success would there be? Yet how could Bruce expect Comyn, after struggling in vain against English rule for five years, now to incur the terrible risk of a new rebellion? and that not for himself, but for another? The case seemed hopeless. What, then, was to be done?

Such thoughts as these, we cannot for a moment doubt, must have passed through Bruce's mind in his journey from Sheen to Scotland, in October and November, 1305. The question seemed to reduce itself within the smallest limits: " Comyn, what will he do? And, supposing he refuses to aid us in a new rebellion, by what means can we thrust him out of our way?"

The answer to this question, the final resolve, we know to have been an evil one. Bruce had already en-

* Tytler, vol. i., p. 213.

tangled himself in the guilt of deception and hypocrisy, but now he must go much further. The great prize of a crown was suspended before him, and he would hesitate at nothing to gain it.

His decision was formed: if Comyn would obstruct his course—if Comyn would neither act nor permit others to act, then Comyn must be got rid of. A settled plan of deliberate assassination was the final result of these long cogitations.

Four of the principal English chroniclers of the time, besides divers others, give us the result.

Walter Hemingford, one of the best of the English historians, says—

"Robert de Brus, grandson of that Brus who had disputed with Baliol the crown of Scotland," "relying on perverse counsel, aspired to the kingdom, and fearing lord John Comyn, a powerful noble, and faithful to the king," "he sent to him with treacherous intent two of his brothers, Thomas and Nigel, asking him to meet him at Dumfries, to treat of certain matters; and he, suspecting no evil, came to him to the church of the Friars' Minors. And when they were conversing, as it seemed, with peaceful words, all at once altering his mien and changing his language, he began to inveigh against him, accusing him of having injured him in the king's estimation. And when Comyn attempted to reply, the other would not hear him, but, *as he had plotted*, he struck him with his foot, and then with his sword; and, retiring, left him to his retainers, who, pressing on him, left him for dead on the pavement of the altar."

The "Chronicle of Lanercost," written at the time and in the neighbourhood, thus records the fact:—

"Lord Robert Brus, earl of Carrick, guilefully sent a message to lord John Comyn, asking him to come and have an interview with him at the house of the Friars' Minors in Dumfries; and when he had come, he slew him in the church, and also lord Robert Comyn, his uncle."

Matthew of Westminster is another contemporary historian, who shows that he had access to the best sources of information. He thus describes the murder :—

"Robert Bruce, earl of Carrick, first secretly, and afterwards more openly, conferred with some of the Scottish nobles, saying, 'Ye know that by right this kingdom belongs to me; and this nation intended to have crowned my grandfather king, had not the cunning of the king of England disappointed them. But now, if ye will crown me king, I will deliver this kingdom and people from the tyranny of the English.' To this many consented. But when he asked John Comyn, a noble and powerful knight, he resolutely replied that he did not consent. He added, 'All the world knows that the king of England has four times subdued our country, and that we all, both knights and clergy, have sworn fealty to him. Far be it from me to consent to this perjury, I will not burden my soul with it.' Bruce begins to persuade, Comyn continues to object; the one threatens, the other withstands. At length, Bruce, drawing his sword, strikes Comyn, who was unarmed. Comyn fell, grasping the sword; Bruce's attendants rushed in and gave Comyn fresh wounds. This took place at Dumfries, in the church of the Friars' Minors."

Peter Langtoft, another writer of the time, thus describes the scene :—

> "He sent for John Comyn, the lord of Badenoch:
> To Dumfries should he come, unto the Minors' kirke:
> A speking there they had: the Comyn will not worke,
> Nor do after the saying of Robert the Bruse.
> Away he 'gan him drawe; his conseil to refuse:
> Robert, with a knife, the Comyn there he smote;

hrough which wound his life he lost, well I wote.
He went to the high altar, and stood and rested him there;
Came Robert's squire, and wounded him well more;
For he will not consent to raise no follye,
Nor do as he meant, to gin to make partie
Against king Edward, Scotland to dereyne."

These four writers are all contemporary witnesses; they all had access to the best sources of information, and they wrote at the very time. Many other and similar accounts might be cited, but these are sufficient.

Almost one hundred years after, the three principal Scottish historians—Barbour, Fordun, and Wyntoun—arose in Scotland. They had to write the history of their country, but their only materials consisted of Scottish traditions and English chronicles. Barbour, the first of these, had a pension granted to him out of the Scottish exchequer, " for compiling the book of the deeds of king Robert the First." The work assigned to him evidently was to represent the Bruce as a hero, and, as far as possible, a " blameless king."

After him followed Fordun and Wyntoun, and, still later, Hector Boece. No one of these could pretend to be a contemporary—all gave from tradition such facts as the Scottish people demanded of them. The general result is a story of this kind:—

That Comyn and Bruce had had conferences, to discuss the prospects of a new rebellion, in which Comyn was to support Bruce, and to receive his, Bruce's, estates as a reward. That this agreement was put into an " endentur," and sealed. That Comyn, being in Scotland, rode off to the king (who, at the time indicated, was in Dorset or Hants) and showed him the " endentur," and left it with him. That thereupon the king summoned a parliament, and Bruce came up from Scotland to attend it. That Edward, having

Bruce in town, was about to seize him, when the earl of Gloucester gave him warning, and he fled. That, on his way to Scotland, he met a messenger, whom he killed, and on whose person he found letters from Comyn to Edward. That, thus armed, and indignant at Comyn's treachery, he went to Dumfries, met Comyn in the church of the Friars' Minors, where he upbraided him, and at last slew him.

Such is the story, which appeared a century after the time in which the events occurred, and from the pen of men engaged to represent Bruce as a hero. We shall give, first of all, a Scottish criticism on the whole romance—the reasonable remarks of Mr. David Macpherson, the editor of *Andrew Wyntoun's Chronicle*:—

"This whole story of the transactions of Bruce with Comyn has much the air of a fable contrived to varnish over the murder, and to make it appear an act of justice in Bruce, whose splendid actions had so prepossessed the people in his favour that they were determined not to believe that he could do wrong. The story has this sure mark of fable— that the later writers give us more circumstances than the earlier ones. Barbour has nothing of the earl of Gloucester, nor of Comyn's messenger being intercepted and put to death, which are found in Fordun. In Bower's time the tale was embellished with the devil's consultation, and his wise scheme of inspiring Comyn to betray Bruce; together with the fall of snow, and the ingenious device of shoeing the horses backward. It was also thought proper to augment his retinue with a groom, and to allow two days more for the journey. Nothing remained for Hector Boece but to turn the earl of Gloucester's pennies into two pieces of gold, and to make a brother for Bruce, whom he calls David."*

* Macpherson's Chronykyl of Andrew Wyntoun, vol. ii., p. 501.

One or two other remarks may be added :—

1. All the Scottish writers speak of a parliament being summoned, in order to bring Bruce back to London.* Now we know that this is a fiction. No such parliament was ever held, or called.

2. Bruce having taken leave of the king, at the end of October, and returned home to Scotland, Comyn, whose presence in England at that time is nowhere to be traced, is said to go to the king, and to show him the " endentur." Whereupon Bruce, who had returned to Scotland, is to be suddenly brought back again, that the king may charge him with his treason. Now the journey, at that time, occupied from fifteen to twenty days. Winchelsey, a few years earlier, described it as requiring twenty. Barbour says that Bruce accomplished it in fifteen.† Here we have, first, Comyn's "riding off to the king"; then, the king's issue of a summons, to be sent to Scotland to Bruce; then, the return of Bruce to England, to attend a parliament; and finally, Bruce's flight back into Scotland—which last, of itself, his own historian says, occupied fifteen days. It cannot be necessary to add that all this riding backward and forward, from England to Scotland, and from Scotland to England, is a romance, not a history.

3. Had the king been warned beforehand of Bruce's treachery, he would have spoken of it. It would have been recorded in some of the English chronicles. No reason can be imagined why such a fact, if known, should have been kept secret by any one. Bruce's flight, too, had it ever happened, would have alarmed Edward, and precautions would have been taken. But it is quite clear that when Edward heard of Bruce's treason, and of the assassination of Comyn, the news came upon him as a surprise. Neither he nor

* Barbour, i., 590; Wyntoun, viii., 18.   † Barbour i., 647.

the people of England had any previous expectation of it. "Nothing," says Dr. Henry, "could exceed the surprise and indignation of Edward, when he heard of this revolution."

4. Comyn, it is alleged, after having been guilty of treachery towards Bruce, is invited to meet him in private conference. Bruce goes there with the dagger by his side; but Comyn, with all his consciousness of having sinned grievously against Bruce, which, according to this story, he must have felt, goes to this conference unarmed. Is this a credible account of the matter.? Must we not rather agree with Dr. Lingard, who says, "There can be little doubt that all this is a fiction, invented to wash the guilt of blood from the character of Bruce, and to justify a transaction which led to the recovery of Scottish independence."* A more recent writer, Mr. Pearson, says, "There can be no reasonable doubt that the crime was, to some extent, *premeditated*, as one in which lay the only hope of safety for a betrayed and desperate man" (vol. ii., p. 437). We believe that the murder was premeditated; but we see no proof of any betrayal.

Mr. Macpherson is doubtless right when he thinks that "this whole story has much the air of a fable," invented long after, "to varnish over the murder of Comyn." We are not at all bound to regard Bruce, as these Scottish writers would have us, as so hardened a hypocrite as to be blandly discussing with Edward, at Sheen, the terms of the "settlement of Scotland," if he had already agreed with Comyn on the mode and manner of a new rebellion. We deem the simple narrative of the English chroniclers who wrote at the time to be both the more probable and also that which casts the least blame upon Bruce. It surely is most probable that the thoughts of a new rebellion only arose in his mind during his homeward journey; that, arrived in Scot-

* Lingard, vol. ii., p. 615.

land, he spent some time, as the English historians tell us, in conferring with the Scottish lords; and that it was only when he found that Comyn would not concur, and that his opposition would be fatal to the whole plan, that his final resolve was taken. He would draw Comyn into a position from which there should be no retreat. It should be, "Consent, or die!"

But the deed was now done. Bruce, by a perfidious device, had effected his purpose, and by one stroke of a dagger, had removed the last remaining obstacle from his path.* "The first noble in the realm," whose opposition would have been fatal to the plan, was slain, and the conspirators had now the ground clear before them. We speak of a conspiracy, although most modern Scottish writers assume the murder to have been committed "in the heat of passion." None, however, of the older Scottish historians so represent it; and the well-known anecdote of Kirkpatrick refutes the idea. All Scottish writers tell us that Bruce came out of the church exclaiming, "I doubt I have killed Comyn!" "You doubt!" exclaims Kirkpatrick, "I'll soon make sure!" (mak siccar). The exclamation is that of a man who expected some such news; not of one who was surprised or shocked. Evidently, Hemingford had ground for his statement. "He struck him with his foot, and then with his sword, *as he had plotted*, and then, retiring, left him to his retainers, who, pressing on him, left him for dead on the pavement."

"The die was now cast," adds Mr. Tytler. "Bruce had, with his own hand, assassinated the first noble in the land, in a place of tremendous sanctity. He had stained the

---

* Sharon Turner says, "On every supposition, it was still the destruction of a competitor by the person who was to be most benefited by the crime; and from this suspicious atrocity the memory of Bruce cannot be vindicated."

high altar with blood, and had directed against himself the resentment of the powerful friends and vassals of the murdered earl." " He must now either become a fugitive and an outlaw, or raise open banner against Edward."

There can be no doubt that Bruce had weighed these chances beforehand. The inveigling his victim into " a place of tremendous sanctity," into which he naturally came unarmed, and there falling upon him, shows clearly a " foregone conclusion." The chief man in England, he well knew, was incapacitated by age and disease, and he had now got rid of the chief man in Scotland. These obstacles removed, for all the rest he relied on his own skill and audacity, his good sword, and his strong right arm. And the issue showed that his calculations were just and accurate; and " the power of intellect without conscience " was once more proved to be sufficient to achieve great earthly and temporary success.

He repaired forthwith to Lochmaben castle, where he was at least safe from any sudden pursuit of the Comyns. From thence he immediately despatched letters to every friend who was likely to give him any aid. Of these, the earls of Athol and Lennox, and the bishops of Glasgow, St. Andrew's, and Athol, and about fourteen others of some rank, as knights or barons, quickly joined his standard. With these few supporters, " he had the courage," says Fordun, " to raise his hand, not only against the king of England and his allies, but *against the whole accumulated power of Scotland.*"

This confession, from the pen of Scotland's first historian—himself a profound admirer of Bruce—decides one question. It was not in obedience to Scotland's call that Bruce took up arms; " the whole accumulated power of Scotland " was opposed to his enterprise. The cause he undertook was simply *his own cause*, not that of Scotland. He had said to the Scottish people—(to use the language of Matthew of Westminster)—"Make me your king, and I will deliver you from the tyranny of the English." The response he received was the adherence of two earls, three bishops, and fourteen knights or barons. The *dissentients* were so numerous as to amount, in Fordun's view, to " the whole accumulated power of Scotland."

Still, however insignificant the support he received, and however evident it might be that the movement had no other origin or purpose than the gratification of his own personal ambition, he had now gone too far to recede. Not even flight could save him, for who in France or Italy would shelter one who had committed such sacrilege? He therefore boldly took the only course which remained open. Three or four weeks sufficed to collect together a sufficient force, and on the 24th or the 25th of March, Bruce rode to Glasgow, and from thence, on the 27th, to Scone, where, in the accustomed spot, he received from the bishops some kind of a coronation. Some robes were provided by the bishop of Glasgow; a slight coronet of gold, " probably borrowed," says Mr. Tytler, supplied the place of the ancient crown of Scotland; and a banner wrought with the royal arms was delivered by Wishart to the new king; who, beneath it, received the homage of his few adherents, as " Robert the first." On the second day after the ceremony a repetition of the scene took place. The earls of Fife had long enjoyed the privilege of placing the kings of Scotland, at their coronation, upon the throne. The present earl was with Edward in England; but his sister, the countess of Buchan, was an enthusiastic partisan of Bruce; and, hearing of the intended ceremony, she rushed to Scone to offer her services in her brother's room. Bruce could not afford to slight or disappoint any adherent; and hence, simply to gratify her, the coronation was performed over again, and she was allowed the privilege upon which she set so much value.

The new king then began a progress through such parts of Scotland as were likely to favour his pretensions; seizing the royal castles, driving away the English officers, and asserting his rights as king wherever he could find an opening. But his party, Mr. Tytler admits, "*was small;* the Comyns possessed the greatest power in Scotland; and many earls and barons, who had suffered in the late war, preferred the quiet of submission to the hazard of insurrection and revolt." In fact, as we have seen Fordun admitting—the rebellion was *not a popular one.* Bruce had a far smaller party than either Wallace or Comyn had gathered, and if a couple of years of life and vigour had been left to Edward, the suppression of this third revolt would have proved an easier task than the defeat of either of the former two. Of Bruce's method of proceeding we have a sample in a document still extant, in which the earl of Strathern describes the mode in which he had been dealt with. This is a memorial, addressed by the earl to king Edward, in explanation of his position. In it the earl states, that as soon as Bruce was made king, he sent letters of credence to the earl, by the abbot of Inchaffrayn. The abbot urged the earl to repair forthwith to Bruce, to perform homage and fealty. "Nay," said the earl, "I have nothing to do with him." Thereupon Bruce and Athol, with a power, entered Strathern, and occupied Foulis. Bruce sent the earl a safe conduct, to repair to him. He did so, and on refusing to pay homage, he was carried to Inchmecolmec. Here he found Sir Robert Boyd, who advised Bruce, in his presence, *to behead him,* the earl, and to grant away the lands of Strathern. On hearing this, he was frightened, and did their will, and then they let him go.*

Tidings of all these proceedings—of Comyn's murder; of Bruce's coronation; and of the treason of Lennox and Athol, of Wishart, and of the two other bishops, reached Edward at Winchester, in Lent, and shortly before Easter in 1306. Had there been any truth in the stories told by Barbour, Fordun, and Wyntoun, of Bruce's escape and flight to Scotland, in the January preceding, we should have found, long before this, traces of Edward's foresight and energy, in the writs and other documents which such occurrences would have drawn forth. But no such traces are to be met with. This of itself abundantly proves that the narratives of Barbour and Fordun are wholly fabulous.

The intelligence came upon the king as a surprise; and it awakened in him feelings of the greatest indignation. As a knight and a soldier, accustomed to the laws of honour, an act of premeditated assassination—the assault of several armed men upon a single nobleman, whom they had induced to come without arms to an amicable meeting, would naturally fill his mind with horror and detestation. As a sincerely religious man, who, in 1289, had abstained from violating the sanctity of a church, even to take a notorious criminal from its protection, the ruthless murder of a nobleman on the steps of the altar must increase, if it were possible, his just indignation. But evidently, that feature of the case which most exasperated him, was the perfidy and treachery which had marked the whole transaction. The two chief actors in this tragedy had been Bruce and Wishart; and it had been to these two men, above all others, that he had looked for the quiet settlement of Scotland. They had come from Scotland professedly to assist him. They had

* Palgrave's Documents, p. cxxxix.

sat at his council-table for weeks together, and, doubtless, had often taken their places at his festive board, and shared with him in the summer enjoyments of his Richmond retirement. And now, it was not merely that they had fallen off from him, but that they had proved, by the desperate course which they adopted immediately on their return, that all their pretended zeal and loyalty in the October preceding, had been utterly false and treacherous. Edward was well versed in the language of the Psalms, and he would naturally be inclined to cry out, with David, "Yea! even mine own familiar friend, in whom I trusted, which did eat of my bread, hath lift up his heel against me."

This perfidy is made the especial charge against both the bishops, in an accusation laid by Edward before the pope. In this document the king recounts a long list of perjuries. Thus, of Wishart, bishop of Glasgow, the king alleges—

That when he, the king, was first called into Scotland, about the matter of the succession, he, the bishop, took the oath to the king, as superior lord, and was appointed by him as one of the guardians of the realm; yet, when Baliol was put into possession of the kingdom, he, the bishop, aided and advised him in making war upon England.

Next, that, upon Baliol's submission, the bishop came to the king at Elgin, and prayed forgiveness; and took an oath on the consecrated host, on the gospels, and upon the black rood of Scotland, that he would be faithful and true to the king, and would never counsel anything to his hurt or damage. And that, at the parliament held at Berwick, he took the oath of fealty for the third time. Yet when the king was gone to Flanders, the bishop abetted Wallace, and came forth into the field against the king.

Again, when the rebellion seemed to decline, the bishop

once more submitted himself to the king, at Irvine, in July, 1297. Yet, in less than a month afterwards, he had again confederated himself with Wallace and the rebels, encouraging them as heretofore.

Next, the king having returned from Flanders, the bishop came before him at Holme Cultram, and prayed the king's grace and mercy, and did then, for the *fourth* time, take the oath of fealty upon the host, gospels, rood, etc., etc. Yet, while this oath was yet fresh, the bishop assembled all his strength, and marched against the king's army.

Again, the rebellion being suppressed, the bishop came before the king at Cambuskenneth, and prayed grace and mercy, and forswore himself a *fifth* time, upon the host, gospels, etc., etc. And at the parliament at St. Andrew's, he took the same oath a *sixth* time. And yet, after all this, within eight days after the murder of Comyn, he gave Bruce plenary absolution—thus showing his approval of the sacrilege and the murder. He also in every way promoted and encouraged the rebellion, in violation of the oath which he had, on six different occasions, taken.

Similar are the complaints made by the king of the perjuries of the bishop of St. Andrew's, and the bishop of Elgin or Moray. To this general faithlessness on the part of the leaders in the rebellion, Wyntoun, in his "Cronykyl," published in the next century, pleads guilty, saying of Wallace's day—

> " For in his time, I heard well say,
> That fickle they were, all time, of fay" (faith).

But the disgust and exasperation which this perpetual perfidy would naturally excite in an honourable mind will be obvious to every one; and we have no doubt that it was this feeling which induced the inscription on the king's tomb—*Pactum serva*—an inscription which doubtless was placed there by his own command.

All the troubles of Edward's life had arisen from the faithlessness of those with whom he was concerned. David of Wales, Philip of France, Balliol, Bruce—all, in their turn, first swore to him, and then shamelessly violated their oaths. Hence, as his last word, he desires this injunction or maxim—"KEEP YOUR COVENANT"—to be engraven on his monument; and there, in Westminster Abbey, it still remains.

Meanwhile, the immediate result of all this perfidy is seen in the entire change which is perceptible in Edward's policy. For thirty years he had been singularly merciful, insomuch that Lingard, as we have just seen, declares it to be "difficult to point out any conqueror who had displayed equal lenity." And our latest historian, Mr. Pearson, concedes to him "the praise of being slow to shed blood."* But there is truth in the maxim, "Beware of the anger of a patient man." Edward was not naturally a patient man, but he had the command of his own spirit; he loved justice tempered with mercy; and one of his chief principles of action had been shown in his hasty exclamation in Segrave's case, implying clearly that to seek his mercy, in all ordinary cases, was to find it. But now he evidently felt that the time for showing lenity was past. There is a degree of sternness, mingled probably with some feeling of exasperation, in the acts of the last year of his life; but his love of justice never varied, and cruelty was a thing to him unknown.

"Although broken in body," says Mr. Tytler, "this great king was, in his mind and spirit, yet vigorous and unimpaired, as was soon evinced by the rapidity and

---

* Pearson's History, vol. i., p. 351.

decision of his orders, and the subsequent magnitude of his preparations. He instantly sent to strengthen the frontier-garrisons of Berwick and Carlisle, with the intention of securing the English borders from invasion; and he appointed the earl of Pembroke, with lord Robert Clifford and Henry Percy, to march into Scotland." It is clear, also, that the whole tone of the king's mind and language was changed, and his purpose was everywhere openly avowed, to take a signal vengeance on all who had in any way been concerned in the murder of Comyn.

Yet the death of that nobleman had deprived him of no favourite,—of no intimate personal friend or counsellor. Between this Scottish baron and the king there had been very little intercourse. For four or five years Comyn had kept the field against Edward, while Bruce had been professing the greatest zeal in his service. But Edward recognized in Comyn a frank and earnest opponent, who carried on the war until submission seemed to be a duty, and then surrendered his sword, accepted peace, gave his fealty to the king, and *kept his covenant*. And Edward saw this nobleman treacherously murdered by that Robert Bruce who had often sat at his table and professed attachment to him;—murdered, too, merely because he would not join in treason. Hence the king's vehement decision seemed at once to be taken, that for Bruce and his abettors there was to be no more mercy. The blood of Comyn should be fully avenged. He often showed his familiarity with the Old Testament, and on this occasion he probably recurred frequently to the language of David concerning Joab: " He shed the blood of war in peace, and put the blood of war upon the girdle that was about his loins, and in the shoes that were on his feet: let not his head go down to the grave in peace."

And it is quite evident that his feelings were generally shared by his people. A grand religious ceremony was announced to take place at Whitsuntide in Westminster Abbey. There the king purposed to confer knighthood on the young prince, and on other young men of rank, his companions. Nearly three hundred of the younger nobility and gentry were candidates for this honour, and eager to take their part in the new enterprise. So vast was the concourse of people in the abbey, that some persons were crushed to death in the throng. The king was scarcely able to perform his part; but at the banquet which followed, he took a solemn oath, according to the laws of chivalry, that he would proceed to Scotland, there to avenge the death of John Comyn, and to punish the perfidy of the Scots; and that, when that work was done, he would embark for the Holy Land, and leave his body in that hallowed soil. Soon after this solemnity, the young prince, with the new-made knights, his companions, and a considerable force of horse and foot, began the march to Scotland, leaving the king, who was now in his sixty-eighth year, to follow more at leisure. The rendezvous was appointed for July 8, at Carlisle.

But before either the king or the prince could arrive in Scotland, the new rebellion seemed nearly to have reached its close. The surprise of Roslyn had been reversed, and a disastrous defeat had reduced Bruce to the condition of a fugitive. The earl of Pembroke commanded a small English force at Perth, then called Johnstown. Bruce, having now gathered to himself something amounting to an army, marched towards the place, and sent a challenge to the earl to come out and fight him. The earl sent him for answer, that the day was now too far advanced, but that he would give him battle on the morrow. The Scotch retired, and incautiously broke up their array, and began to prepare their suppers. Suddenly, the cry was heard that the enemy was upon them. Pembroke, on second thoughts, disliking to appear backward, had marshalled his forces, and marched out to find the Scots. Bruce, still a young commander, had neglected all the usual precautions, and his troops, taken entirely by surprise, were thrown into utter confusion. Six or seven men of note were taken prisoners, and the loss of the Scotch is said to have been seven thousand men; in fact, the army, such as it was, was annihilated. Bruce himself, with a few friends, escaped to the coast, and fled to hide themselves in the western isles. Here, says Fordun, " he was reduced to such necessity, that he passed a long period without any other food than herbs, and roots, and water. He wandered barefoot, now hiding alone in some of the islands, now chased by his enemies, and despised and ridiculed by his own vassals."* " He and his friends," says Mr. Tytler, " began to feel the miseries of outlaws. Compelled to harbour in the hills, deprived of the common comforts of life, he and his followers presented a ragged and wretched appearance. Their shoes were worn off their feet by constant toil; and hunting, instead of pastime, became a necessity." † The English army, scouring the country, picked up all the fugitives they could find, and the chief power of Scotland was opposed to the insurrection. The lord of Lorne beset the passes, and had nearly captured Bruce. The earl of Rosse seized Bruce's wife and daughter, and handed them over to the English. The bishops of Glasgow and St. Andrews, the abbot of Scone, the lord

---

* " Bruce was so beaten by ill-fortune, that he was left alone to take passage to the Isles with two mariners in a boat, who asked him 'if he had any tidings of Robert Bruce?'"—*Scala Chronica*, App. p. 287.

† Tytler's Hist., vol. i., p. 222.

Seton, the earl of Athol, and the countess of Buchan, all were successively found, and brought in as prisoners. The king had, meanwhile, arrived at Dumfries, and the prince, after scouring the country, came to Perth. Bruce, now wholly disheartened, sent messengers to the young Edward to learn whether his submission would be accepted; but the king, when he heard of it, was incensed with the prince for holding any correspondence with "that traitor." We thus see the distinction drawn between his case and Wallace's. Wallace, after all his cruelties, was "to be received, if he chose to submit himself;" but Bruce's perfidy, his sacrilege, and his treacherous murder of Comyn, had put him beyond the pale of mercy. The king had sworn to avenge Comyn's murder, and hence with Bruce no communication was to be held.

There was now no visible insurrection in Scotland, the chief rebel being a mere fugitive among the hills. Hence, in October, we find the king at Lanercost, in Cumberland, where a council was held, and a deliberate sentence passed, with reference to the rebellion and its chief abettors.

This ordinance, in which various Scottish writers profess to find cruelty, is merely identical with what, *under the like circumstances*, would be passed at the present day. The parties arraigned had most of them been rebels in past years, and had found mercy. They had, in most cases, sworn fealty to Edward again and again, and had asked and received pardon. Their lives and their lands had been forfeited, and the forfeiture had not been exacted. Yet, after all this lenity, they were again found in rebellion, and now with the added guilt of murder and sacrilege. They had slain the first nobleman in Scotland, treacherously and perfidiously, and "in a place of tremendous sanctity." What in our own time would be the judgment passed on such criminals? or, rather, what *has been* the punishment adjudged to such criminals, within the last twenty years, in our Indian possessions?

The Ordinance of Lanercost declared—1. "That all who were guilty or were abettors of the murder of John Comyn should be hanged, and that all who advised or assented to such murder should have the same punishment." 2. "And that all who were aiding or assisting Robert Bruce, or were procuring or persuading the people to rise contrary to law, should be imprisoned during the king's pleasure."

Could queen Victoria, *under like circumstances*, be advised to pursue any less severe course? Yet, for this mere administration of justice, is the king charged by some writers with "cruelty!"

Doubtless he had now deliberately laid aside that singular lenity with which, for ten years past, he had treated the Scotch, and had become convinced that, with respect to some among them at least, mercy would be no longer consistent with a proper regard to justice. Yet, surely, the second of these provisos, which merely ordains for actual rebels "imprisonment during the king's pleasure," is one seldom equalled for its temperance and lenity. There was also perceptible, in some of his decisions, that notion of apportioning the punishment to the offence, which was observable in former actions of the king's life. Thus, the countess of Buchan had, careless of Bruce's perfidy and recklessness of crime in the murder of Comyn, rushed forward with zeal to take part in his coronation. She was now a prisoner. The king said, "Since she has not struck with the sword, let her not be stricken with the sword; but as a penalty for the treasonable coronation in which she took part, let her be shut up in a cage made in the form of a crown, that she may be a spectacle and a reproach."* The wife of Bruce, being also a prisoner, was sent to England as a captive. These two instances of severity are fastened upon by some writers as showing "vindictiveness." Yet the countess of Buchan was plainly guilty of treason; and to have allowed Bruce's wife to return free into Scotland, would evidently have been an act of imprudence. But the censors of Edward's conduct neglect to remark that the countess's cage was ordered "to have all the conveniences of a handsome chamber;" and that Bruce's wife was sent to the king's manor of Bruntwick; with seven attendants, and liberty to ride out whenever she chose.†

But with the male prisoners the Ordinance of Lanercost was carried into effect. Nigel Bruce was brought to trial at Berwick, hanged, and beheaded. Christopher and Alexander Seton, both Englishmen, shared the same sentence. These had been all concerned, in various ways, in the murder. The earl of Athol had taken part in the coronation of Bruce, and had been in arms at the affair of Johnstown. He attempted to escape by sea, but was driven back by a storm, and captured. Sir Simon Fraser was the same person who had cruelly murdered Ralph the cofferer at the battle of Roslyn, in 1302. He had received pardon for the offences of that period, but was now found again in arms. These two were tried in Westminster Hall, and executed, and their heads placed on London Bridge. "If we consider these men," says Lingard, "as champions of freedom, they may demand our pity; but their execution cannot substantiate the charge of cruelty against Edward. Some were murderers, all had repeatedly broken their oaths of fealty, and had repeatedly been admitted to pardon."

The winter now reigned, and Bruce was hidden in the

* Matthew of Westminster.   † Palgrave's Documents, p. clxxxix.

little isle of Rachrin. On the approach of spring he surprised the isle of Arran, and from thence sent spies into his own country of Annandale. The English in and near Turnberry Castle were cantoned in careless security, hearing nothing of any enemy; and it was not difficult to take them by surprise. Lord Henry Percy shut himself up in the castle; but he was soon relieved by the arrival of Sir Roger St. John with a thousand men. About this time two of Bruce's brothers, Thomas and Alexander, having collected about seven hundred men in Ireland, landed in Galloway. But they were met on landing by Macdowal, a Scottish chief, who remained true to his oath. The Irish auxiliaries were routed and scattered, and both the Bruces, with Sir Reginald Crawford, were taken prisoners. They were sent to Carlisle, and, having been concerned in Comyn's murder, were immediately brought to trial and executed. The whole of the executions on the scaffold, which took place in consequence of this rebellion, included about sixteen or eighteen persons. Most of these had been concerned in Comyn's murder, either as actual parties, or as accessories. Yet is it insisted upon by some writers that these punishments partook of cruelty. These critics, however, have no censure to spare for such atrocities as "the Douglas larder," which was perpetrated on Palm Sunday. Sir James Douglas, one of Bruce's adherents, surprised the English garrison of Douglas *while in church.* He butchered them all, after Wallace's manner, and as he had no strength wherewith to hold the castle, he raised a great pile of wood, threw the bodies of the English garrison upon it, and then setting it on fire, consumed the whole.* Such deeds as these were not calculated to soften the king's disposition, or to dispose him to lenity when any of Bruce's immediate accomplices

* Tytler, vol. i., p. 235.

fell into his hands. Yet, when was such a rebellion as this suppressed—as, during Edward's lifetime, it *was* suppressed —with so small an amount of judicial punishment? Four centuries later, another Scottish rebellion was quelled, while England was guided by the councils of Pelham, Hardwicke, Stephen Fox, Granville, and the elder Pitt. And these statesmen did not shrink from exhibiting, in various places, eighty ghastly heads; or from beheading, on Tower Hill, lords Kilmarnock and Balmerino, and finally, lord Lovat, a man whose years were fourscore!*

The spring of 1307 was now advancing, and Bruce, whose valour and personal prowess were of the highest order, found many opportunities of harassing the English, by surprises and sudden encounters. His success, however, was not unvaried. On one occasion he lost his banner, and was in the greatest peril of capture or death. In May he ventured to stand the assault of the earl of Pembroke, and by strongly posting his men, armed with long spears, he defeated the earl's attempt to break his line, and drove back the English, who had only cavalry to oppose to his spears. Three days after, he encountered the earl of Gloucester, whose force he also routed, and who retreated into the castle of Ayr. But the king, hearing that Bruce was in the field, sent a force from Carlisle, before which the rebel chief retreated. "He then took refuge in the marshes and forests, where the English found it impossible to follow him."† And thus stood matters at the opening of July, 1307.

But now drew near that great event for which, there can be no doubt, Bruce had long been eagerly looking, and which entirely changed the whole position of affairs. The king, as our readers will probably have observed, had never made his appearance in the field during the whole of the

* See Appendix. † Matthew of Westminster, 1307.

fifteen months which had elapsed since the first outbreak of the rebellion. He had found it possible to get as far as Carlisle and Dumfries, but Bruce knew full well that his active career as a military commander was for ever terminated. The last few months of his life presented merely a painful struggle between a still vigorous mind and a decaying body. During all the spring of 1307, a dysentery had detained and weakened him, and the natural ardour of his temperament must have conspired with the disease. His very longing for the active life to which he had been so long accustomed, supplied fuel to the inward fire which was already consuming him. Bruce's reappearance in the field, and his occasional successes, made any longer delay appear intolerable. Persuading himself, at the beginning of July, that his disease was abating, he offered up the litter in which he had hitherto travelled, in the cathedral of Carlisle, and mounted his horse for a new expedition into Scotland; but the decaying body was unable to answer the call of that powerful spirit. The effort merely brought on at once that termination of his disease which might otherwise have been delayed for months. In the course of the next two or three days, he was unable to proceed more than some six or seven miles; reaching the village of Burgh on the Sands, where he probably halted at the close of the first or second day's march, and where, on the seventh of that month, he died.

His last hours were spent in vainly endeavouring to impress upon his son some obvious lessons of prudence and firm resolve—lessons which were indeed greatly needed, but which the young prince seemed mentally incapable of receiving. He enjoined upon him never to permit the return of Gaveston. He urged him forthwith, and once for all, to put down the Scottish revolt, the means of which were all prepared and ready to his hand. So earnestly and enthusiastically did he dwell upon this point, that he desired his son to carry, after his death, his bones at the head of his army; so that he, before whose charge no Scottish army had been able to stand, might, even after death, be still in some sort present in the first shock of the battle.

But he spoke to ears which had already been closed, by luxury and dissipation, against all high and noble counsels. Not one of his commands was obeyed. The young king no sooner saw the opulence and splendour of royalty within his grasp, than he turned his back at once on the calls of honour and duty. The great and all-important object of putting down the insurrection in Scotland was disregarded. The forward march was countermanded, the anticipations of Bruce were fully realized, and the union of the two kingdoms—the great object of Edward's labours during the last ten years—was forgotten and practically abandoned. The remains of the greatest king that England had ever seen were, after some delay, removed to Westminster, and were placed near to his father Henry and to his beloved Eleanor. A simple tomb received that noble heart, with the brief inscription :—

> Edvardus Primus: Scotorum Malleus:
> Hic Est: mcccviii.*
> Pactum Serva.

---

* This was evidently the date of the erection of the tomb. The king had died in July, 1307, and had been buried in Westminster in October. The tomb was naturally completed in the following year.

The death of Edward may be said to have ensured the ultimate success of Bruce's ambitious enterprise. "The two greatest (*i.e.*, most puissant) knights in Europe at that period," says Froissart, "were king Edward and Robert Bruce." Edward being removed, Bruce found no equal in the field. Not only so, but there was opposed to him, in Edward's room, the weakest and most incompetent monarch that ever sat on the throne of England. It was nearly inevitable, therefore, that he should entirely succeed in the enterprise to which he had devoted himself. He decided the question of Scottish independence at Bannockburn, inflicting on the English the greatest defeat they had received since the battle of Hastings. This victory established him on the throne of Scotland, of which he held entire possession for the remainder of his life.

One very serious and very deplorable mistake has been made in modern times, in misinterpreting all these events, and, instead of seeing in them another successful Norman enterprise,—regarding them as an effort of the highest "patriotism." Thus Bruce is described by Sir Walter Scott as "the vindicator of his country's liberty"—as one who had adopted "the unalterable resolution, either to free his country or to perish in the attempt;"* while Hume unhesitatingly tells us, that "Bruce had long harboured in his breast the design of freeing his enslaved country;" and a writer of our own day styles him "the most heroic, as well as the most patriotic, monarch which Scotland has ever produced."

It is difficult to imagine a greater abuse of language than this. Patriotism is a love of country ; and a real patriot will

* Sir Walter Scott's History of Scotland, vol. i., p. 87. Sir Walter forgot here that, before six months had passed, Bruce sent messengers to the young prince to ask if his submission would be accepted.

labour and suffer, and, if needful, will die for his country; but Robert Bruce conspired against his country, fought against his country, and, in the end, inflicted upon his country the most grievous injuries. If this be "patriotism," then words have lost their meaning.

"Bruce was an Englishman;"—we quote the words of a volume put forth by a committee of Scottish gentlemen, "Bruce by descent was an Englishman, and probably so by affection as well as interest."*

The son of a great Yorkshire baron, and heir to ninety-four English lordships and to two Scottish estates, he was born, as we have seen, in the metropolis of England, a few weeks before Edward's coronation. We entirely accept, therefore, the statement of the *Wallace Documents*, that "Bruce was an Englishman;"—but we read with hesitation the rest of the sentence—"and probably so by affection as well as interest." We believe that Sir Walter Scott formed a more accurate estimate of these matters when he wrote, concerning the Norman knights who were settled in Scotland, that "Two or three generations had not converted Normans into Scots; in fact, *the Normans were neither by birth nor manners accessible to the emotions which constitute patriotism.*" "The ideal perfection of the knight-errant was, to wander from land to land in quest of renown; to gain earldoms, *kingdoms*, nay, empires, by the sword; and to sit down a settler on his acquisitions, without looking back on the land which gave him life."† This vivid sketch seems as if it had been meant to describe a Robert de Brus.

Still, so long as Edward could keep the field, the young aspirant remained in quietness; but when he had seen

* Wallace Documents, Maitland Club, Glasgow, 1841, p. 48.
† History of Scotland, vol. i., p. 68.

distinctly that the great captain's campaigns were ended, Bruce came boldly to the front, and soon won a kingdom for himself. Such honour and credit as belong to a feat of this kind ought to be awarded to Bruce; but this sort of merit should not be confounded with the far higher virtue of real "patriotism."

Bruce's success made him to all succeeding ages a hero. "So long as thou doest well unto thyself," says the Psalmist, "men will speak good of thee." With this sort of popular and vulgar applause we shall not quarrel, but the more serious and thoughtful students of history should pause before they award a nobler kind of praise to a mere knight-errant of the Norman breed.

His success placed him on the throne of Scotland, and maintained him on that throne to the end of his life; and yet it may be questioned whether, even on the lowest view, of mere material and personal advantage, his success was such as a man might look back upon with satisfaction. He was crowned king at Scone in March, 1306. Edward's death assured to him the quiet possession of that throne, and he did, in fact, retain it until 1331, when he died. Fourteen years of uncertain warfare, and then eleven years of settled dominion, made up the whole of his kingly career. He had indeed succeeded, but such a success was scarcely better than failure. His family had been destroyed. Of a brotherhood of five gallant knights who took part in the murder of Comyn, he, the king, was, in 1318, the sole survivor. Three of his brothers had perished on the scaffold before a year had been completed from Comyn's death; and the fourth, endeavouring to find for himself a throne in Ireland, died in the attempt; and he, the beginner of the strife, was now left alone. His wife for several years was held in captivity in England; he himself died of leprosy in 1331, and his son spent a large portion of his life in an English prison. On the son's death the line of Bruce ended, and that of Stewart came in its stead—a line scarcely to be paralleled in history for disaster, wretchedness, and disgrace.* This being the measure of Bruce's success, it may be questioned whether failure would not have been on the whole preferable, so far as he personally was concerned.

But what of Scotland? Are the usual phrases of "deliverance," "independence," "freedom from a foreign yoke," etc., properly applied to this case? In the year 1603, Scotland became permanently united to England, and has ever since been ruled by governments sitting at Westminster. Has this change been calamitous for Scotland? Is there a Scotchman living, whose opinion is worth a straw, who would desire to see Bruce's enterprise repeated, and a new Scottish monarchy established?

No, Scotland was very far from benefiting by this greatly-lauded "deliverance." A separation of the northern and southern districts of this island had indeed been effected, but that separation was not then, any more than it would be now, for the good of either section.

In mere military glory, the advantage could not long remain on the Scottish side. "Never," says Alison, "at any subsequent period, was Scotland able to withstand the more powerful arms of the English yeomanry. Thenceforward, her military history is little more than a melancholy catalogue of continued defeats."

The discomfitures of Halidon-hill, of Dupplin-moor, of Durham, of Hamildon-hill, of Flodden, and of Pinkie, soon

* Robert III. died of a broken heart; James I. was murdered; James II. accidentally killed; James III. murdered; James IV. died on Flodden-field; James V. of a broken heart. Then followed Mary, who died on the scaffold, James's troubled reign, Charles's bloody death, and, finally, the expulsion of the family.

left Bannockburn the one solitary triumph amidst a long history of disaster. These six battles are computed to have inflicted on the Scots a loss of one hundred thousand men. Allow one-half or one-third of this number for the English losses, and then add to the reckoning the perpetual drain arising from skirmishes and " border-raids," and we shall see that this irrational idea of " Scottish independence " must have cost the two nations, from Bruce's day to Elizabeth's, at least a quarter of a million of valuable lives. The loss of property and of material prosperity during the same period cannot easily be estimated.

An unfriendly critic remarks of Edward, that, with statesmanlike sagacity, " he saw that, before England could mount very high in the scale of nations, the whole island must be one undivided power, instead of three." This aim and object was a noble one, and if pursued by honourable means—as we believe that it was—it casts lustre on the sovereign's name. But how, then, shall we praise the man who, from the far lower motive of mere personal ambition, withstood and finally frustrated the great king's purpose?

Scotland was not benefited by Bruce's success. Her independence, as we have just remarked, brought upon her a long train of calamitous wars and ruinous defeats. The uniform custom of France, whenever she quarrelled with England, was, to send to Scotland, and to incite her to attack her neighbour on the northern side, as a diversion in favour of the war beginning in the south: but Scotland, so allied with France, was merely the dwarf going to battle by the side of the giant. Of the hard blows she received a full share; but the glory and the profit, when there were any, usually fell to the lot of her ally.

Nor did Scotland gain, by her desired " self-government," any recompence for what she lost in her external relations? All Scottish historians of any credit admit, that Edward's mode of government was liberal, mild, and upright. Mr. Tytler confesses that "the measures he adopted were equally politic and just." "No wanton or unnecessary act of rigour was committed, no capricious changes introduced." And when, in 1304—5, a new "settlement of Scotland" was required, the king called on the most active of the Scottish prelates, Wishart, upon Mowbray, and upon Bruce, and placed the matter wholly in their hands.

Could Scotland obtain, then, in recompense for all the losses she suffered in this home-warfare, any solid advantages, springing out of "home-government," which could counterbalance long years of carnage and desolation? History gives no affirmative answer. We will ask the Scottish writers, and them only. Describing a period only sixty years after Bruce's death, Sir Walter Scott says: "To use a scriptural expression, 'every one did that which was right in his own eyes,' as if there had been no king in Scotland." A little later he says: "If we look at Scotland generally during the minority, it forms a dark and disgusting spectacle." And Mr. Tytler uses similar language. In one place he says: "The nation had been reduced to the lowest pitch of impoverishment in every branch of public wealth" (vol. ii. p. 75); in another, "The pride and power of the feudal barons had risen to a pitch destructive of all regular subordination" (p. 85); and again, "Scotland seemed to be rapidly sinking under her accumulated distresses" (p. 94). No—the "recovery of her independence" had been no gain to Scotland; to each district of the island—to Scotland as well as to England—it had brought merely weakness, distraction, and loss. Edward's desire to create one united Britain was wise and statesmanlike. Had Llewellyn and Balliol co-operated with him, each of them might have preserved his throne. But Bruce's enterprise, commencing with an atrocious murder, was strictly one of personal ambition. If he ever really dreamed that he was conferring a benefit on Scotland, he fell into a grievous error; but if his self-consciousness prevented this, and he merely used "independence" as a popular cry,—a device, then his scheme and his effort, from first to last, was a grievous crime. Let us leave this part of the subject, however, and try to take a fitting leave of the great sovereign whose reign we have endeavoured to describe. And here we must remember that, at each point of the story, we have freely expressed an opinion—have endeavoured to meet hostile attacks, and to place Edward's character in the fullest light of truth. We must not now repeat all these arguments. We prefer, for obvious reasons, to gather into one view the judgments formed by many eminent writers, both of past times and of our own day, and thus to collect, by degrees, the verdict of a very competent jury.

Two very different and, in fact, opposite beliefs have obtained currency in England during the last five centuries. For four hundred years Englishmen formed their own opinions, and spoke of Edward as they knew him, or as their forefathers had known him. Then, for one hundred years, they submitted to have a different view forced upon them; and they received in silence, until they gradually came to believe it—the estimate of Edward which was formed by the admirers of Bruce and of Wallace;—of Bruce the false and of Wallace the ferocious. Thus, strangely enough, the people of England learned to think, in the eighteenth century, quite differently of the greatest of their kings from what their forefathers had done, during at least ten or twelve generations.

The men of his own day admired and venerated Edward. Hemingford speaks of him as "the most excellent, wise, and sagacious king." Rishanger tells us of "his infinite labours and manifold troubles," and of "his numberless good deeds." Wykes dwells on "his wonderful mercy towards transgressors," "a mercy which not only relinquished revenge, but freely granted pardon."

This estimate, this character of him, had gone abroad. Uberti, an Italian poet of Edward's own time, condemns his father, Henry, but adds—

"Yet there's some good to say of him, I grant,
Because of him was the good Edward born,
Whose valour still is famous in the world."*

A little later another foreigner, Froissart, uses the same language, describing him as he who was "called the good king Edward, who was brave, wise, and fortunate in war."

During four centuries our own chroniclers and historians continue to use the same language. Fabyan, in 1494, describes him as "slow to all manner of strife; discreet, and wise, and true of his word; in arms a giant." Holinshed speaks of him as "wise and virtuous, gentle and courteous." John Foxe, the puritan, terms him "valiant and courageous, pious and gentle." Prynne, another puritan, speaks of him as "the most illustrious,—our glorious king Edward." Camden, in Elizabeth's days, describes him as "a monarch most renowned, in whose valiant soul the spirit of God seemed evidently to dwell; so that he justly merited the character of one of the greatest glories of Britain." And when we turn to Rapin, who wrote towards the end of the seventeenth century, and who was, like Froissart, a foreigner, and wholly impartial—we find him giving this deliberate judgment:—"Edward joined to his bodily perfections

* Rossetti's translation.

a solid judgment, a great penetration, and a prudence which rarely suffered him to make a false step. Besides this, he had principles of justice, honour, and honesty, which restrained him from countenancing vice. He was also of an exemplary chastity, a virtue seldom found in sovereigns. All these noble qualities bred in the hearts of his subjects a love and esteem which greatly contributed to the peace of his kingdom."*

Thus, through a period of several succeeding centuries, Englishmen, with one consent, regarded this great sovereign with veneration—not so much for his valour or his prowess, in which the Conqueror, or him of the "lion heart," might, perhaps, equal him, as for his wisdom, his statesmanlike qualities, his "legislative mind," and, still more, for his uprightness, his truthfulness, his merciful disposition, and his various moral excellences. In their eyes he was indeed "great," but, still more remarkably, he was "good."

But in the eighteenth century, new histories, brought up to more recent times, were needed, and English attempts to supply the want generally failed. Brady, in 1685, Tyrrell, in 1700, and Carte, in 1747, were laborious and dull. To supply the want, which could not but be felt, two Scotchmen, of unquestionable talent, offered themselves, and the histories written by Hume and by Henry soon became the favourite authorities. An Anglo-Irishman, Goldsmith, was content to follow in their track. Other Scotchmen of high merit—Mackintosh, Scott, Macfarlane, Tytler, and Chambers—have succeeded Hume and Henry; and of three generations it may be said with truth, that Englishmen have been content to learn the history of their own land from the lips and pens of the natives of Caledonia.

Now, for the greater part of the story, this might occur without any injurious consequences; but how would it affect

* Rapin's History, vol. i., p. 385.

that part of the narrative which described the wars between England and Scotland? Above all, how were the enthusiastic admirers of Bruce and Wallace to discuss impartially the deeds of him who had twice conquered Scotland, and who had sent Wallace and three of the family of Bruce to the scaffold? That they should do so was evidently impossible. Yet they gained almost entire possession of the public ear, and then they utterly changed the public feeling as to this, the greatest of all the English kings.

They could not deny—they did not attempt to deny—his claim to *greatness* in the lower acceptation of the term. He was "the model of a politic and warlike king," says Hume. He was "a great statesman and commander," says Mackintosh. But all the higher qualities of mental and moral excellence were denied to him. Hume speaks of his "barbarous policy," and declares that "never were the principles of equity violated with less scruple or reserve," adding that "the iniquity of his claim was apparent, and was aggravated by the most egregious breach of trust." Dr. Henry speaks of Edward's "unrelenting selfishness," of his "cruelty and iniquity," and, again, of his "injustice and cruelty." Sir James Mackintosh tells how he had "skilfully inveigled the Scotch into his snares," adding that "his ambition tainted all his acts," and that "a conqueror is a perpetual plotter against the safety of all nations." And Sir Walter Scott speaks of him as "bold and crafty," "a subtle and unhesitating politician." Following such leaders as these, it is no wonder that all our school histories, for almost a century past, have taught the youth of England to regard this king as an able and valiant, but withal an unprincipled man.*

* Thus, in the most popular of our school histories, Mrs. Markham's, the scholar is told of Edward's "violent acts," of his fatal thirst of conquest, of his "mad ferocity," of his "injustice and violence," of the "infinite misery" he inflicted on "many thousands" of people.

Such was the position of affairs, a few years back, when a volume made its appearance * which challenged the justice of this verdict, and called, with warmth and earnestness, for a reconsideration of the case. It was a hasty production; it had many palpable faults; it was, not unnaturally, charged with "a partisan spirit," but in its main object it has been entirely successful. It induced many men of literary eminence to take up the question of this great king's real character. They went to the only source of truth on all such questions—to contemporary testimony. They examined and weighed it, and the result has been, a reversal of the verdict.

Do we speak with too' much confidence on this point ? Let the reader peruse the following declarations :—

In Trinity Term, in 1864, a meeting was held of " The Oxford Historical Society,"—its president, professor Goldwin Smith, in the chair—for the consideration of the volume aforesaid ("The Greatest of the Plantagenets "). A paper or elaborate criticism, was read by professor Montagu Burrows, on that volume. In it, he said,—

"This work demands our attention, because it is a bold and, on the whole, successful attempt to reclaim for him, who is perhaps the only sovereign of England since the Conquest who has a right to the title of ' Great,' that position of which he has been deprived for more than a century, —deprived by a number of causes almost unparalleled for the way in which they have combined towards such a result."

After a lengthened review of the work, in which professor Burrows spoke of the writer's "masterly narrative of the facts attending the double conquest of Scotland," and added, " He has conclusively disposed of the leading Scotch fables, and recovered as much of the truth as we shall probably ever know. The great outlines of the story, which

* "The Greatest of the Plantagenets."

form the groundwork of the Scottish Iliad, have been for the first time thoroughly marked out by the help of every available authority;"—the professor concluded his review in the following manner:—

"This king was called by the writers of the next generation 'Edward the Good,' and it has been to our shame as a nation that we have been so careless of a royal reputation, and that so little effort has been made to restore him his rights. If the highest perfection as a soldier, and all but the highest as a general; if patience, fortitude, prudence, mental activity, largeness of mind, public spirit; if a correct private life, a conscientious sense of duty, and a consistent religious character go to make up a great man,—Edward I. is entitled to the name. Place him by the side of those sovereigns who, since the time of Charlemagne and Alfred, have received the title of 'Great,' and how insignificant do they appear. Perhaps the time may come when a more enlightened public opinion shall repair this omission. And among those to whom a very considerable share of credit will be due, will be the author of the work we have just been considering."

The president, Mr. Goldwin Smith, summed up the matter in a few concluding words. These words have weight, as coming from a man who could never have been brought to approve a course of "iniquity," "selfishness," "vindictiveness," "violence," and "ferocity." He said that "So far from Edward's invasion being intended to reduce Scotland to slavery, its object was to introduce the same regular and constitutional quiet which England enjoyed, and to rescue the Scotch from the anarchy resulting from the oppression of the most oppressive of the feudal oligarchies. The kingdom of Scotland was previously in an almost hopeless state of feudal anarchy. One of the first things Edward did was to summon a free Parliament, and he left them with all their independence, and with all their rights as a nation. The short period when he had possession of the kingdom, was the only glimpse they ever had of a lawful, regular, and beneficent government. Wallace was more truly represented, he thought, by the author of 'The Greatest of all the Plantagenets' than by professor Burrows.* He was an irregular rebel, like the Neapolitan brigands of the present day."†

Mr. Goldwin Smith quitted England, and his successor in the Regius professorship at Oxford was Mr. Stubbs. That gentleman has recently given to the world a volume of much value, "On the Early English Charters." Having occasion to speak of Edward I., he thus characterizes him :—

"This great monarch, whose commanding spirit, defining and organizing power, and thorough honesty of character, place him in strong contrast not merely with his father, but with all the rest of our long line of kings, was not likely to surrender, without a struggle, the position which he had inherited. For more than twenty years he reigned as Henry II. had done, showing proper respect for constitutional forms, but exercising the reality of despotic power. He loved his people, and therefore did not oppress them; they knew and loved him, and endured the pressure of taxation, which would not have been imposed if it had not been necessary. He admits them to a share, a large share, in the process of government; he developes and defines the constitution in a way which Simon de Montfort had never contemplated. The organization of parliament is completed until it seems as perfect as it is at the present day; and the legislation is so full that the laws of the next three centuries are little more than a necessary expansion of it." He adds,

* The professor had suggested some apology for Wallace's violence and cruelty.
† "Proceedings of Oxford Historic lSociety, Trinity term, 1864."

of the king himself, that "His own personal character was high, pure, and true." Finally, in closing his investigation, he says: "We stop at Edward I. because the machinery is now completed; the people are now at full growth. And the attaining this point is to be attributed to the defining genius, the political wisdom, and the honesty of this great king."*

We turn to a fourth writer of the same class;—to the Regius professor of Modern History at Belfast, Mr. Yonge. He concludes his review of this reign with these words:—

"Among the rulers of mankind who have won for themselves a conspicuous and honourable place in the history of their country, Edward has no superior, and scarcely an equal. Personal prowess, which in other heroes makes up the greater part of their renown, was in him so overshadowed by more valuable qualities as to be scarcely entitled to notice; and the invincible knight is lost in the consummate general, the wise lawgiver, the far-sighted statesman." "It was no personal or vulgar ambition that prompted his attacks on Wales and Scotland, but a judicious perception of the advantages to be derived, not by England alone, but by the invaded countries, from their union into one kingdom. He was ambitious, not so much of being the conqueror, as the benefactor, of the whole island." "Kings are subjected to a more rigid tribunal than ordinary men, from the fact of their conspicuous position; and we have no right to expect that faultlessness in a sovereign which we know it to be vain to look for in others. But as long as the equitable rule prevails of balancing men's virtues against their faults, and looking at the general results of their conduct, so long will the splendid and universal abilities of Edward I., and the great and lasting benefits which his country has derived from them, secure him a leading, if not

* Prof. Stubbs' Select Charters, 1870, p. 35, 51.

the very first, place among those monarchs who have left an example to be revered by their countrymen and imitated by their successors."*

Sir E. Creasy expresses a similar opinion, but with more brevity, closing his review of Edward's reign with one decisive sentence :—

"If we take a comprehensive and unprejudiced view of his whole career, we shall rest satisfied that few greater men have ever reigned; and that there has been hardly any man, royal or subject, to whom Englishmen ought to look with more gratitude than Edward, as the promoter of our power, and the ordainer of our laws and our constitution." †

A sixth writer, of our own day, who has carefully investigated these questions, is Mr. C. H. Pearson. There is not a trace of partiality in the portrait which he draws; yet a sincere and warm admiration draws from him such expressions as these :—

"Brave almost to insanity, the king was also a consummate general, able to discipline raw levies, and to carry out engineering works with singular audacity and resource.' He was also "large-minded towards mere personal enemies, but never pardoning baseness or broken faith."

Mr. Pearson notices also "a strong love of justice," "a slowness to shed blood," and "a greatness of nature which carried him through every difficulty." "His people knew that he did everything for England; and he inspired trust, for he never broke his word." He was "our first truly English king;" he was "the greatest of his race;" and, finally, "among those of our kings whom we really know, there is, perhaps, no greater name than that of Edward I."

* Yonge's History of England, p. 113.
† Creasy's History of England, p. 485.

And, just as this sheet is passing through the press, a seventh testimony of no small value is given by Mr. E. A. Freeman.* He discusses, in one of his Essays, the whole merits of the Scottish controversy of 1290—1307, and he declares, that "if any man's conduct ever was marked by thorough justice and disinterestedness, that of king Edward was so marked throughout the whole business." "His conduct was throughout honest and above-board." Of Wallace he says, "It is impossible to deny the fiendish brutalities practised by him in England,—brutalities which fully explain the intense hatred with which every English writer speaks of him":—And of Bruce, that "he\ treacherously and sacrilegiously murdered John Comyn, the heir of the Scottish crown." He adds, "that all who were concerned in this murder met with their merited punishment, who can wonder?—it is certain that Edward punished no man who would not be held liable to punishment at the present moment." As to Edward himself, Mr. Freeman's opinion is briefly summed up in a very few words: He was "the greatest and noblest king that England has seen for eight hundred years."

Such have been the independent and deliberate judgments of seven different writers of high rank within the last few years. Let us endeavour, then, in conclusion, to group together all the various characteristics, ascribed to Edward by writers of various countries and different ages, many of whom regarded his general career with unconcealed dislike. Praise from this latter class must be allowed to have a peculiar value.

Edward, then, was,—"A great statesman and commander; the model of a politic and warlike king; the most

* Historical Essays, by E. A. Freeman, D.C.L., late Fellow of Trinity College, Oxford, 1871.

sagacious and resolute of English princes; uniting legislative wisdom with heroic valour. In him the state possessed a centre and a chief, who knew how to concentrate and direct all the forces of society. No man was more acute in counsel, more fervid in eloquence, more self-possessed in danger, more cautious in prosperity, more firm in adversity. He was unequalled by any since the Conqueror for prudence, valour, and success." Such are the admissions of severe critics;—of Mackintosh, Hume, Scott, Alison, Guizot, Sharon Turner, and Hallam.

But he was more than wise and strong; he was upright, he was thoroughly honest; he was merciful and good.

"He was ambitious, not so much of being the conqueror as the benefactor of the whole island. He could demand confidence, for his people knew that he did everything for England; he inspired trust, for he never broke his word; he was as careful in performing his obligations as in exacting his rights.* He had a strong love of justice, a legislative mind; he was one of the best legislators and greatest politicians that ever filled the English throne. Large-minded towards mere personal enemies; he was a wise lawgiver, a far-sighted statesman. He was slow to shed blood; —never was a conquest more merciful than his in Wales. Finally, he was the greatest and noblest king that England has seen for eight hundred years."

Such are the deliberate judgments of professor Yonge, of Mr. Pearson, Mackintosh, Dr. Henry, and Mr. Freeman.

* During the last thirty years a dozen Histories of England have been published in London, all of which servilely followed Hume, describing Edward as "unscrupulous," "perfidious," and "unprincipled." But in the course of the last seven years, all the writers whom we have just quoted have re-examined the subject, and they all unite in declaring the king to have been honest, just, truthful, and disinterested.

They go far to form a complete character. But one more feature,—the interior and personal, remains to be added.

"His character as a son, as a husband, and as a father was without stain; in his private relations he was beyond reproach. A man of deep and earnest piety, whose heart was replete with the sentiment of religion. He displays as a legislator a genuine anxiety for the real interests of the church; but he was equally resolved that his clergy should have no privileges incompatible with the civil order of the realm. He found England the most priest-ridden country in Europe, and he raised a barrier against church aggrandizement which neither monk nor pope could overstep."

These are the testimonies of Sir Edward Creasy, of Dean Hook, and of Mr. Pearson. Surely, we need desire to say nothing more. We have drawn the character of Edward from thirteen different writers, of various times and countries; and to their testimony we have no wish to add a single word.

It is the breadth and completeness of this character which chiefly claims our admiration. Men of power,—men of remarkable talents, are met with again and again in the world's history; but, unhappily, most of the greatest are also found among the meanest; while too many of the good are obliged to ask for our pity or our indulgence. We perceive Edward's character to be one of unusual excellence, so soon as we begin to search for a superior or an equal.

We naturally think, in the first place, of the great Saxon king, who, four centuries before Edward's day, did so much to raise England out of the slough of ignorance and semi-barbarism in which she was grovelling. But we can no more institute a comparison between Alfred and Edward, than we can weigh the respective merits of Alfred and of

Arthur. The hero of the sixth century can only be clearly discerned through the thick darkness of that gloomy period. Alfred might be better seen and more truly appreciated; but it was but partially and doubtfully; as we strive to discern objects through the mists of the early dawn. He fought battles and gained victories; but of the places so distinguished, we know next to nothing. He died, and was buried, we believe, at Winchester, but " his grave no man knoweth." * How can we, then, rationally institute a comparison between a hero who is so imperfectly delineated, and a king whose words and actions are as familiar to us as those of Elizabeth or the third William?

Still, if any one prefers to maintain the belief that Alfred was the greatest of all kings, and almost of all men, we shall not quarrel with his opinion. We merely express a doubt, whether our knowledge is sufficient to warrant such positive language. We think that it is not.

As to the other " heroes " of ancient, or mediæval, or modern days, they seem to us to fall far below Edward's standard. An Alexander, at the head of his irresistible phalanx, can march through Asia, no enemy being able to stand before him; but his own passions conquer him in turn. Two friends are put to death on suspicion, and a

---

* All the best biographers of Alfred are obliged to use, at every turn, the phrases, "It is said," and "Tradition reports." Thus, Mr. Pearson writes: " Probably nothing has been attributed to him without some real fact *underlying the mythical narrative*, but it is not always easy to disentangle the one from the other" (p. 173). Mr. Wright thus speaks: " It is *probable* that the king, during the period he remained at Athelney, was actively engaged in watching the movements of the Danes. *Another legend* represents him," etc. (p. 388). And Mr. Hughes, the latest biographer of the great king, says of one fact, " This is related by Asser to have happened," " *which is clearly impossible.*" In another place, " Any attempt to remove the miraculous element would take all life out of the story." A third story is described as " a sad tangle, which *no man can unravel.*"

third is slain by his own hand in the excitement of drunkenness. Cæsar infinitely surpassed Alexander. He killed a million of men for his own aggrandizement. He was great as a soldier, and still greater as a statesman. But Cæsar knew neither religion nor morals. He believed this life to be the end of man; and naturally he indulged in sensual pleasures "without shame or scruple."* We will not do Edward the injustice to compare him with such men as these.

Coming nearer to his own age, we find a Charlemagne, unquestionably great in council and in war. But the historian cannot help censuring "his cruelty and his excessive dissoluteness."† In private life he was utterly licentious, and in war he could massacre four thousand men—not in a battle, or in the storming of a city, but like a butcher in a slaughter-house.

Another Charles, of great power and great success, arose in Europe after a lapse of two centuries. But what shall we say of a man who, after a successful, but an immoral and treacherous life, brought himself to the grave at the age of fifty-eight, by excessive gluttony?

Still later, at the opening of the present century, we saw a greater soldier and a greater statesman than either Charlemagne or Charles V. In Napoleon we had a loftier genius than either Alexander or Cæsar,—a conqueror who marched from Rome to Poland, from Madrid to Moscow; and who, at Dresden, in 1812, "was waited upon by a crowd of obsequious kings or princes, who accepted every word that fell from his lips, as if an oracle had spoken."‡ And yet it has been truly observed that this autocrat of Europe " had

---

* Merivale, vol. i., 119, 490.
† Robertson's Church History, vol. ii., p. 136.
‡ Gleig.

HIS CHARACTER. 345

not the merit of common truth and honesty; he would steal, slander, assassinate, as his interest dictated. He was intensely selfish; he was perfidious. In short, when you had penetrated through all this immense power and splendour, you found that you were dealing with an impostor and a rogue."*

We cannot measure or balance the king of whom we have been writing, with such characters as these. He is altogether of another class. Casting our eyes among men of honour,—men of conscience, men worthy of our respect, in our search for a superior or an equal, we have not yet succeeded in our quest. We relinquish the task, therefore, here, and hand it over to our readers.

* Emerson.

APPENDIX.

I., *page* 93.

A YEAR'S EXPENDITURE OF THE KING.

It is now more than eighty years since the Society of Antiquarians published " The Account of the Comptroller of the Wardrobe, of the twenty-eighth year of king Edward I., A.D. 1299-1300 ;" and it is probable that few of the readers of this volume have ever seen that publication. It seems desirable, therefore, to give, in this place, a brief sketch of that Account, the whole details of which form a quarto volume. We shall confine ourselves to a few general heads.

I.

The Keeper or treasurer of the Wardrobe acknowledges the receipt, from various sources, of a total sum, within the year, of - - - - £58,155 16s. 2d.

II.

He then gives an account of his disbursements, under twelve heads, as follows :—

1. Alms and oblations, for the relief of the poor, £ s. d
or as religious offerings. The payments fill
thirty-one quarto pages, and are of every
description. The total for the year - - 1,166 14 9

APPENDIX.

		£	s.	d.
2. The next head is that of necessaries bought for the use of the king's household, and for charges and expenses of ambassadors, messengers, etc.—the total being	-	3,338	19	3
3. Then follows the victualling and stores for the king's army in Scotland, and for the supplies for the garrisons of his castles in that country		18,638	1	8
4. Next, gifts and rewards; and payment for horses lost by knights and others in the king's service	-	4,386	4	5
5. Allowances to knights of the king's household; and of foreign troops retained in the king's service	-	3,077	19	0
6. Wages of the engineers, archers, and sergeants-at-arms of the household	-	1,038	10	7
7. Wages of foot-soldiers, archers, artificers, and workmen	-	4,446	9	11
„ Wages to seamen of the Cinque Ports and other towns	-	1,233	9	8
8. Expenses of king's messengers	-	87	11	1
9. Wages and expenses of the huntsmen, falconers, hawks, etc.	-	77	6	11
10. Allowances to knights, bannerets, etc. of the household, for robes	-	714	3	4
11. Goldsmiths' and jewellers' accounts	-	253	15	6
12. Includes cloth, furs, wax, and other things for the use of the household	-	4,391	19	0
Wines and other liquors for the use of the household	-	6,934	6	0
Separate account of the queen	-	3,668	2	9
Costs and charges of the king's Chancery	-	581	9	0
		£54,035	2	7

To which is added, for some current expenses of the household, the particulars of which do not appear to have been preserved, the sum of £10,969 16s. 0d.

So that the treasurer, on this account, would appear to have been in advance. But there was, doubtless, money daily coming in, and he probably had some bills not yet discharged.

The calculations of Bishop Fleetwood's tables show the value of money to have been fifteen times as great at that day as it is now. This would make the royal revenue to amount to about £800,000 per annum. Out of which the king paid, in 1300, what would now be about £500,000, for his troops, seamen, garrisons, etc.; about £270,000 for the expenses of his household, exclusive of robes, jewels, huntsmen, and charities; which last item, of alms and oblations, in the money of our time, would be equal to nearly £18,000 a-year.

II., *page* 165.

EDWARD'S OBTESTATION.

At first sight, remembering the constant and earnest attention to religious duties shown by Edward, we were inclined to doubt whether the chronicler might not be in error in ascribing this oath to the king; the more especially since the person addressed was named BIGOD; so that it would be easy to fall into such an error. But, looking a little further, we found the pope himself, in a public reception of Edward's ambassadors, asseverating "per Deum," that he would do the king justice. So that it seems tolerably clear that even religious men, in those days, thought it lawful to use language similar to that employed by Abraham (Gen. xxiv. 3), by Joab (2 Sam. xix. 7), and by Nehemiah (xiii. 25). As to Edward himself, his whole character assures us, that he never used the Divine name lightly or irreverently.

III., *page* 239.

PARLIAMENT OF LINCOLN.

The requests preferred by the barons, and accorded by the king, were the Ist, IInd, IIIrd, IVth, and Vth, the VIIIth, IXth, Xth, and XIth. Those which he did not concede, were the following:—

VI.

" E ce ke mespris est par nul ministre soit amende solom ce ke le trespas le demaunde par auditours a ceo assignez qe ne soient pas suspecionus des Prelates, Contes, e Barons de la terre solom ceo kil mesmes ainz ces houres ad fet e qe ce seit meintenant mis en oevre."

" Dominus Rex vult providere aliud remedium super hoc sed non per tales auditores."

VII.

" E qe Viscontes de cest houre en avant respoignet des issues solom ce kil soleient fere en tens son Pere les queles issues unt este e uncore ore sunt a grand apovrissement du peuple. E ke Viscontes ne soient plus haut chargez."

" Placet Dominus Rege quod de communi consilio provideatur super hoc quam cito commode poterit remedium optimum."

XII.

" E par ceste choses suzdites ne pount ne osent pas les Prelates de seinte Eglise assenter ke contribucion seit fete de lur biens ne de biens de la clergie en contre le defens le Apostoille."

" Non placuit Regi : sed communitas Procerium approbavit."

IV., *page* 320.

On the general question, of the character of Edward's rule, it is quite undeniable that *there is no reign in English history* which can compare with it for clemency.

If we turn to that of his weak and unworthy successor, we find it full of hurried executions. Thus, when he took Ledes Castle, he hanged up the governor and eleven knights. When he captured the earl of Lancaster, the earl was immediately sent to the scaffold ; and with him fourteen knights and fourteen knights-banneret.

In the reign of Edward III., we have the execution of the earl of Kent, "son of the great Edward," of Mortimer and Bereford, and of the earl of Menteith.

In Richard II.'s reign, we find Tresillian and Brambre, Burley and Beauchamp, Berners and Salisbury, and the earl of Arundel, sent to the scaffold.

In Henry IV.'s reign we hear of the execution of the earls of Kent and Salisbury, of lords Lumley and Despencer, of the earl of Huntingdon, of the earl of Worcester, of lord Kinderton, of Sir Richard Vernon, of the earl of Westmoreland, and of the archbishop of York.

Now Edward I.'s reign was not a calm or peaceful one. He had wars abroad and at home, conspiracies, and earls and archbishops opposed to him. Yet, during thirty years, and until the assassination of Comyn, we find, as we have just said, but three political executions—1. David of Snowdon, who in time of peace had stormed a castle, committing high-treason and murder; 2. Turberville, who had covenanted to assist the landing of the French; and 3. Wallace, who had ravaged two counties with fire and sword, "sparing neither sex nor age." Say we not truly, then, that for clemency, Edward's sway is almost without a parallel.

For half a century past, we have had a popular cry for "the abolition of the punishment of death"; and, very naturally, in our popular histories we meet with expressions of indignation, because Edward, in the course of thirty years, brought three persons to trial, and sent them to the scaffold; and because he, in the last year of his reign, capitally punished sixteen or eighteen others for their participation in a murder.

Yet every one of these persons was brought to a fair and open trial, and condemned by fit and competent judges. We censure the king now, believing that in the advance of civilization we have grown vastly more humane. Yet, what is our custom in this gentle and merciful reign of Queen Victoria?

In India, a few years since, we had to deal with some rebel princes, hardly better, but scarcely worse, than David of Snowdon. And how did we treat them? Here is the published narrative of one of the English officers engaged in suppressing the Sepoy rebellion.

Major Hodson writes, from India, in 1857 :—" The next day I

got permission to go and bring in the king (of Delhi) and his favourite wife and her son. This was successfully accomplished. I then set to work to get hold of the villain princes. I started for the tomb of the Emperor Humayoon, where they had taken sanctuary. After two hours of wordy strife, they appeared, and I sent them away under a guard. . . . . I then went to look after my prisoners, who, with their guard, had moved towards Delhi. I came up just in time, and seizing a carbine from one of my men, I deliberately shot them one after another. I then ordered the bodies to be taken into the city and thrown out on the Chiboutre, in front of the Kotwallu. In twenty-four hours, therefore, I had disposed of the principal members of the house of Timur the Tartar." This narrative is published without the least expression of regret by a clergyman of Trinity College, Cambridge.

Fourteen years more have passed away, and we have now a Republic established in France, professing, of course, universal philanthropy, benevolence, and kindness. And what is one of its latest acts? It has tried deliberately, and has deliberately sentenced to death, a Paris *litterateur*, for writing seditious articles in a newspaper!

And yet our great king is to be stigmatized as "vindictive" and "cruel," because he sent to the scaffold a deceitful rebel, on whom he had conferred many favours, and who had attacked a castle, slaying its defenders;—a marauder, who had ravaged two English counties, "sparing neither sex nor age;" and a knot of Scottish traitors, who had assassinated the first noble in Scotland in a church, because he stood in the way of their treasonable purposes.